THE PERFECT
CHRISTMAS

THE PERFECT CHRISTMAS

HOW TO PLAN AND ENJOY THE BEST CELEBRATION EVER

Carolyn Bell

HERMES HOUSE

This edition published by Hermes House, an imprint of
Anness Publishing Limited, Hermes House, 88–89 Blackfriars Road, London SE1 8HA
Tel: 020 7401 2077; fax: 020 7633 9499

www.hermeshouse.com; www.annesspublishing.com

If you like the images in this book and would like to investigate using them for publishing, promotions or
advertising, please visit our website www.practicalpictures.com for more information.

Publisher: Joanna Lorenz
Project Editor: Felicity Forster
Photography: Karl Adamson, Edward Allwright, Steve Baxter, Steve Dalton, James Duncan, Michelle Garrett,
Nelson Hargreaves, Amanda Heywood, Janine Hosegood, Don Last, Patrick McLeavey,
Debbie Patterson, Anthony Pickhaver, Peter Williams, Mark Wood, Polly Wreford
Recipes: Carla Capalbo, Jacqueline Clark, Carole Clements, Roz Denny, Nicola Diggins, Joanna Farrow,
Christine France, Silvana Franco, Christine Ingram, Judy Jackson, Elizabeth Lambert Oritz, Wendy Lee,
Janice Murfitt, Jane Stevenson, Laura Washburn, Pamela Westland, Steven Wheeler, Elizabeth Wolf-Cohen
Craft Projects: Michael Ball, Fiona Barnett, Petra Boase, Penny Boylan, Marion Elliot, Tessa Evelegh, Emma Hardy,
Christine Kingdom, Mary Maguire, Terence Moore, Isabel Stanley, Sally Walton, Pamela Westland
Jacket Photography: John Freeman
Editor: Judy Cox
Designer: Ian Sandom
Editorial Reader: Jonathan Marshall
Production Controller: Steve Lang

ETHICAL TRADING POLICY

Because of our ongoing ecological investment programme, you, as our customer, can have the pleasure and reassurance of knowing that a tree
is being cultivated on your behalf to naturally replace the materials used to make the book you are holding. For further information about
this scheme, go to www.annesspublishing.com/trees

© Anness Publishing Limited 2000, 2009

Previously published as *The Complete Book of Christmas*

For all recipes, quantities are given in both metric and imperial measures and, where appropriate, measures are also given in standard cups and
spoons. Follow one set of measures, but not a mixture, because they are not interchangeable. Standard spoon and cup measures are level.
1 tsp = 5ml, 1 tbsp = 15ml, 1 cup = 250ml/8fl oz. Australian standard tablespoons are 20ml. Australian readers should use 3 tsp in place
of 1 tbsp for measuring small quantities of gelatine, cornflour, salt, etc. American pints are 16fl oz/2 cups.
American readers should use 20fl oz/2.5 cups in place of 1 pint when measuring liquids.. Electric oven temperatures in this book are for
conventional ovens. When using a fan oven, the temperature will probably need to be reduced by about 10–20°C/20–40°F.
Since ovens vary, you should check with your manufacturer's instruction book for guidance.
Medium eggs are used unless otherwise stated.

$\mathscr{C}$ONTENTS

INTRODUCTION

Christmas is a rich, warm, magical time of year, when friends and family come together and exchange what the Victorians called "tokens of affection". Many of the customs we observe today date back thousands of years, while others, such as the Christmas tree, were only introduced in the nineteenth century.

One of the main features of our celebrations is a lavish Christmas dinner, to which we may invite the extended family, friends and neighbours. This tradition of hospitality, in the form of a large feast, was, in the past, a Christmas responsibility for those with extensive lands or large households.

The feast was held in the main hall and consisted of two courses, each comprising many dishes. A ceremonial boar's head was usually the most important dish, carried in by the master of the household on a large platter – turkey didn't replace boar and beef as the main Christmas dish in England until late in the nineteenth century.

At the end of the meal, a small group of honoured guests would be invited into a separate room to share exquisite sweetmeats, made of expensive imported sugar and spices. The centrepiece was often a "marchpane", a large disc of iced almond paste, which is the origin of our modern marzipan. This was

ABOVE: *These eye-catching and realistic fruits make perfect gifts for lovers of marzipan.*

RIGHT: *It's great fun watching friends and family discover treats inside their Christmas crackers.*

OPPOSITE: *Who could resist a traditional Christmas dinner with all the trimmings?*

elaborately decorated with three-dimensional figures made of almond paste or cast sugar, painted inscriptions and gold leaf. Sugar-plate, similar to today's fondant icing, was used in many of the dishes for the banquet and was moulded to make visual jokes, such as bacon and eggs.

Evergreens have been gathered for thousands of years, long before the era of Christianity, and brought into the home as decoration in the dark mid-winter. The fact that these green branches seemed to stay alive when other plants and trees had apparently died gave them mystical power, symbolic of ever-lasting life. Ivy, holly, mistletoe and

ABOVE: *One candle of the Advent ring is lighted on each of the four Sundays before Christmas.*

BELOW: *Bringing evergreens indoors creates a wonderfully scented Christmas decoration.*

yew produce berries in winter and this fruit made them even more potent a symbol of fertility for the year ahead. The wreaths and garlands we hang on our doors and walls at Christmas continue this tradition and their circular, never-ending shape is a sign of hospitality and welcome to our guests.

Games were always a popular element of the Christmas festivities. Medieval times were notorious for the Lords of Misrule, when one member of the household was elected to preside as master over the rowdy celebrations, but this gradually turned into more modern parlour games. A popular game in the eighteenth century was Bullet Pudding, which involved a pile of flour heaped into a cone with a bullet on top.

ABOVE: *A memory game such as Pelmanism requires very little preparation: players have to memorize small items from around the home.*

Players attempted to cut slices of the pudding without the bullet falling and the poor person who finally did let it fall had to retrieve it from among the flour with their teeth.

At the end of the eighteenth century and during the first decades of the nineteenth century, Twelfth Night became a major celebration harking back to the Lords of Misrule and involving an elaborate game rather like our modern Charades. Fanny Knight, Jane Austen's niece, described Twelfth Night in 1809: "we had such frightful masks, that it was enough to kill one with laughing at putting them on and altogether it went off very well and quite answered our expectations." Confectioner's shops in London competed with each other to display magnificent Twelfth-cakes decorated with gilded paper, ribbons, laurel leaves and figures made of paper or sugar paste, and for the less well-off there were iced Twelfth-buns. The Twelfth-cakes slowly changed into Christmas cakes, with the "marchpane" or marzipan layer underneath the icing. Today, our only memory of Twelfth Night is that we leave the Christmas decorations up until January 6th.

Christmas was completely transformed during the reign of Queen Victoria into the festival we celebrate today. Prince Albert was so enthusiastic about adopting the German custom for a Christmas tree for his own royal family that the fashion quickly spread and flourished. The simple decorations of the German trees were soon replaced with innumerable small gifts, such as tambourines, drums, trumpets,

paintboxes, dolls and toy furniture. Trays, baskets and "bonbonniers" for sweetmeats were suspended between the wax tapers that lit the tree, the whole effect being quite magical and alluring.

The Christmas card was a purely English invention. Sir Henry Cole, director of the Victoria and Albert Museum in London, hit on the idea of mass-producing cards to save time, and by the 1880s they were a runaway success. Elaborate three-dimensional and joke cards were popular, and ornamental cards were decorated with

ABOVE: *Christmas cards like these began to be mass-produced in the Victorian Era.*

LEFT: *Christmas would not be Christmas for a great many families without a traditional fruit cake. No matter how sumptuous the Christmas dinner, only the most resolute guest will refuse a slice of rich fruit cake covered with almond paste and frosted with royal icing. This traditional Christmas cake glitters with silver dragées – edible confections you can buy in specialist cake shops.*

delicate paper-lace borders and pressed flowers. Victorian cards are widely collected today and can often provide inspiration when you are making your own handmade Christmas cards.

Before the Victorians, presents were given at New Year rather than Christmas. Fresh produce and other food delicacies were the most common gifts, sent by relatives to the town or country where these luxuries were

BELOW: *A beautifully wrapped gift shows that time, thought and great care have been taken to offer someone a bit of extra happiness at Christmas.*

scarce. At the end of the nineteenth century Father Christmas and Santa Claus emerged into popular conscious-ness, originally as two separate figures. Father Christmas had been known since medieval times as the personification of the spirit of Christmas, bringing good-will rather than gifts. Santa Claus was the Dutch-American descendant of St Nicholas, a Christian martyred by the Romans. On the eve of December 6th Dutch children put out shoes or clogs filled with straw for St Nicholas' white horse and if they had been good they

were rewarded in the morning by finding the straw replaced by sweets. If the child had not been good, the straw was untouched and a birch rod was left as a warning. Our modern image of Father Christmas comes largely from a poem written in 1822 by an American, Clement Clarke Moore, called "A Visit from St Nicholas". Meanwhile, the Dutch tradition of children putting out clogs for St Nicholas' horse evolved into hanging a stocking at the foot of the bed.

Christmas today is the ideal time to blend traditional customs with modern materials and ideas from other cultures.

If we decide to make an evergreen wreath or mantelpiece swag, as people have done for centuries, we can add exotic dried fruit, such as pomegranates, to give it a modern twist. Instead of a shop-bought centrepiece for the Christmas table, we can pile up a pyramid of fresh pineapples, grapes and roses, just as the Victorians would have done, except that their table fruits were grown in hothouses staffed by teams of gardeners. We have so many ingredients and materials at our disposal and Christmas is the perfect time to experiment with some of the more unusual ones.

LEFT: *A garland of evergreens adorned with golden wheat stalks and fir cones is the perfect seasonal decoration to transform a room.*

ABOVE: *A vine wreath entwined with dried hops may decorate the home from Thanksgiving through to Christmas.*

Lighting is an important part of the Christmas experience, creating the right mood and accentuating shimmering sequins and silver and gold decorations. Dim the central lights and instead use lamps and candles of all kinds on side tables and windowsills. Place candle arrangements in front of a mirror so that the candlelight is magnified around the room. For real Christmas spirit, nothing beats an impressive chandelier hanging from the ceiling or a candelabra on the dinner table.

ABOVE: *Candles create a special Christmas mood.*

In this age of convenience you will not want to attempt to do everything yourself, but you will certainly gain enormous satisfaction from the personal touches you do make for your family and friends. The traditional spirit of Christmas has always been about sharing good food and hospitality, about decorating the home with symbols of life and cheer in the midst of winter, and this tradition still lives on today.

13

COUNTDOWN TO CHRISTMAS

This at-a-glance timetable will help you to plan and organize a perfect Christmas. Prepare as much as possible ahead so that you enjoy Christmas as much as your family and friends.

THROUGHOUT THE YEAR

Save left-over wool (yarn) and fabric from knitting and sewing projects to use in decorations, such as the Country Angel. Look out for interesting buttons in junkshops and markets to make tree ornaments, such as the Button Garland, and to decorate other designs. Collect seashells when you visit the seaside.

OCTOBER

Make a selection of preserves and relishes, such as Crab-apple and Lavender Jelly or Christmas Chutney, to serve with cold meats and pies.

Pick seedheads, such as poppies and Chinese lanterns (winter cherry) and ornamental grasses, and hang them up to dry.

Stitch embroidery decorations and gifts such as the Needlepoint Pincushion.

ABOVE: *You can make Christmas decorations at any time of year.*

NOVEMBER
First week

Begin to make Christmas tree decorations, using all the non-perishable materials you have collected, such as aluminium foil, papier-mâché and sequins.

ABOVE: *Plum pudding should be made at the end of November.*

Second week
Make Moist and Rich Christmas Cake.

Third week
Feed Christmas Cake.

Fourth week
Make Traditional Christmas Pudding.
Plan the Christmas Dinner: consider the number of guests and their food preferences before you plan the menu.
Order turkey, goose, beef or ham.
Continue to feed Moist and Rich Christmas Cake.
Gather fir cones and twigs in the woods for decorations, such as the Willow Twig Napkin Rings.
Make Advent Calendar.

DECEMBER
First week
Make Light Jewelled Fruit Cake.
Make mincemeat for De Luxe Mincemeat Tart.
Continue to feed Moist and Rich Christmas Cake.

ABOVE: *Preserves can be made well in advance, and, covered with coloured gingham circles and raffia, make lovely gifts.*

Compile complete shopping list for main Christmas meals under headings for different stores or for the various counters at the supermarket.
Continue to make decorations for the Christmas tree and table. Make your own Christmas cards and gift-wrap. Help children to make cards, gifts and decorations, such as the Snowstorm Shaker.

Second week
Make Almond Paste to cover Moist and Rich Christmas Cake. Shop for dry goods, such as rice, dried fruits and flour.
Order special bread requirements. Order milk, cream and other dairy produce.
Make Cumberland Rum Butter. Decorate the Christmas tree. Put up paper chains and other decorations indoors. Pick ever-greens, such as ivy and blue pine (spruce), and make a wreath for the front door.
Make orange pomanders. Decide on the theme for your Christmas table and make place cards, gift bags and crackers to match the tablecloth and napkins.

ABOVE: *Use leftover trimmings from your Christmas tree to make an evergreen wreath for the fireplace.*

ABOVE: *You don't always have to ice your Christmas cake. This one simply has nuts and glacé cherries on top.*

Third week
Make Roquefort Tartlets and other pastry-type cocktail savouries and freeze them. Cover Moist and Rich Christmas Cake with Royal Icing, leave one day, then cover and store. Bake Gingerbread Plaques for edible tree decorations. Make candle pots and candle displays using dried grasses and seedheads.

Fourth week
Shop for chilled ingredients. Buy wines and other festive drinks.
Decorate the mantelpiece with evergreens and candles, as in the Mantelpiece Decoration or Mantelpiece Swag.
Wrap presents in handmade paper and gift boxes and place under the tree. Display decorations with chocolates and candies.

21 DECEMBER
Check thawing time for frozen turkey, duck, beef or other meat. Large turkeys (11.5kg/25lb) need 86 hours (3½ days) to thaw in the refrigerator, or 40 hours at room temperature.

Make a note to take the meat from the freezer at the appropriate time.

23 DECEMBER
Shop for fresh vegetables, if not possible to do so on 24 December. Make Cheese and Spinach Flan and freeze if not making on Christmas Day.
Make Crunchy Apple and Almond Flan.

24 DECEMBER
Shop for fresh vegetables, if possible.
Assemble Christmas Salad and refrigerate dressing separately. Make stuffing for poultry. Cook poultry giblets to make gravy.
Defrost cocktail pastries. Prepare bacon rolls by threading them on to cocktail sticks. Place Santa's Toy Sack on the hearth and hang stockings at the foot of the beds. Fill gift bags for each table setting.
Prepare paper, pens and other materials for the party games.

ABOVE: *Add gingerbread shapes to the tree for a last-minute finishing touch.*

CHRISTMAS DAY

This timetable is planned for Christmas Dinner to be served at 2.00pm.

If you wish to serve it at a different time, adjust the times accordingly.

Choose between turkey with a joint of ham, traditional Victorian goose or beef.

8.30AM Stuff the turkey or goose. Make forcemeat balls with any left-over stuffing, or spoon it into greased ovenproof dishes.
Set the table, using a festive tablecloth and napkins. Add a place card, gift bag or cracker at each place setting. Put a table centrepiece in position, if using.

9.00AM Put a steamer or large saucepan on the cooker and bring water to the boil. Put the Christmas Pudding on to steam.

TO COOK A 4.5KG/10LB TURKEY
9.05AM Set the oven to 220°C/425°F/Gas 7.
9.25AM Put turkey in the oven.
9.45AM Reduce the heat to 180°C/350°F/Gas 4.
Baste the turkey now and at frequent intervals.
12.15PM Put potatoes around the meat.
Remove the foil from the turkey and baste again.
12.45PM Increase the heat to 200°C/400°F/Gas 6.
Put any dishes of stuffing in the oven.
Turn the potatoes.

1.45PM Remove the turkey and potatoes from the oven, put on a heated dish, cover with foil and keep warm.
Make gravy and grill some bacon rolls.

TO COOK A 2KG/4½LB HAM JOINT
EARLY MORNING Bring to the boil, discard the water. Put in a pan with fresh water, boil for 1 hour 35 minutes.
Glaze.
Bake for 15 minutes while the oven is set at 180°C/350°F/Gas 4.
Reheat Cumberland Sauce.

ABOVE: *Set the table early, leaving the rest of the morning free for cooking.*

LEFT: *Try to have most of your ingredients ready to hand before you start preparing the meal.*

To Cook a 5kg/11lb Goose

8.55am Set the oven to 230°C/450°F/Gas 8.

9.15am Put goose in the oven.

9.35am Reduce the heat to 180°C/350°F/Gas 4. Pour off the fat from the roasting tin. Turn the goose and baste it now and at regular intervals.

11.05am Pour off the fat from the roasting tin. Turn the goose and baste it now and at intervals.

12.15pm Put a dish of red cabbage in the oven.

1.25pm Arrange whole apples around the goose, or in a separate dish.

1.35pm Steam some small new potatoes.

1.45pm Turn off the oven. Remove the goose, potatoes and apples from the oven, arrange on a warmed serving dish, cover with foil and keep warm.
Fry any forcemeat balls.
Fry some apple slices.

To Cook a 2.5kg/5.5lb Forerib of Beef

11.00am Set the oven to 230°C/450°F/Gas 8. (for well-done)
or

11.15am (for medium)
or

11.30am (for rare)

11.20am Put beef in the oven.
or

11.35am
or

11.50am

11.30am Reduce the heat to 180°C/350°F/Gas 4.
or

11.45am
or

12noon

12.15pm Put potatoes around meat.

1.45pm Remove the beef and potatoes from oven, put them on a warm serving dish, cover with foil and keep warm.

To Cook a Vegetarian Meal

11.15am Make pastry for the Cheese and Spinach Flan, if not cooking from frozen. (If you are making Christmas Pie, begin 20 minutes earlier to allow time to chill the assembled pie.)

11.45am Put the pastry in the fridge and chill. Prepare the sprouts for Festive Brussels Sprouts.

12.15pm Pre-heat the oven for the Cheese and Spinach Flan. Remove the pastry from the fridge and assemble. (For Christmas Pie, chill the assembled dish for 20 minutes before baking. Preheat the oven 10 minutes before removing the pie from the fridge.)

1.00pm Put flan or pie in the oven.

1.20pm Simmer the chestnuts for 10 minutes.

1.30pm Simmer the sprouts for 5 minutes.

1.35pm Simmer the carrots for 5 minutes.

1.40pm Gently reheat all the vegetables together.

1.45pm Remove the flan or pie from the oven.

2.00pm Serve the first course.

ABOVE: *Before carving, allow the meat to stand for 10 minutes.*

ABOVE: *Serve sauces in bowls handed round separately.*

ABOVE: *Keep vegetables warm by covering them with foil.*

Cooking for Christmas

Entertaining and hospitality are at the heart of the Christmas celebrations and there are many occasions for cooking delicious meals, as well as on Christmas Day itself. Experiment with new recipes from around the world to add to the traditional family favourites and delight your family and friends. Many of the following recipes can be prepared in advance, leaving you free to be with your guests and to enjoy the Christmas season as much as they do. There are also plenty of mouth-watering ideas for buffets and parties, taking you right through to the New Year in great style.

*I*NTRODUCTION

*C*hristmas is the time for high spirits and good cheer, a time for giving and sharing. Food plays an essential part in the festive season – the gathering of friends and family around a table laden with rich and lavish fare goes hand-in-hand with our idea of what Christmas is all about.

While all cooks know the importance of good food at Christmas, they also know that great demands will be made on their time. The secret of a carefree Christmas lies in the planning. Thinking ahead and preparing in advance mean that decision-making under pressure is avoided. As the holiday gets closer,

the list of things to do gets longer – planning meals and menus, shopping for the freshest and choicest ingredients, followed by all the roasting, chopping, kneading and baking. The preparation of Christmas foods is as much a part of Christmas as the eating and can be just as much fun, so include the whole family by delegating tasks. The excitement mounts as each task is crossed off the list.

ABOVE: *Some vegetarian dishes, such as this Chestnut and Mushroom Loaf, can be prepared ahead and frozen before baking.*

LEFT: *A Buck's Fizz is a perfect, refreshing Christmas cocktail.*

LEFT: *Instead of turkey, you could try roast goose served with apples and blanched young asparagus.*

BELOW: *Small bottles of flavoured vinegars make lovely gifts when decorated with herbs and ribbons.*

This section is packed with inspirational ideas and valuable advice to take the cook smoothly through the festive season. There are over 200 recipes to choose from, including all the traditional favourites plus a range of tempting alternative dishes, which are every bit as festive as the customary fare.

Before you start, make sure you have everything you need in front of you, and decide which recipes you will be making. To help you, this section begins with

a handy guide to the basic cookery equipment you will need, as well as a selection of sample menus for Christmas Day and other festive occasions, including a Boxing Day lunch and

a New Year's Eve party. Involve everyone in your cooking preparations, ensuring that Christmas is a happy and memorable one for the cook and the whole family.

RIGHT: *This elaborate Iced Praline Torte is made from a delicious caramel and nut mixture.*

EQUIPMENT

Look after your equipment well and it should never need replacing.

Keep metal cutters, tins and utensils in a warm, dry place.

BAKING SHEET
Good-quality steel sheets without sides are best.

CHOPPING BOARD
Made of wood or acrylic. Acrylic is non-stick and therefore good for working with marzipan.

COOLING RACK
Wide and narrow mesh racks in a variety of sizes are needed for drying and cooling cakes.

CUTTERS
Used to cut out biscuits, pastry or icing shapes.

FLOWER AND LEAF CUTTERS
Tiny metal cutters are available in almost any shape and size.

FLOWER MAT
Invaluable for giving sugar flowers and leaves a natural shape.

GLAZING BRUSH
Used for glazing cakes, brushing pastry and greasing tins.

GRATER
Available with a variety of grating sizes.

JAM FUNNEL
Invaluable for filling jars without spillage or drips.

JELLY BAG
This will ensure that the jelly is crystal clear.

KNIVES
Choose a long-bladed knife for slicing, a medium one for chopping and a small knife for paring.

MEASURING CUPS
For measuring dry ingredients in American cup sizes.

MEASURING JUG
For accurate measuring of liquids.

MEASURING SPOONS
For measuring spoon sizes.

MIXING BOWLS
Keep different sizes, including heatproof bowls, for whisked mixtures and sugar syrup.

MODELLING TOOLS
Used for cake decoration.

PAINTBRUSHES
For painting on food colourings and sticking sugar pieces together.

PALETTE KNIVES
Available with small, medium and large blades.

POTATO PEELER
Used to pare rind from fruit and make chocolate curls.

PRESERVING JAR
Essential for storing preserves.

ROLLING PIN
Used for pastry, dough and icing.

SAUCEPAN
Choose a saucepan with a tight-fitting lid and sturdy bottom.

SIEVE
Used for sieving and straining ingredients and mixtures.

TINS
Good-quality tins will not bend or warp.

jelly bag

measuring jug

modelling tools

measuring cups

tins

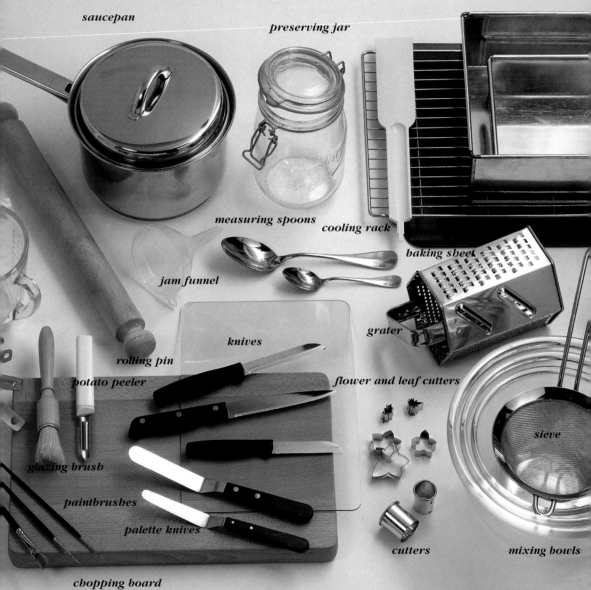

saucepan

tins

preserving jar

measuring spoons

cooling rack

jam funnel

baking sheet

grater

rolling pin

knives

potato peeler

flower and leaf cutters

sieve

glazing brush

paintbrushes

palette knives

cutters

mixing bowls

chopping board

Suggested Menus

Christmas Dinner
for 8 People

Roquefort Tartlets

*Roast Turkey, stuffing balls, chipolata sausages,
bacon rolls and gravy*

Festive Brussels Sprouts

Traditional Christmas Pudding

Vegetarian Christmas Dinner
for 8 People

Christmas Salad with bought mini bread rolls

Cheese and Spinach Flan or Vegetarian Christmas Pie

Garden Vegetable Terrine or Festive Brussels Sprouts

Crunchy Apple and Almond Flan

Boxing Day Lunch
for 12 People

Warm Prawn Salad with bought herb and garlic bread

Baked Gammon with Cumberland Sauce

Vegetable Gnocchi

De Luxe Mincemeat Tart

Hot Fork Supper
for 12 People

Roquefort Tartlets and Filo Vegetable Pie

Chicken with Red Wine Vinegar

Sweet and Sour Red Cabbage

Iced Praline Torte and Ruby Fruit Salad

Cold Buffet Lunch
for 12 People

Layered Salmon Terrine

Fillet of Beef with Ratatouille

Turkey Rice Salad

*Ginger Trifle and Almond
Mincemeat Tartlets*

New Year's Eve Party
for 8 People

Smoked Salmon Salad

Roast Goose with Caramelized Apples

Gratin Dauphinois and Sweet and Sour Red Cabbage

Chocolate and Chestnut Yule Log

Festive Starters

*C*hristmas is all about anticipation: the people you will
see, the gifts you will receive and, of course, the Christmas
meals you eat together. A Christmas meal is like a good novel –
a tempting starter that builds to an exciting middle and leads on
to a satisfying ending. All of the festive starters in this chapter will
tempt the senses, and the trick is to make a good match between
the colours, textures and richness of all your courses. Virtually
any will complement the traditional turkey, but keep in mind
Pumpkin Soup for a beautiful colour contrast, or Oriental Duck
Consommé for an exotic touch. Farmhouse Pâté will balance
lighter fish or chicken lunches, while Grilled Brie and Walnuts
or Roquefort Tartlets will suit beef or lamb dishes.

CARROT AND CORIANDER SOUP

Nearly all root vegetables make excellent soups as they purée well and have an earthy flavour which complements the sharper flavours of herbs and spices. Carrots are particularly versatile, and this simple soup is elegant in both flavour and appearance.

INGREDIENTS

450g/1lb carrots, preferably young and tender
15ml/1 tbsp sunflower oil
40g/1½oz/3 tbsp butter
1 onion, chopped
1 celery stick, plus 2–3 pale leafy celery tops
2 small potatoes, chopped
1 litre/1¾ pints/4 cups chicken stock
10–15ml/2–3 tsp ground coriander
15ml/1 tbsp chopped fresh coriander
200ml/7fl oz/⅞ cup milk
salt and freshly ground black pepper

Serves 4–6

1 Trim the carrots, peel if necessary and cut into chunks. Heat the oil and 25g/1oz/2 tbsp of the butter in a large flameproof, casserole or heavy-based saucepan and fry the onion over a gentle heat for 3–4 minutes until slightly softened, but not browned.

2 Cut the celery stick into slices. Add the celery and potatoes to the onion in the pan, cook for a few minutes and then add the carrots. Fry over a gentle heat for 3–4 minutes, stirring, and then cover. Reduce the heat and sweat for 10 minutes. Shake the pan occasionally so that the vegetables do not stick.

3 Add the stock, bring to the boil and then partially cover and simmer for a further 8–10 minutes until the carrots and potatoes are tender.

4 Remove 6–8 tiny celery leaves for use as a garnish and finely chop the remaining celery tops (about 15ml/1 tbsp once chopped). Melt the remaining butter in a small saucepan and fry the ground coriander for about 1 minute, stirring constantly.

5 Reduce the heat and add the finely chopped celery and fresh coriander and fry over a gentle heat for about 1 minute. Set aside.

6 Process the soup in a food processor or blender until smooth and pour into a clean saucepan. Stir in the milk, coriander mixture and seasoning. Heat gently, taste and adjust the seasoning as necessary. Serve the soup garnished with the reserved celery leaves.

> COOK'S TIP
>
> *For a more piquant flavour, add a little lemon juice to the soup just before serving.*

CREAM OF MUSHROOM SOUP

A good mushroom soup makes the most of the subtle and sometimes rather elusive flavour of mushrooms.

Button mushrooms are used here for their pale colour; chestnut or, better still, field mushrooms give

a fuller flavour but will turn the soup a darker shade of brown.

INGREDIENTS

275g/10oz/3¼ cups button mushrooms
15ml/1 tbsp sunflower oil
40g/1½oz/3 tbsp butter
1 small onion, finely chopped
15ml/1 tbsp plain flour
450ml/¾ pint/1¾ cups vegetable stock
450ml/¾ pint/1¾ cups milk
pinch of dried basil
30–45ml/2–3 tbsp single cream (optional)
fresh basil leaves, to garnish
salt and freshly ground black pepper

Serves 4

1 Pull the mushroom caps away from the stalks. Finely slice the caps and finely chop the stalks, keeping the two piles separate.

2 Heat the sunflower oil and half the butter in a heavy-based saucepan and add the chopped onion, mushroom stalks and ½–¾ of the sliced mushroom caps. Fry for about 1–2 minutes, stirring frequently, and then cover and sweat over a gentle heat for 6–7 minutes, stirring occasionally.

3 Stir in the flour and cook for about 1 minute. Gradually add the stock and milk to make a smooth, thin sauce. Add the basil, and season with salt and pepper. Bring to the boil and then simmer, partly covered, for 15 minutes.

4 Allow the soup to cool slightly and then pour into a food processor or blender and process until smooth. Melt the remaining butter in a heavy-based frying pan, and fry the remaining mushrooms over a gentle heat for 3–4 minutes until they are just tender.

5 Pour the soup into a large, clean saucepan and stir in the sliced mushrooms. Heat until very hot but not boiling and add salt and ground black pepper to taste. Add a little of the single cream, if using. Ladle the soup into 4 warmed bowls and serve the soup at once, sprinkled with the fresh basil leaves.

Pumpkin Soup

The sweet flavour of pumpkin is good in soups, teaming well with other more savoury

ingredients such as potatoes to make a warm and comforting dish.

INGREDIENTS
15ml/1 tbsp sunflower oil
25g/1oz/2 tbsp butter
1 large onion, sliced
675g/1½lb pumpkin, cut into large chunks
450g/1lb potatoes, sliced
600ml/1 pint/2½ cups vegetable stock
good pinch of nutmeg
5ml/1 tsp chopped fresh tarragon
600ml/1 pint/2½ cups milk
about 5–10ml/1–2 tsp lemon juice
salt and freshly ground black pepper

Serves 4–6

1 Heat the sunflower oil and butter in a frying pan and fry the onion for 4–5 minutes until softened. Stir frequently.

2 Transfer the onions to a saucepan and add the pumpkin and potato. Stir well, then cover with the lid and sweat over a low heat for about 10 minutes until the vegetables are almost tender. Stir the vegetables occasionally to prevent them from sticking to the pan.

3 Stir in the stock, nutmeg, tarragon and seasoning. Bring the liquid to the boil and then simmer for about 10 minutes until the vegetables are completely tender.

4 Allow the liquid to cool slightly away from the heat, then pour into a food processor or blender and process until smooth. Pour back into a clean saucepan and add the milk. Heat gently and then taste, adding the lemon juice and extra seasoning if necessary. Serve piping hot with crusty brown bread rolls.

COOK'S TIP

Pumpkins are readily available in supermarkets throughout the winter months. Other unusual vegetables, such as squashes, can also be used to make tempting Christmas soups.

ORIENTAL DUCK CONSOMMÉ

Christmas need not be about just traditional European flavours. This soup is both light

and rich at the same time and has intriguing flavours of Southeast Asia.

INGREDIENTS

1 duck carcass (raw or cooked), plus 2 legs or any giblets, trimmed of fat
1 large onion, unpeeled, with root end trimmed
2 carrots, cut into 5cm/2in pieces
1 parsnip, cut into 5cm/2in pieces
1 leek, cut into 5cm/2in pieces
2–4 garlic cloves, crushed
2.5cm/1in piece fresh root ginger, peeled and sliced
15ml/1 tbsp black peppercorns
4–6 thyme sprigs, or 5ml/1 tsp dried thyme
1 small bunch coriander (6–8 sprigs), leaves and stems separated

For the Garnish
1 small carrot
1 small leek, halved lengthways
4–6 shiitake mushrooms, thinly sliced
soy sauce
2 spring onions, thinly sliced
watercress or shredded Chinese leaves
freshly ground black pepper

Serves 4

1 Put the duck carcass, with the legs or giblets, the onion, carrots, parsnip, leek and garlic in a large saucepan or flameproof casserole. Add the ginger, peppercorns, thyme and coriander stems, cover with cold water and bring to the boil over a medium-high heat. Skim off any foam on the surface.

2 Reduce the heat and simmer gently for 1½–2 hours, then strain through a muslin-lined sieve into a bowl, discarding the bones and vegetables. Cool the stock and chill for several hours or overnight. Skim off any congealed fat and carefully blot the surface with kitchen paper to remove any traces of fat.

3 For the garnish, cut the carrot and leek into 5cm/2in pieces and then lengthways in thin slices. Stack and slice into thin julienne strips. Place in a saucepan with the mushrooms. Pour over the stock and add a few dashes of soy sauce and some pepper.

4 Bring to the boil over a medium heat, skimming off any foam that rises to the surface. Adjust the seasoning. Stir in the spring onions and watercress or Chinese leaves. Serve the consommé sprinkled with the coriander leaves.

Warm Prawn Salad with Spicy Marinade

Most of the ingredients for this salad can be prepared in advance, but wait until just before serving to cook

the prawns and bacon. Spoon them over the salad and serve with hot herb and garlic bread.

INGREDIENTS

225g/8oz/2 cups large, cooked, shelled prawns
225g/8oz smoked streaky bacon, chopped
mixed lettuce leaves, washed and dried
30ml/2 tbsp snipped fresh chives

For the Lemon and Chilli Marinade
1 garlic clove, crushed
finely grated rind of 1 lemon
15ml/1 tbsp lemon juice
60ml/4 tbsp olive oil
1.5ml/1¼ tsp chilli paste, or a large pinch dried ground chilli
15ml/1 tbsp light soy sauce
salt and freshly ground black pepper

Serves 8

1 In a glass bowl, mix the prawns with the garlic, lemon rind and juice, 45ml/3 tbsp oil, the chilli paste and soy sauce. Season with salt and pepper. Cover with clear film and leave to marinate for at least one hour.

2 Gently cook the bacon in the remaining oil until crisp. Drain well.

3 Tear the lettuce into bite-size pieces and arrange on plates.

4 Just before serving, put the prawns with their marinade into a frying pan, bring to the boil, add the bacon and cook for one minute. Spoon over the salad and sprinkle with snipped chives.

SMOKED SALMON SALAD

This recipe works equally well using smoked trout in place of salmon. The dressing can be made in

advance and stored in the fridge until you are ready to eat.

INGREDIENTS

4 thin slices white bread
oil, for frying
paprika, for dusting
mixed lettuce leaves
25g/1oz Parmesan cheese
225g/8oz smoked salmon, thinly sliced
1 lemon, cut into wedges

For the Vinaigrette Dressing
90ml/6 tbsp olive oil
30ml/2 tbsp red wine vinegar
1 garlic clove, crushed
5ml/1 tsp Dijon mustard
5ml/1 tsp runny honey
15ml/1 tbsp chopped fresh parsley
2.5ml/½ tsp fresh thyme
10ml/2 tsp capers, chopped
salt and freshly ground black pepper

Serves 8

1 First make the dressing. Put all the ingredients into a screw-top jar and shake the jar well. Season to taste.

2 With a small star-shaped cutter, stamp out shapes from the bread. Heat 2.5cm/1in oil in a shallow frying pan until the oil is almost smoking (test it with a cube of bread: it should sizzle on the surface and brown within 30 seconds). Fry the croûtons in batches until golden brown. Remove the croûtons and drain on kitchen paper. Dust with paprika and leave to cool.

3 Wash the lettuce, dry the leaves and tear them into small bite-size pieces. Wrap the leaves in a clean, damp tea towel and keep the lettuce in the fridge until ready to serve.

4 Slice the Parmesan cheese into wafer-thin flakes with a vegetable peeler. Put the flakes into a dish and cover with clear film.

5 Cut the salmon into 1cm/½in strips no more than 5cm/2in long.

6 Arrange the lettuce on individual plates, scatter over the Parmesan flakes and arrange the salmon strips on top. Shake the dressing vigorously again and spoon over the salad. Scatter over the croûtons and place a lemon wedge on the side of each plate.

Christmas Salad

A light and simple first course that can be prepared ahead and assembled just before serving.

INGREDIENTS

Mixed red and green lettuce leaves
2 sweet pink grapefruit
1 large or 2 small avocados, peeled and
cubed

For the Dressing
90ml/6 tbsp light olive oil
30ml/2 tbsp red wine vinegar
1 garlic clove, crushed
5ml/1 tsp Dijon mustard
salt and freshly ground black pepper

For the Caramelized Orange Peel
4 oranges
50g/2oz/4 tbsp caster sugar
60ml/4 tbsp cold water

Serves 8

1 For the caramelized peel, using a vegetable peeler, remove the rind from the oranges in thin strips and reserve the fruit. Scrape away the white pith from the rind with a sharp knife, and cut the rind in fine shreds.

2 Put the sugar and water in a small pan and heat gently until the sugar has dissolved. Then add the shreds of orange rind, increase the heat and boil steadily for 5 minutes, until the rind is tender. Using two forks, remove the orange rind from the syrup and spread it out on a wire rack to dry. (This can be done the day before.) Reserve the syrup to add to the dressing.

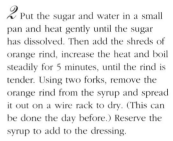

3 Wash and dry the lettuce and tear the leaves into bite-size pieces. Wrap them in a damp tea towel and chill. Over a bowl, cut the oranges and grapefruit into segments, removing the pith.

4 Put the dressing ingredients into a screw-top jar and shake vigorously to emulsify the dressing. Add the reserved orange-flavoured syrup and adjust the seasoning to taste. Arrange the salad ingredients on individual plates with the avocados, spoon over the dressing and scatter on the caramelized peel.

Wild Mushroom Polenta

The wild mushrooms used here have a wonderful flavour and texture, which combine well

with polenta to make an unusual starter dish or light snack.

INGREDIENTS

450g/1lb small new potatoes
1.3 litres/2¼ pints/5½ cups light
vegetable stock
175g/6oz young carrots, trimmed and
peeled
175g/6oz sugar snap peas
50g/2oz/4 tbsp unsalted butter
75g/3oz Caesar's mushrooms or
hedgehog fungus, trimmed and sliced
5 horn of plenty fungus, fresh, chopped
250g/9oz/1½ cups fine
polenta or cornmeal
2 shallots or 1 small onion, chopped
2 fist-size pieces of cauliflower fungus or
15g/½oz/¼ cup, dried
115g/4oz chicken of the woods, trimmed
and sliced
150ml/¼ pint/⅔ cup single cream
3 egg yolks
10ml/2 tsp lemon juice
salt and cayenne pepper

Serves 4

1 Lightly oil a 23cm/9in loaf tin and line with a sheet of greaseproof paper. Set aside. Cover the potatoes with boiling water in a pan, add a pinch of salt and cook for 20 minutes. Bring the vegetable stock to the boil, add the carrots and peas and cook for 3–4 minutes. Remove the vegetables with a slotted spoon and keep warm. Add 25g/1oz/2 tbsp of the butter and all of the mushrooms to the stock and simmer for 5 minutes.

2 Introduce the polenta to the saucepan in a steady stream and stir for 2–3 minutes until thickened. Turn the polenta into the prepared tin, cover and allow to become firm.

3 For the sauce, melt the remaining butter, add the shallots or onion and cook gently. Add the cauliflower fungus, cut into bite-size pieces, with the chicken of the woods, and cook for 2–3 minutes. Add the cream and the reserved cooked vegetables and simmer to eliminate any moisture.

4 Remove from the heat, stir in the egg yolks and allow residual heat to slightly thicken the sauce. The sauce must not boil at this stage. Add the lemon juice, then season with salt and a dash of cayenne pepper.

5 To serve, turn the warm polenta out onto a board, slice with a wet knife and arrange on four warmed serving plates. Spoon the mushroom and vegetable sauce over the polenta. If preferred, the polenta loaf can be prepared in advance and stored in the freezer.

Goat's Cheese Soufflé

Make sure everyone is seated before the soufflé comes out of the oven because it will begin to deflate-almost

immediately. This recipe works equally well with strong blue cheeses such as Roquefort.

INGREDIENTS

25g/1oz/2 tbsp butter
25g/1oz/2 tbsp plain flour
175ml/6fl oz/¾ cup milk
1 bay leaf
freshly grated nutmeg
grated Parmesan cheese, for sprinkling
40g/1½oz herb and garlic soft cheese
150g/5oz firm goat's cheese, diced
6 egg whites, at room temperature
1.5ml/¼ tsp cream of tartar
salt and freshly ground black pepper

Serves 4–6

1 Melt the butter in a heavy saucepan. Add the flour and cook until golden, stirring. Pour in half the milk, stirring vigorously until smooth, then stir in the remaining milk and add the bay leaf. Season with a pinch of salt and plenty of pepper and nutmeg. Reduce the heat, cover and simmer for about 5 minutes, stirring occasionally.

2 Preheat the oven to 190°C/375°F/ Gas 5. Generously butter a 1.5 litre/ 2½ pint/6¼ cups soufflé dish and sprinkle with Parmesan cheese.

3 Remove the sauce from the heat and discard the bay leaf. Stir in both cheeses until melted.

4 In a clean, grease-free bowl, using an electric mixer or balloon whisk, beat the egg whites slowly until they become frothy. Add the cream of tartar, increase the speed and continue beating until they form soft peaks, then stiffer peaks.

5 Stir a spoonful of beaten egg white into the cheese sauce to lighten it, then pour the cheese sauce over the remaining whites. Using a metal spoon, gently fold the sauce into the whites until the mixtures are just combined, cutting down to the bottom, then along the side of the bowl and up to the top.

6 Gently pour the soufflé mixture into the prepared dish and bake for 25–30 minutes until puffed and golden brown. Serve at once.

GRILLED BRIE AND WALNUTS

This unusual cheese recipe will impress your guests as it looks as though it has been made

professionally. You'll be pleased to know that it requires almost no preparation.

INGREDIENTS

*15g/½oz/1 tbsp butter, at room
temperature
5ml/1 tsp Dijon mustard
675g/1½lb wheel of Brie or
Camembert cheese
25g/1oz/¼ cup chopped walnuts
French stick, sliced and toasted to serve*

Serves About 16–20

2 Sprinkle the surface with the walnuts and grill for 2–3 minutes longer until the nuts are golden. Serve immediately with the French bread toasts. Allow your guests to help themselves as the whole grilled Brie makes an attractive centrepiece.

1 Preheat the grill. In a small bowl, cream together the butter and Dijon mustard, and spread evenly over the surface of the cheese. Transfer the cheese to a flameproof serving plate, and grill 12–15cm/4–6in from the heat for 3–4 minutes until the top just begins to bubble.

ROQUEFORT AND CUCUMBER MOUSSE

This refreshingly cool mousse makes a perfect starter to prepare ahead and store in

the fridge. If you prefer, other blue-veined French cheeses, such as Bleu d'Auvergne

or Fourme d'Ambert, may be used instead of Roquefort.

INGREDIENTS

18cm/7in piece cucumber
10ml/2 tsp powdered gelatine
75ml/5 tbsp cold water
100g/3½oz Roquefort cheese
200g/7oz full-, medium- or low-fat soft
cheese
45ml/3 tbsp crème fraîche or soured
cream
cayenne or white pepper
seedless red and green grapes and fresh
mint leaves, to garnish

Serves 6

1 Using a sharp kitchen knife, cut the cucumber lengthways into quarters. Remove the seeds and cut the cucumber strips into 2.5cm/1in pieces. Chop the cucumber pieces finely.

2 Sprinkle the gelatine over the cold water in a small heatproof bowl. Let the gelatine stand to soften for about 2 minutes, then place the bowl in a shallow pan of simmering water. Heat until the gelatine is dissolved, stirring occasionally.

3 In a mixing bowl (or in a food processor fitted with a metal blade) mix both types of cheese with the crème fraîche or cream until smooth. Add the dissolved gelatine and blend. Add the chopped cucumber to the bowl, mixing well without reducing the cucumber to a purée. Season to taste with cayenne or white pepper.

4 Rinse a 1.5 litre/2½ pint/6¼ cups dish or mould with cold water to prevent the mousse from sticking to the mould when turned out. Carefully spoon the mixture into the dish or mould and tap gently to remove air bubbles. Chill for 4–6 hours or overnight until well set.

5 To turn out, run a knife around the edge of the dish or mould, dip in hot water for 10–15 seconds and wipe the wet base. Place a large plate over the top of the dish and invert both together, shaking firmly to release the mousse. Garnish with the grapes and fresh mint leaves.

COOK'S TIP

The delicate taste and elegant appearance mean that this mousse would make a great addition to any buffet supper or party menu.

FOIE GRAS PÂTÉ IN FILO CUPS

This is an extravagantly rich hors d'oeuvre so it is perfect for special occasions such as Christmas Day.

Any other fine liver pâté may be used if foie gras is unavailable.

INGREDIENTS

3–6 sheets fresh or defrosted filo pastry
40g/1½oz/3 tbsp. butter, melted
225g/8oz tinned foie gras pâté or other
fine liver pâté, at room temperature
50g/2oz/4 tbsp butter, softened
30–45ml/2–3 tbsp Cognac or brandy
(optional)
chopped pistachios, to garnish

Makes about 24

COOK'S TIP

The pâté and pastry are best eaten soon after preparation. If preparing ahead and refrigerating, be sure to bring back to room temperature before serving.

1 Preheat the over to 200°C/400°F/ Gas 6. Grease a bun tray with 24 x 4cm/1½in cups. Stack the filo sheets on a work surface and cut into 6cm/ 2½in squares. Cover with a damp towel to prevent the pastry from drying out.

2 Keeping the rest of the filo squares covered, place one square on a work surface and brush lightly with melted butter, then turn over and brush the other side. Butter a second square and place it over the first at an angle. Butter a third square and place at a different angle over the first two sheets to form an uneven edge.

3 Press the pastry layers into the cups of the bun tray. Continue with the remaining pastry and butter until all the cups are filled.

4 Bake the filo cups for 4–6 minutes until crisp and golden, then remove and cool in the pan for 5 minutes. Carefully remove each filo cup to a wire rack and cool completely.

5 In a small bowl, beat the pâté with the softened butter until smooth and well blended. Add the Cognac or brandy to taste, if using. Spoon into a piping bag fitted with a medium star nozzle and pipe a swirl into each cup. Sprinkle with pistachio nuts. Refrigerate until ready to serve.

CHICKEN LIVER MOUSSE

This mousse makes an elegant yet easy first course. The onion marmalade make a delicious accompaniment, along with a salad of chicory or other bitter leaves.

INGREDIENTS

450g/1lb chicken livers
175g/6oz/¾ cup butter, diced
1 small onion, finely chopped
1 garlic clove, finely chopped
2.5ml/½ tsp dried thyme
30–45ml/2–3 tbsp brandy
salt and freshly ground black pepper
green salad, to serve

For the Onion Marmalade
25g/1oz/2 tbsp butter
450g/1lb red onions, thinly sliced
1 garlic clove, finely chopped
2.5ml/½ tsp dried thyme
30–45ml/2–3 tbsp red wine vinegar
15–30ml/1–2 tbsp clear honey
40g/1½oz/¼ cup sultanas

Serves 6–8

1 Use a sharp knife to trim the chicken livers, cutting off any green spots and removing any filaments or fat.

2 In a heavy-based frying pan, melt 25g/1oz/2 tbsp of the butter. Add the finely chopped onion and cook for 5–7 minutes over a gentle heat until soft and golden, then add the garlic to the pan and cook for 1 minute more. Increase the heat and add the chicken livers, thyme, salt and freshly ground black pepper. Cook for 3–5 minutes until the livers are coloured, stirring frequently; the livers should remain pink inside, but not raw. Add the brandy, stirring, and cook for a further minute.

3 Using a slotted spoon, transfer the livers to a food processor fitted with a metal blade. Pour in the cooking juices and process for 1 minute, or until smooth, scraping down the sides once. With the machine running, add the remaining butter, a few pieces at a time, until it is incorporated.

4 Press the mousse mixture through a fine sieve with a wooden spoon or rubber spatula until it has a creamy smooth consistency.

5 Line a 475ml/16fl oz/2 cup loaf tin with clear film, smoothing out as many wrinkles as possible. Pour the mousse mixture into the lined tin. Cool, then cover and chill until firm.

6 To make the onion marmalade, heat the butter in a frying pan, add the onions and cook for 20 minutes until softened and just coloured. Stir in the chopped garlic, thyme, vinegar, honey and sultanas and cook, covered, for 10–15 minutes, stirring occasionally, until the onions are completely soft and jam-like. Spoon into a serving bowl and allow to cool to room temperature.

7 To serve, dip the loaf tin into hot water for 5 seconds, wipe dry and invert. Lift off the tin, peel off the clear film and smooth the surface with a palette knife. Serve sliced, with the onion marmalade and a green salad.

Farmhouse Pâté

This pâté is full of flavour and can be cut into slices for easy serving. You can make the pâté in

individual dishes or in a larger container, if you are expecting an unspecified number of guests.

INGREDIENTS

8 slices rindless streaky bacon
2 x 175g/6oz chicken breasts
225g/8oz chicken livers
1 onion, chopped
1 garlic clove, crushed
2.5ml/½ tsp salt
2.5ml/½ tsp freshly ground black pepper
5ml/1 tsp anchovy essence
5ml/1 tsp ground mace
15g/1 tbsp chopped fresh oregano
75g/3oz/1 cup fresh white breadcrumbs
1 egg
30ml/2 tbsp brandy
150ml/¼ pt/⅔ cup chicken stock
10ml/2 tsp gelatine

To Garnish
strips of pimento and black olives

Makes 450g/1lb

1 Preheat the oven to 160°C/325°F/
Gas 3. Press the bacon slices flat with
a knife to stretch them slightly. Line
the base and sides of each dish with
bacon and neatly trim any excess off
the edges.

2 Place the chicken breasts and
livers, onion and garlic into a food
processor. Process until smooth.
Add the salt, pepper, anchovy
essence, mace, oregano, breadcrumbs,
egg and brandy. Process until smooth.

3 Divide the mixture between the
dishes. Cover the dishes with a double
thickness of foil and stand them in a
roasting tin. Add enough hot water to
come halfway up the sides of the tin.

4 Bake in the centre of the oven for
1 hour or until firm. Remove the foil to
release the steam. Place a weight on top
of each dish to flatten until cool.

5 Pour the juices from each dish into a
measuring jug and make up to 150ml/
¼ pint/⅔ cup with chicken stock. Heat in
a pan until boiling. Blend the gelatine
with 30ml/2 tbsp water and pour into
the stock, stirring. Allow to cool.

6 Garnish the pâté when cold, then
spoon the gelatine mixture over the top.
Chill until set. Cover with clear film.

BAKED EGGS WITH CREAMY LEEKS

This wonderful recipe can also be prepared using other vegetables, such as puréed spinach

or ratatouille, as a base. For such an elegant dish, it needs very little preparation time.

INGREDIENTS

15g/½oz/1 tbsp butter, plus extra for
greasing
225g/½lb, about 2 cups, small leeks, thinly
sliced
75–90ml/5–6 tbsp whipping cream
freshly grated nutmeg
4 eggs
salt and freshly ground black pepper

Serves 4

1 Preheat the oven to 190°C/375°F/
Gas 5. Generously butter the base
and sides of four ramekins or
individual soufflé dishes.

2 Melt the butter in a small frying pan
and cook the leeks over a medium
heat, stirring frequently, until softened
but not browned.

3 Add 45ml/3 tbsp of the whipping
cream and cook over a gentle heat
for about 5 minutes until the leeks are
very soft and the cream has thickened
a little. Add plenty of salt, freshly
ground black pepper and nutmeg
to the frying pan, to season.

4 Arrange the ramekins or soufflé
dishes in a small roasting tin and divide
the leeks among them. Break an egg
into each, spoon 5–10ml/1–2 tsp of
the remaining cream over each egg
and season lightly.

5 Pour boiling water into the baking
dish to come halfway up the sides of
the ramekins or soufflé dishes. Bake
in the preheated oven for about 10
minutes, until the egg whites are set
and the yolks are still quite soft, or a
little longer if you prefer your eggs
more well cooked.

ROQUEFORT TARTLETS

These can be made in shallow tartlet tins to serve hot as a first course. You could also make them

in tiny cocktail tins, to serve warm as bite-size snacks with a drink before a meal.

INGREDIENTS

175g/6oz/1½ cups plain flour
large pinch of salt
115g/4oz/½ cup butter
1 egg yolk
30ml/2 tbsp cold water

For the Filling
15g/½oz/1 tbsp butter
15g/1½oz/1 tbsp flour
150ml/¼ pint/⅔ cup milk
115g/4oz Roquefort cheese, crumbled
150ml/¼ pint/⅔ cup double cream
2.5ml/½ tsp dried mixed herbs
3 egg yolks
salt and freshly ground black pepper

Makes 12

1 To make the pastry, sift the flour and salt into a large mixing bowl and rub the butter into the flour until it resembles breadcrumbs. Mix the egg yolk with the water and stir into the flour to make a soft dough. Knead until smooth, wrap in clear film and chill for 30 minutes.

2 Melt the butter, stir in the flour and then the milk. Boil to thicken, stirring continuously. Off the heat, beat in the cheese and season. Allow to cool. Bring the cream and herbs to the boil. Reduce the mixture to 30ml/2 tbsp. Beat into the sauce with the egg yolks.

3 Preheat the oven to 190°C/375°F/ Gas 5. On a lightly floured work surface, roll out the pastry 3mm/⅛in thick. Stamp out rounds with a fluted cutter and use to line the tartlet tins.

4 Divide the filling between the tartlets so they are two-thirds full. Stamp out smaller fluted rounds or star shapes and lay on top of each tartlet. Bake for 20–25 minutes, or until golden brown.

Main Dinners

*F*or purists, there can be no other main course than
Turkey on Christmas Day, but an equally festive
main dish of pheasant, goose or duck will provide such
an attractive centrepiece that even traditionalists at the
table won't object. And who's to say that the seasonal
celebration can't be marked with a seafood alternative
like Lobster Thermidor or Sea Bass with Citrus Fruit?
Of course, venison, lamb or pork tenderloin all have their
appeal, so the choice may be a difficult one. If you're
not having a big crowd for dinner, try adding together main
dishes such as Roast Beef with Roasted Sweet Peppers or Chicken
with Morels, and see which has less left over afterwards.

ROASTING AND CARVING A TURKEY

Allow about 350g/8 oz of dressed (plucked and oven-ready) bird per head. A good-sized turkey to buy

for Christmas is 4.5kg/10lb. This will serve about 12 people, with leftovers for the following day.

Thaw a frozen turkey, still in its bag, on a plate at room temperature (18–21°C/65–70°F) until the legs are flexible and there are no ice crystals in the cavity of the bird. Remove the giblets from the cavity as soon as the bird has thawed enough.

Oven-ready weight	Thawing time	Number of servings	Cooking time
3.5kg/8lb	18 hours	8–10 people	2½–3½ hours
4.5kg/10lb	19 hours	12–14 people	3½–4 hours
5.5kg/12lb	20 hours	16–18 people	3¼–4½ hours
6.5kg/14lb	24 hours	18–20 people	4–5 hours

3 Carve the leg into slices.

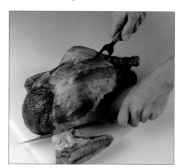

4 Remove the wing, cutting through the joint in the same way as for the leg.

These times apply to a turkey weighed after stuffing and at room temperature. Set the oven to 220°C/425°F/Gas 7. Cook the turkey, covered with butter and bacon rashers and loosely covered with foil, for 20 minutes, then reduce the temperature to 180°C/350°F/Gas 4. Increase the heat to 200°C/400°F/Gas 6 for the last hour of the specified cooking time.

To test whether the turkey is fully cooked, push a skewer into the thickest part of the leg and press the flesh; the juices should run clear and be free from any blood. The legs take longer than the breast to cook; keep the breast covered with foil until the legs are cooked. The foil can be removed for the final hour of cooking to brown and crisp the skin. The turkey should be basted with the juices from the roasting tin every hour of cooking.

Plan for the turkey to be ready 15–20 minutes before you want to serve dinner. Remove it from the oven and allow the flesh to relax before carving it.

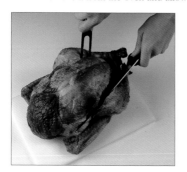

1 First remove the leg by cutting the skin between the breast and leg. Press the leg flat, to expose the joint. Cut between the bones through the joint.

2 Cut the leg in two, through the joint.

5 Carve the breast in thin slices, working your way from the front to the back of the breast.

Making Bacon Rolls

If you want to wrap stoned prunes or chicken livers inside each rasher,

cut the bacon rashers in half after stretching them.

1 Remove the rind from the rashers of bacon and stretch them with the back of a large knife.

2 Roll the rashers up neatly.

3 Skewer the bacon rolls with cocktail sticks. Grill the rolls until crisp, turning them halfway through cooking.

Roasting Potatoes

Floury potatoes make the best crisp roast potatoes. Garlic or rosemary can be added to the oil,

to flavour the potatoes during cooking.

1 Preheat the oven to 200°C/400°F/ Gas 6. Peel the potatoes and cut large ones in half. Parboil them for 10 minutes. Drain. Score the surface of each potato with a fork. Roll them in flour and tap them to remove any excess. Heat 2.5cm/1in olive oil in a shallow roasting tin until smoking hot.

2 Put the potatoes in the hot oil and baste them to coat them in oil. Roast for about an hour.

3 Baste and turn the potatoes twice during cooking. Drain them on kitchen paper and sprinkle them with salt.

ROAST GOOSE WITH CARAMELIZED APPLES

Choose a young goose with a pliable breast bone for the best possible flavour.

INGREDIENTS

*4.5–5.5kg/10–12lb goose, with giblets
(thawed overnight, if frozen)
salt and freshly ground black pepper*

For the Apple and Nut Stuffing
*225g/8oz/2 cups prunes
150ml/¼ pint/⅔ cup port or red wine
675g/1½lb cooking apples, peeled, cored
and cubed
1 large onion, chopped
4 celery sticks, sliced
15ml/1 tbsp mixed dried herbs
finely grated rind of 1 orange
goose liver, chopped
450g/1lb pork sausagemeat
115g/4oz/1 cup chopped pecans
2 eggs*

For the Caramelized Apples
*50g/2oz/4 tbsp butter
60ml/4 tbsp redcurrant jelly
30ml/2 tbsp red wine vinegar
8 small dessert apples, peeled and cored*

For the Gravy
*30ml/2 tbsp plain flour
600ml/1 pint/2½ cups giblet stock
juice of 1 orange*

Serves 8

1 The day before you want to cook
the goose, soak the prunes in the port
or the red wine. After the soaking time,
remove each prune from the marinade
and stone each one and cut it into four
pieces. Reserve the port or red wine
and set aside.

2 The next day, mix the prunes with
all the remaining stuffing ingredients
and season well. Moisten with half the
reserved port.

3 Preheat the oven to 200°C/400°F/
Gas 6. Stuff the neck-end of the goose,
tucking the flap of the skin under and
securing it with a small skewer.
Remove the excess fat from the cavity
and pack it with the stuffing. Tie the
legs together to hold them in place.

4 Weigh the stuffed goose to calculate
the cooking time: allow 15 minutes for
each 450g/1lb. Put the bird on a rack
in a roasting tin and rub the tin with
salt. Prick the skin all over to help the
fat run out. Roast for 30 minutes, then
reduce the heat to 180°C/350°F/Gas 4
and roast for the remaining cooking
time. Pour off any fat produced during
cooking into a bowl. The goose is
cooked if the juices run clear when the
thickest part of the thigh is pierced with
a skewer. Pour a little cold water over
the breast to crisp the skin.

5 Meanwhile, prepare the apples. Melt
the butter, redcurrant jelly and vinegar
in a small roasting tin or a shallow
ovenproof dish. Put in the apples, baste
them well and cook in the oven for
15–20 minutes. Baste the apples halfway through the cooking time. Do not
cover them or they will collapse.

6 Lift the goose onto the serving dish
and let it stand for 15 minutes before
carving. Pour off the excess fat from
the roasting tin, leaving any sediment
in the bottom. Stir in the flour, cook
gently until brown, and then blend in
the stock. Bring to the boil, add the
remaining reserved port, orange juice
and seasoning. Simmer for 2–3 minutes.
Strain into a gravy boat. Surround the
goose with the caramelized apples and
spoon over the redcurrant glaze.

Roast Turkey

Serve this classic Christmas roast with stuffing balls, bacon rolls, roast potatoes, Brussels sprouts and gravy.

INGREDIENTS

*4.5kg/10lb oven-ready turkey, with giblets
(thawed, if frozen)
1 large onion, peeled and studded with
6 whole cloves
50g/2oz/4 tbsp butter, softened
10 chipolata sausages
salt and freshly ground black pepper*

For the Stuffing
*225g/8oz rindless streaky bacon, chopped
1 large onion, finely chopped
450g/1lb pork sausagemeat
25g/1oz/¼ cup rolled oats
30ml/2 tbsp chopped fresh parsley
10ml/2 tsp dried mixed herbs
1 large egg, beaten
115g/4oz dried apricots, finely chopped*

For the Gravy
*25g/1oz/2 tbsp plain flour
450ml/¾ pint/1⅞ cups giblet stock*

Serves 8

1 Preheat the oven to 200°C/400°F/ Gas 6. Adjust the spacing of the shelves to allow for the size of the turkey. To make the stuffing, cook the bacon and the chopped onion together over a gentle heat in a heavy-based frying pan until the bacon is crisp and the onion is tender but not browned. Transfer the cooked bacon and onion to a large mixing bowl and add in all the remaining stuffing ingredients. Season well with plenty of salt and freshly ground black pepper and mix well to blend.

2 Stuff the neck end of the turkey only, tucking the flap of skin under and securing it with a small skewer or stitching it in place with a thread. Do not overstuff the turkey or the skin will burst during cooking. Reserve any remaining stuffing and set aside.

3 Put the onion studded with cloves in the body cavity of the turkey and tie the legs together with string to hold them in place. Weigh the stuffed bird and calculate the cooking time: allow 15 minutes per 450g/1lb plus 15 minutes over. Place the turkey in a large roasting tin.

4 Brush the turkey with the butter and season well with salt and pepper. Cover it loosely with foil and cook it for 30 minutes. Baste the turkey with the pan juices. Then lower the oven temperature to 180°C/350°F/Gas 4 and cook for the remainder of the calculated time. Baste the turkey every 30 minutes or so.

5 With wet hands, shape the remaining stuffing into small balls or pack it into a greased ovenproof dish. Cook in the oven for 20 minutes, or until golden brown or crisp. About 20 minutes before the end of cooking, put the chipolata sausages into an ovenproof dish and put them in the oven. Remove the foil from the turkey for the last hour of cooking and baste. The turkey is cooked if the juices run clear when the thickest part of the thigh is pierced with a skewer.

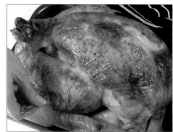

6 Transfer the turkey to a serving plate, cover it with foil and let it stand for 15 minutes before carving. To make the gravy, spoon off the fat from the roasting pan, leaving the meat juices. Blend in the flour and cook for 2 minutes. Gradually stir in the stock and bring to the boil. Check the seasoning and pour into a sauce boat. Remove the skewer and pour any juices into the gravy. To serve, surround the turkey with chipolata sausages, bacon rolls and stuffing.

ROAST PHEASANT WITH PORT

Roasting the pheasant in foil helps to keep the flesh particularly moist and succulent. This recipe

is best for very young birds and, if you have a choice and an obliging butcher, you should

request the more tender female birds.

INGREDIENTS

vegetable oil
2 oven-ready hen pheasants
(about 675g/1½lb each)
50g/2oz/4 tbsp unsalted butter, softened
8 fresh thyme sprigs
2 bay leaves
6 streaky bacon rashers
15 ml/1 tbsp plain flour
175ml/6fl oz/¾ cup game or chicken stock
15ml/1 tbsp redcurrant jelly
45–60ml/ 3–4 tbsp port
freshly ground black pepper

Serves 4

1 Preheat the oven to 230°C/450°F/Gas 8. Line a large roasting tin with a sheet of strong foil large enough to enclose both of the pheasants. Lightly brush the foil with vegetable oil.

2 Wipe the pheasants with damp kitchen paper and remove any extra fat or skin. Using your fingertips, carefully loosen the skin of the breasts. With a round-bladed knife or small palette knife, spread the butter between the skin and the breast meat of each bird. Tie the legs securely with string then lay the thyme sprigs and a bay leaf over the breast of each bird.

3 Lay bacon rashers over the breasts, place the birds in the foil-lined tin and season with plenty of ground black pepper. Bring together the long ends of the foil, fold over securely to enclose, then twist firmly together to seal.

4 Roast the birds for 20 minutes then reduce the oven temperature to 190°C/375°F/Gas 5 and cook for a further 40 minutes. Uncover the birds and roast 10–15 minutes more or until they are browned and the juices run clear when the thigh of each of the birds is pierced with a skewer. Transfer the birds to a board and leave to stand, covered with clean foil, for 10 minutes before carving.

5 Pour the juices from the foil into the roasting tin and skim off any fat. Sprinkle the flour in to the juices and cook over a medium heat, stirring continuously until the mixture is smooth. Whisk in the stock and the redcurrant jelly and bring to the boil. Simmer until the sauce thickens slightly, adding more stock if needed, then stir in the port and adjust the seasoning to taste. Strain the sauce and serve at once, with the pheasants.

VARIATION

Other game birds which would be suitable for this type of cooking include guinea fowl and partridge.

CHICKEN WITH RED WINE VINEGAR

These chicken breasts with their slightly tart taste are inspired by a famous French chef and make an

original, light and tasty Christmas meal. You could substitute tarragon vinegar, if you prefer.

INGREDIENTS

*4 skinless boneless chicken breasts,
200g/7oz each
50g/2oz/4 tbsp unsalted butter
freshly ground black pepper
8–12 shallots, trimmed and halved
60ml/4 tbsp red wine vinegar
2 garlic cloves, finely chopped
60ml/4 tbsp dry white wine
120ml/4fl oz/½ cup chicken stock
15ml/1 tbsp chopped fresh parsley
green salad, to serve*

Serves 4

1 Using a sharp kitchen knife cut each chicken breast in half crossways to make eight pieces.

2 Melt half the butter in a heavy-based frying pan over a medium heat. Add the chicken and cook for 3–5 minutes until golden brown, turning once, then season with pepper.

3 Add the shallot halves to the pan, cover and cook over a low heat for 5–7 minutes, shaking the pan and stirring the pieces occasionally.

4 Transfer the chicken pieces to a plate. Add the vinegar and cook, stirring frequently, for about 1 minute until the liquid is almost evaporated. Add the garlic, wine and stock and stir.

5 Return the chicken to the pan with any accumulated liquid. Cover and simmer for 2–3 minutes until the chicken is tender and the juices run clear when the meat is pierced with a knife or skewer.

6 Transfer the chicken and the shallots to a serving dish and cover to keep warm. Increase the heat and rapidly boil the cooking liquid until it has reduced by half.

7 Off the heat, gradually add the remaining butter, whisking until the sauce is slightly thickened and glossy. Stir in the parsley and pour the sauce over the chicken pieces and shallots. Serve at once with a green salad.

CHICKEN WITH MORELS

Morels are among the most tasty dried mushrooms and, although expensive, a little goes a long way.

Use fresh morels (about 275g/10oz), if you prefer, or chanterelles, shiitake or oyster mushrooms.

INGREDIENTS

40g/1½oz dried morel mushrooms
250ml/8fl oz/1 cup chicken stock
50g/2oz/4 tbsp butter
5 or 6 shallots, thinly sliced
100g/3½oz button mushrooms, sliced
1.5ml/¼ tsp dried thyme
175ml/6fl oz/¾ cup double cream
175ml/6fl oz/¾ cup brandy
4 skinless boneless chicken breasts about 200g/7oz each
15ml/1 tbsp vegetable oil
175ml/6fl oz/¾ cup Champagne or dry sparkling white wine
salt and freshly ground black pepper

Serves 4

1 Put the morels in a strainer and rinse well under cold running water, shaking to remove as much sand as possible. Put them in a large heavy-based saucepan with the stock and bring to the boil over a medium-high heat. Remove the pan from the heat and leave to stand for 1 hour.

2 Remove the morels from the cooking liquid and strain the liquid through a very fine sieve or muslin-lined strainer and reserve for the sauce. Reserve a few whole morels and slice the rest.

3 Melt half the butter in a frying pan over a medium heat. Add the shallots and cook for 2 minutes until softened, then add the morels and mushrooms and cook, stirring frequently, for 2–3 minutes. Season well with salt and ground black pepper and add the thyme, 100ml/3½fl oz/⅓ cup of cream and the brandy. Reduce the heat and simmer 10–12 minutes until any liquid has evaporated, stirring occasionally. Remove the morel mixture from the frying pan and set aside.

4 Pull off the fillets from the chicken breasts. (The fillet is the finger-shaped piece on the underside of the breast.) Wrap the fillets tightly in clear film and freeze, to reserve for another use. Make a pocket in each chicken breast by cutting a slit with a sharp knife along the thicker edge, taking care not to cut all the way through the meat.

5 Using a small spoon, fill each pocket with one-quarter of the mushroom mixture, then close and, if necessary, secure with a cocktail stick to hold the stuffing inside the chicken.

6 Melt the remaining butter with the oil in a frying pan over a medium heat and cook the chicken breasts on one side for 6–8 minutes. Transfer to a plate. Add the Champagne or sparkling wine to the pan and boil to reduce by half. Add the strained morel cooking liquid and boil to reduce by half again.

7 Add the remaining cream and cook over a medium heat for 2–3 minutes until the sauce thickens and coats the back of a spoon. Season. Return the chicken to the pan with any juices and the reserved whole morels, and simmer for 3–5 minutes over a medium-low heat until the juices run clear when the meat is pierced with a skewer.

DUCK WITH ORANGE SAUCE

Commercially-raised ducks tend to have more fat than wild ducks. In this recipe, the initial slow cooking

and pricking the skin of the duck help to draw out the excess fat.

INGREDIENTS

2kg/4½lb duck
2 oranges
100g/3½oz/½ cup caster sugar
90ml/6 tbsp white wine vinegar or cider
vinegar
120ml/4fl oz/½ cup Grand Marnier or
orange liqueur
salt and freshly ground black pepper
watercress and orange slices, to garnish

Serves 2–3

1 Preheat the oven to 150°C/300°F/ Gas 2. Trim off all the excess fat and skin from the duck and prick the skin all over with a fork. Generously season the duck inside and out with salt and freshly ground black pepper, and tie the legs together with string to hold them in place.

2 Place the duck on a rack in a large roasting tin. Cover tightly with foil and cook in the preheated oven for 1½ hours. Using a vegetable peeler, remove the rind in wide strips from the oranges, then stack up two or three strips at a time and slice into very thin julienne strips. Squeeze the juice from the oranges and set it aside.

3 Place the caster sugar and vinegar in a small heavy-based saucepan and stir to dissolve the sugar. Boil over a high heat, without stirring, until the mixture is a rich caramel colour. Remove the pan from the heat and, standing well back, carefully add the freshly squeezed orange juice, pouring it down the side of the pan. Swirl the pan to blend, then bring back to the boil and add the orange rind and liqueur. Simmer for 2–3 minutes.

4 Remove the duck from the oven and pour off all the fat from the roasting tin. Raise the oven temperature to 200°C/ 400°F/Gas 6.

5 Roast the duck, uncovered, for 25–30 minutes, basting three or four times with the caramel mixture, until the duck is golden brown and the juices run clear when the thigh is pierced with a skewer.

6 Pour the juices from the cavity into the casserole and transfer the duck to a carving board. Cover loosely with foil and leave to stand for 10–15 minutes. Pour the roasting juices into the pan with the rest of the caramel mixture, skim off the fat and simmer gently. Serve the duck with the orange sauce, garnished with sprigs of watercress and orange slices.

ROAST LEG OF VENISON

The marinade for this recipe forms the base for a deliciously tangy, slightly sweet sauce which

complements perfectly the richness of roasted venison.

INGREDIENTS

1 onion, chopped
1 carrot, chopped
1 celery stick, chopped
3 or 4 garlic cloves, crushed
4–6 fresh parsley sprigs
4–6 fresh thyme sprigs
2 bay leaves
15ml/1 tbsp peppercorns, lightly crushed
750ml/1¼ pints/3 cups red wine
60ml/4 tbsp vegetable oil, plus more for
brushing
1 young venison haunch, about 2.75kg/
6lb, trimmed
30ml/2 tbsp plain flour
250ml/8fl oz/1 cup beef stock
1 unwaxed orange
1 unwaxed lemon
60ml/4 tbsp redcurrant or raspberry jelly
60ml/4 tbsp ruby port or Madeira
15ml/1 tbsp cornflour, blended with
30ml/2 tbsp water
15ml/1 tbsp red wine vinegar
fresh herbs, to garnish

Serves 6–8

1 Place the onion, carrot, celery, garlic, parsley, thyme, bay leaves, peppercorns, wine and oil in a dish large enough to hold the venison, then add the venison and turn to coat. Cover the dish with clear film and leave to marinate in the fridge for 2–3 days, turning occasionally.

2 Preheat the oven to 180°C/350°F/ Gas 4. Remove the meat from its marinade and pour the marinade into a saucepan. Pat the meat dry, then brush with a little oil and wrap in foil.

3 Roast the venison for 15–20 minutes per 450g/1lb for rare to medium meat. About 25 minutes before the end of the cooking time, remove the foil, sprinkle the venison with the flour and baste.

4 Add the stock to the marinade and boil until reduced by half, then strain and set aside.

5 Using a vegetable peeler, remove the rind from the orange and half the lemon. Cut the pieces into thin julienne strips. Bring a saucepan of water to the boil and add the orange and lemon strips. Simmer them for 5 minutes, then drain and rinse under cold water.

6 Squeeze the juice of the orange into a medium saucepan. Add the redcurrant or raspberry jelly and cook over a low heat until melted, then stir in the port or Madeira and the reduced marinade and simmer gently for 10 minutes, stirring.

7 Stir the blended cornflour mixture into the marinade and cook, stirring frequently, until the sauce is slightly thickened. Add the vinegar and the orange and lemon strips and simmer for a further 2–3 minutes. Keep warm, stirring occasionally, to keep the fruit strips separated.

8 Transfer the venison to a board and allow to stand, loosely covered with foil, for 10 minutes before carving. Garnish with your chosen fresh herbs and serve with the sauce.

FILET MIGNON WITH MUSHROOMS

This haute cuisine French dish was originally made with truffle slices but large mushroom caps

are less expensive and look just as attractive, especially when they are fluted.

INGREDIENTS

4 thin slices white bread
120g/4oz pâté de foie gras or mousse de
foie gras
4 large mushroom caps
70g/2½oz/5 tbsp butter
10ml/2 tsp vegetable oil
4 fillet steaks, about 2.5cm/1in thick
45–60ml/3–4 tbsp Madeira or port
125ml/4fl oz/½ cup beef stock
watercress, to garnish

Serves 4

1 Cut the bread into rounds about the same diameter as the steaks, using a large round cutter or by cutting into squares, then cutting off the corners. Toast the bread and spread with the foie gras, dividing it evenly. Place the bread on warmed plates.

2 Flute the mushroom caps using the edge of a knife blade. Melt about 25g/1oz/1 tbsp of the butter and sauté the mushrooms until golden. Transfer the mushrooms to a plate and keep warm.

3 In the same pan, melt another 25g/1oz/1 tbsp of the butter with the oil, swirling to combine. When the butter just begins to brown, add the steaks and cook for 6–8 minutes, turning once, until cooked as preferred (medium-rare meat will still be slightly soft when pressed, medium will be springy and well-done firm). Place the steaks on the bread and top with the cooked mushroom caps.

4 Add the Madeira or port to the pan and boil for 20–30 seconds. Add the stock and boil until reduced by three-quarters. Swirl in the remaining butter. Pour a little sauce over each steak, then garnish with sprigs of watercress.

CHATEAUBRIAND WITH BÉARNAISE SAUCE

Chateaubriand is a lean and tender cut of beef from the thick centre of the fillet that is

pounded to give it its characteristic shape. This portion is usually served for two people and

would be perfect for a romantic Christmas meal for two.

INGREDIENTS

150g/5oz/⅔ cup butter, cut into pieces
25ml/1½ tbsp tarragon vinegar
25ml/1½ tbsp dry white wine
1 shallot, finely chopped
2 egg yolks
450g/1lb beef fillet, about 12.5–15cm/
5–6in long, cut from the thickest part of
the fillet
15ml/1 tbsp vegetable oil
salt and freshly ground black pepper
Sautéed Potatoes, to serve

Serves 2

1 Clarify the butter by melting in a saucepan over a low heat; do not boil. Skim off any foam and set aside.

2 Put the vinegar, wine and shallot in a small heavy saucepan over a high heat and boil to reduce until the liquid has almost evaporated. Remove from the heat and cool slightly. Add the egg yolks and whisk for 1 minute. Place the saucepan over a very low heat and whisk constantly until the yolk mixture begins to thicken and the whisk begins to leave tracks on the base of the pan, then remove the pan from the heat.

3 Whisk in the butter, slowly at first, then more quickly, until the sauce thickens. Season and keep warm.

4 Place the meat between two sheets of greaseproof paper or clear film and pound with the flat side of a meat pounder or roll with a rolling pin to flatten to about 4cm/1½in thick. Season with plenty of salt and pepper.

5 Heat the vegetable oil in a heavy-based frying pan over a medium-high heat. Add the meat and cook for about 10–12 minutes, turning once, until cooked as preferred (medium-rare meat will be slightly soft when pressed, medium will be springy and well-done will be firm).

6 Transfer the steak to a board and, using a very sharp kitchen knife, carve in thin, diagonal slices. If you prefer a smooth sauce, strain it through a fine sieve then serve with the steak, accompanied by Sautéed Potatoes.

Roast Beef with Roasted Sweet Peppers

This substantial and warming dish makes an ideal dinner for cold winter nights.

INGREDIENTS

1.5kg/3–3½lb piece of sirloin
15ml/1 tbsp olive oil
450g/1lb small red peppers
115g/4oz/¾ cup mushrooms
175g/6oz thick-sliced pancetta, cubed
50g/2oz/2 tbsp plain flour
150ml/¼ pint/⅔ cup full-bodied red wine
300ml/½ pint/1¼ cups beef stock
30ml/2 tbsp Marsala
10ml/2 tsp mixed dried herbs
salt and freshly ground black pepper

Serves 8

1 Preheat the oven to 190°C/375°F/ Gas 5. Season the meat. Heat the oil in a pan, then brown the meat. Place in a roasting tin and cook for 1¼ hours.

2 Put the red peppers in the oven to roast for 20 minutes (or roast for 45 minutes if using larger peppers).

3 Near the end of the meat's cooking time, prepare the gravy. Roughly chop the mushroom caps and stems.

4 Heat the pan again and add the pancetta. Cook until the fat runs from the meat. Add the flour to the pan and cook for a few minutes until browned.

5 Stir in the red wine and stock and bring to the boil. Lower the heat and add the Marsala, herbs and seasoning.

6 Add the mushrooms and heat through. Remove the sirloin from the oven and leave to stand for 10 minutes. Serve with the peppers and hot gravy.

ROAST STUFFED LAMB

This lamb is stuffed with a tempting blend of kidneys, spinach and rice.

INGREDIENTS

1.8–2kg/4–4½ lb boneless leg or shoulder of lamb (not tied)
25g/1oz/2 tbsp butter, softened
15–30ml/1–2tbsp plain flour
120ml/4fl oz/½ cup white wine
250ml/8fl oz/1 cup chicken or beef stock
salt and freshly ground black pepper
watercress, to garnish
Sautéed Potatoes, to serve

For the Stuffing
65g/2½oz/5 tbsp butter
1 small onion, finely chopped
1 garlic clove, finely chopped
50g/2oz/⅓ cup long grain rice
150ml/¼ pint/⅔ cup chicken stock
2.5ml/½ tsp dried thyme
4 lamb kidneys, halved and cored
275g/10oz young spinach leaves, well washed
salt and freshly ground black pepper

Serves 6–8

1 To make the stuffing, melt 25g/1oz/ 2 tbsp of the butter in a saucepan over a medium heat. Add the onion and cook for 2–3 minutes until just softened, then add the garlic and rice and cook for about 1–2 minutes until the rice appears translucent, stirring constantly. Add the stock, salt and pepper and thyme and bring to the boil, stirring occasionally, then reduce the heat and cook for about 18 minutes, covered, until the rice is tender and the liquid is absorbed. Tip the rice into a bowl and fluff with a fork.

2 In a frying pan, melt 25g/1oz/2 tbsp of the remaining butter over a medium-high heat. Add the kidneys and cook for 2–3 minutes, turning once, until lightly browned but still pink inside, then transfer to a board and leave to cool. Cut the kidneys into pieces and add to the rice, season with salt and pepper and toss to combine.

3 In a frying pan, heat the remaining butter over a medium heat until foaming. Add the spinach leaves and cook for 1–2 minutes until wilted, drain off excess liquid, then transfer the leaves to a plate and leave to cool.

4 Preheat the oven to 190°C/375°F/ Gas 5. Lay the meat skin-side down on a work surface and season with salt and pepper. Spread the spinach leaves in an even layer over the surface, then spread the stuffing in an even layer over the spinach. Roll up the meat like a Swiss roll and use a skewer to close the seam. Tie the meat at 2.5cm/1in intervals to hold its shape, then place in a roasting tin, spread with the butter and season.

5 Roast for 1½–2 hours until the juices run slightly pink when pierced with a skewer, or until a meat thermometer inserted into the thickest part of the meat registers 57–60°C/135–140°F (for medium-rare to medium). Transfer the meat to a carving board, cover with foil and leave for about 20 minutes.

6 Skim off the fat from the roasting tin. Place the tin over a medium heat and bring to the boil. Sprinkle over the flour and cook for 3 minutes until browned, stirring and scraping the base of the tin. Whisk in the wine and stock and bring to the boil. Cook for 5 minutes until the sauce thickens. Season and strain. Garnish the meat with watercress and serve with the gravy and potatoes.

BAKED GAMMON WITH CUMBERLAND SAUCE

Serve this delicious cooked meat and sauce either hot or cold.

INGREDIENTS

*2.25kg/5lb smoked or unsmoked gammon
joint
1 onion
1 carrot
1 celery stick
bouquet garni sachet
6 peppercorns*

For the Glaze
*whole cloves
50g/2oz/4 tbsp soft light brown or
demerara sugar
30ml/2 tbsp golden syrup
5ml/1 tsp English mustard powder*

For the Cumberland Sauce
*juice and shredded rind of 1 orange
30ml/2 tbsp lemon juice
120ml/4fl oz/½ cup port or red wine
60ml/4 tbsp redcurrant jelly*

Serves 8–10

1 Soak the gammon overnight in a cool place in enough cold water to cover. Discard this water. Put the joint into a large pan and cover it with more cold water. Bring the water to the boil slowly and skim off any scum that rises to the surface.

2 Add the vegetables and seasonings, cover the pan and simmer over a gentle heat for 2 hours.

3 Leave the meat to cool in the liquid for 30 minutes. Then remove it from the liquid and strip off the skin neatly with the help of a knife (use rubber gloves if the gammon is too hot).

4 Score the fat in diamonds with a sharp knife and stick a clove in the centre of each diamond.

5 Preheat the oven to 180°C/350°F/ Gas 4. Put the sugar, golden syrup and mustard powder in a small pan and heat gently to melt them. Place the gammon in a roasting tin and spoon over the glaze. Bake it until golden brown, about 20 minutes. Put it under a hot grill, if necessary, to get a good colour. Allow to stand in a warm place for 15 minutes before carving.

6 For the sauce, put the orange and lemon juice into a pan with the port or red wine and jelly, and heat to melt the jelly. Pour boiling water on to the orange rind, drain, and add to the sauce. Cook for 2 minutes. Serve in a sauce boat.

TENDERLOIN OF PORK WRAPPED IN BACON

This easy-to-carve "joint" is served with an onion and prune gravy.

INGREDIENTS

3 large pork fillets, weighing about 1.2kg/2½lb in total
225g/8oz rindless streaky bacon
25g/1oz/2 tbsp butter
150ml/¼ pint/⅔ cup red wine

For the Prune Stuffing

25g/1oz/2 tbsp butter
1 onion, very finely chopped
115g/4oz mushrooms, finely chopped
4 ready-to-eat prunes, stoned and chopped
10ml/2 tsp mixed dried herbs
115g/4oz/2 cups fresh white breadcrumbs
1 egg
salt and freshly ground black pepper

To Finish

16 ready-to-eat prunes
150ml/¼ pint/⅔ cup red wine
16 pickling onions
30ml2 tbsp plain flour
300ml/½ pint/1¼ cups chicken stock

Serves 8

1 Preheat the oven to 180°C/350°F/Gas 4. Trim the fillets, removing any sinew and fat. Cut each fillet lengthways, three-quarters of the way through, open them out and flatten.

2 For the stuffing, melt the butter and cook the onion until tender, add the mushrooms and cook for 5 minutes. Transfer to a bowl and mix in the remaining stuffing ingredients. Spread the stuffing over two of the fillets and sandwich together with the third fillet.

3 Stretch each rasher of bacon with the back of a large knife.

4 Overlap the rashers across the meat. Cut lengths of string and lay them at 2cm/¾in intervals over the bacon. Cover with a piece of foil and hold in place, and roll the "joint" over. Fold the bacon rashers over the meat and tie the string to secure them in place. Roll the "joint" back on to the bacon joins and remove the foil.

5 Place in a roasting tin and spread the butter over the joint. Pour the wine around the meat and cook for 1¼ hours, basting occasionally with the liquid in the roasting tin, until evenly browned. Simmer the remaining prunes in the red wine until tender. Boil the onions in salted water for 10 minutes, or until just tender. Drain and add to the prunes.

6 Transfer the pork to a serving plate, remove the string, cover loosely with foil and leave to stand for 10–15 minutes, before carving into slices. Remove any fat from the roasting tin, add the flour to the sediment and juices and cook gently for 2–3 minutes. Then blend in the stock, bring to the boil and simmer for 5 minutes. Adjust the seasoning to taste. Strain the gravy on to the prunes and onions, reheat and serve in a sauce boat with a ladle.

Sea Bass with Citrus Fruit

Try this recipe using fresh sea bass for friends or family who would appreciate an

alternative to meat or poultry at Christmas time; it would be an ideal choice for

a New Year's Eve dinner. The delicate flavour of the fish is complemented

perfectly by the citrus fruits and olive oil.

INGREDIENTS

1 small grapefruit
1 orange
1 lemon
1 sea bass, about 1.35kg/3lb, cleaned and scaled
6 fresh basil sprigs
plain flour, for dusting
45ml/3 tbsp olive oil
4–6 shallots, peeled and halved
60ml/4 tbsp dry white wine
15g/½oz/1 tbsp butter
salt and freshly ground black pepper
fresh dill, to garnish

Serves 6

1 With a vegetable peeler, remove the rind from the grapefruit, orange and lemon. Cut into julienne strips, cover and set aside. Peel off the white pith from the fruits and, working over a bowl to catch the juices, cut out the segments from the grapefruit and orange and set them aside for the garnish. Slice the lemon thickly.

2 Preheat the oven to 190°C/375°F/ Gas 5. Wipe the fish dry inside and out and season the cavity with salt and pepper. Make three diagonal slashes on each side. Reserve a few basil sprigs for the garnish and fill the cavity with the remaining basil, the lemon slices and half the julienne strips of citrus rind.

3 Dust the fish lightly with flour. In a roasting tin or flameproof casserole large enough to hold the fish, heat 30ml/2tbsp of the olive oil over a medium-high heat and cook the fish for about 1 minute until the skin just crisps and browns on one side. Add the halved shallots to the roasting tin.

4 Place the fish in the preheated oven and bake for about 15 minutes, then carefully turn the fish over and stir the shallots. Drizzle the fish with the remaining oil and bake for a further 10–15 minutes until the flesh is opaque throughout.

5 Carefully transfer the fish to a heated serving dish and remove and discard the cavity stuffing. Pour off any excess oil and add the wine and 30–45ml/ 2–3 tbsp of the fruit juices to the pan. Bring to the boil over a high heat, stirring. Stir in the remaining julienne strips of citrus rind and boil for 2–3 minutes, then whisk in the butter. Spoon the shallots and sauce around the fish and garnish with fresh dill and the reserved basil and grapefruit and orange segments.

VARIATION

When sea bass is not available, a whole grey mullet or large trout would make a good alternative.

SOLE WITH PRAWNS AND MUSSELS

This luxurious dish is a classic seafood recipe. It is a true feast for fish lovers at any time

of the year and would make a welcome change at Christmas.

INGREDIENTS

75g/3oz/6 tbsp butter
8 shallots, finely chopped
300ml/½ pint/1¼ cups dry white wine
1kg/2¼lb mussels, scrubbed and
debearded
225g/8oz button mushrooms, quartered
250ml/8fl oz/1 cup fish stock
12 skinless lemon or Dover sole fillets,
about 75–150g/3–5oz each
30m1/2 tbsp plain flour
60ml/4 tbsp crème fraîche or double
cream
225g/8oz/2 cups cooked, peeled prawns
salt and white pepper
fresh parsley sprigs, to garnish

Serves 6

1 In a large heavy flameproof casserole, melt 15g/½oz/1 tbsp of the butter over a medium-high heat. Add half the shallots and cook for about 2 minutes until they are softened, but not browned. Stir the shallots frequently. Add the white wine and bring to the boil, then add the mussels and cover tightly. Cook the mussels over a high heat, shaking and tossing the pan occasionally, for 4–5 minutes until the shells open. Discard any mussels that do not open.

2 Transfer the mussels to a large bowl. Strain the mussel cooking liquid through a muslin-lined sieve and set aside. When cool enough to handle, reserve a few mussels in their shells for the garnish. Then remove the rest from their shells and set aside, covered.

3 Melt half the remaining butter in a large heavy-based frying pan over a medium heat. Add the remaining shallots and cook for 2 minutes until just softened, stirring frequently. Add the mushrooms and fish stock and bring just to simmering point. Season the fish fillets with salt and pepper. Fold or roll them and slide gently into the stock. Cover and poach for 5–7 minutes until the flesh is opaque. Transfer thé fillets to a warmed serving dish and cover tightly to keep warm. Increase the heat and boil the liquid until it has reduced by one-third.

4 Melt the remaining butter in a small saucepan over a medium heat. Add the flour and cook for 1–2 minutes, stirring constantly; do not allow the flour mixture to brown. Gradually whisk in the reduced fish cooking liquid, the reserved mussel liquid and pour in any liquid from the fish, then bring to the boil, stirring constantly.

5 Reduce the heat to medium-low and cook the sauce for 5–7 minutes, stirring frequently. Whisk in the crème fraîche or double cream and keep stirring over a low heat until the sauce is well blended. Adjust the seasoning to taste, then add the reserved mussels and the cooked prawns to the sauce. Cook gently for 2–3 minutes to heat through, then spoon the sauce over the fish and serve garnished with fresh parsley sprigs and the mussels in their shells.

LOBSTER THERMIDOR

Lobster Thermidor is a rich and delicious dish that is luxurious enough

to serve at Christmas-time. Serve one lobster per person as a main course or

one filled shell each for a starter.

INGREDIENTS

2 live lobsters, about 675g/1½lb each
20g/¾oz/1½ tbsp butter
30ml/2 tbsp plain flour
30ml/2 tbsp brandy
120ml/4fl oz/½ cup milk
90ml/6 tbsp whipping cream
15ml/1 tbsp Dijon mustard
lemon juice, salt and white pepper
grated Parmesan cheese, for sprinkling
fresh parsley and dill, to garnish

Serves 2–4

1 Boil the lobsters in a large saucepan of salted water for 8–10 minutes.

2 Cut the lobsters in half lengthways and discard the dark sac behind the eyes, then pull out the string-like intestine from the tail. Remove the meat from the shells, reserving the coral and liver, then rinse the shells thoroughly under running water and wipe dry. Cut the meat into bite-size pieces.

3 Melt the butter in a heavy saucepan over a medium-high heat. Stir in the flour and cook, stirring, until slightly golden. Pour in the brandy and milk, whisking vigorously until smooth, then whisk in the cream and mustard.

4 Push the lobster coral and liver through a sieve into the sauce and whisk briskly to blend. Reduce the heat to low and simmer gently for about 10 minutes, stirring frequently, until thickened. Season the sauce with salt, if needed, then add pepper and lemon juice.

5 Preheat the grill. Arrange the lobster shells in a gratin dish or shallow flameproof baking dish.

6 Stir the lobster meat into the sauce and divide the mixture evenly among the shells. Sprinkle with Parmesan cheese and grill until golden. Serve piping hot, garnished with fresh herbs.

Salmon Steaks with Sorrel Sauce

Salmon and sorrel are a traditional combination – the sharp flavour of the sorrel balances the richness

of the fish. If sorrel is not available, use finely chopped watercress instead.

Ingredients

2 salmon steaks (about 225g/8oz each)
5ml/1 tsp olive oil
15g/½oz/1 tbsp butter
2 shallots, finely chopped
45ml/3 tbsp whipping cream
100g/3½oz fresh sorrel leaves, washed and patted dry
salt and freshly ground black pepper
fresh sage, to garnish

Serves 2

1 Season the salmon steaks with salt and freshly ground black pepper. Brush a non-stick frying pan with oil.

2 Place the frying pan over a medium heat until hot. Add the salmon steaks and cook for about 5 minutes, until the flesh is opaque next to the bone. If you're not sure, pierce with the tip of a sharp knife; the juices should run clear.

3 Meanwhile, in a small saucepan, melt the butter over a medium heat and fry the shallots, stirring frequently, until just softened. Add the cream and the sorrel to the shallots and cook, stirring constantly, until the sorrel is completely wilted. Arrange the salmon steaks on two warmed plates, garnish with fresh sage and serve at once, with the sorrel sauce.

> ### Cook's Tip
>
> *If preferred, cook the salmon steaks in a microwave oven for about 4–5 minutes, tightly covered, or according to the manufacturer's guidelines.*

Vegetarian Dishes
& Vegetables

*I*n any Christmas celebration today, it's likely that
you'll have some vegetarian guests, and they'll appreciate
more than just the leftover vegetables. Many recipes here, such
as Vegetarian Christmas Pie or Cheese, Rice and Vegetable
Strudel can stand alone as vegetarian main courses or can
make a wonderful accompaniment to the turkey in place of
traditional vegetables and potatoes. There is a strong ethnic
element in vegetarian cooking, and Pumpkin Gnocchi or
Spiced Vegetable Couscous will bring an international
element to the Christmas table. And what would Christmas
be without Brussels sprouts, parsnips and potatoes, all cooked
in ways to make them extra special.

VEGETARIAN CHRISTMAS PIE

A sophisticated mushroom flan with a cheese-soufflé topping. Serve hot with cranberry relish

and Brussels sprouts with chestnuts and carrots.

INGREDIENTS

225g/8oz/2 cups plain flour
175g/6oz/¾ cup butter
10ml/2 tsp paprika
115g/4oz Parmesan cheese, grated
1 egg, beaten with 15ml/1 tbsp cold water
15ml/1 tbsp Dijon mustard

For the Filling
25g/1oz/2 tbsp butter
1 onion, finely chopped
1–2 garlic cloves, crushed
350g/12oz/5 cups mushrooms, chopped
10ml/2 tsp mixed dried herbs
15ml/1 tbsp chopped fresh parsley
50g/2oz/1 cup fresh white breadcrumbs
salt and freshly ground black pepper

For the Cheese Topping
25g/1oz/2 tbsp butter
25g/1oz/2 tbsp plain flour
300ml/½pint/1¼ cups milk
25g/1oz Parmesan cheese, grated
75g/3oz Cheddar cheese, grated
1.5ml/¼ tsp English mustard powder
1 egg, separated

Serves 8

2 For the filling, melt the butter and cook the onion until tender. Add the garlic and mushrooms and cook, uncovered, for 5 minutes, stirring occasionally. Increase the heat and drive off any liquid in the pan. Remove the pan from the heat and stir in the dried herbs, parsley, breadcrumbs and seasoning. Allow to cool.

3 Preheat the oven to 190°C/375°F/ Gas 5. Put a baking tray in the oven. On a lightly floured surface, roll out the pastry and use it to line a 23cm/ 9in loose-based flan tin, pressing the pastry well into the edges and making a narrow rim around the top edge. Chill for 20 minutes.

4 For the cheese topping, melt the butter in a pan, stir in the flour and cook for 2 minutes. Gradually blend in the milk. Bring to the boil to thicken and simmer for 2–3 minutes. Remove the pan from the heat and stir in the cheeses, mustard powder and egg yolk, and season well. Beat until smooth. Whisk the egg white until it holds soft peaks. Then, using a metal spoon, fold the egg white into the topping.

5 To assemble the pie, spread the Dijon mustard evenly over the base of the flan case with a palette knife. Spoon in the mushroom filling and level the surface by tapping the case firmly on the work surface.

6 Pour over the cheese topping and bake the pie on the hot baking tray for 35–45 minutes until the topping is set and golden. If you tap on the bottom of the flan case it should sound hollow. Serve at once or freeze until needed.

1 To make the pastry, sift the flour into a bowl and rub in the butter until the mixture resembles fine breadcrumbs. Stir in the paprika and the Parmesan cheese. Bind to a soft pliable dough with the egg and water. Knead until smooth, wrap in clear film and chill for 30 minutes.

Vegetable Gnocchi

This delicious vegetarian main course can be assembled well ahead of time – always a bonus at Christmas.

INGREDIENTS

450g/1lb frozen spinach
15g/½oz/1 tbsp butter
1.5ml/¼ tsp grated nutmeg
225g/8oz/1 cup ricotta or curd cheese
115g/4oz Parmesan cheese, grated
2 eggs, beaten
115g/4oz/1 cup plain flour
50g/2oz Cheddar cheese, grated
salt and freshly ground black pepper

For the Sauce
50g/2oz/4 tbsp butter
50g/2oz/4 tbsp plain flour
600ml/1 pint/2½ cups milk

For the Vegetable Layer
25g/1oz/2 tbsp butter
2 leeks or onions, sliced
4 carrots, sliced
4 celery sticks, sliced
4 courgettes, sliced

Serves 8

1 Put the spinach in a large saucepan with the butter and heat gently to defrost it. Using a wooden fork, carefully break up the spinach to help it thaw out, then increase the heat to drive off any moisture. Season well with salt, freshly ground black pepper and the grated nutmeg. Turn the spinach into a large bowl and mix in the ricotta or curd cheese, Parmesan cheese, eggs and flour. Beat the mixture well until it is smooth.

2 Shape the mixture into ovals with two dessert spoons and place them on a light floured tray. Chill for 30 minutes.

3 Have a large shallow pan of simmering, salted water ready. Cook the gnocchi in two batches, for about 5 minutes. As soon as the gnocchi rise to the surface, remove them with a slotted spoon and drain on a clean tea towel.

4 Preheat the oven to 180°C/350°F/ Gas 4. For the sauce, melt the butter in a pan, add the flour and blend in the milk. Boil until thickened and season.

5 For the vegetable layer, melt the butter and cook the leeks, carrots and celery. Add the courgettes, season and stir. Turn into a 2.4 litre/4 pint/ 10 cup ovenproof dish.

6 Place the drained gnocchi on top, spoon over the sauce and sprinkle with grated cheese. Bake for 30 minutes, until golden brown. Grill if necessary.

Vegetable Gougère

This makes a light vegetarian supper or a main meal served with baked potatoes.

INGREDIENTS

50g/2oz/4 tbsp butter
150ml/¼ pint/⅔ cup water
65g/2½oz/⅔ cup plain flour
2 eggs, beaten
1.5ml/¼ tsp English mustard powder
50g/2oz Gruyère or Cheddar cheese, cubed
salt and freshly ground black pepper
10ml/2 tsp chopped fresh parsley, to garnish

For the Filling
25g/1oz/2 tbsp butter
1 onion, sliced
1 garlic clove, crushed
225g/8oz/3 cups sliced mushrooms
15ml/1 tbsp plain flour
400g/14oz can tomatoes plus their juice
5ml/1 tsp caster sugar
225g/8oz courgettes, thickly sliced

For the Topping
15ml/1 tbsp grated Parmesan cheese
15ml/1 tbsp breadcrumbs, toasted

Serves 4

1 Preheat the oven to 200°C/400°F/ Gas 6. To make the choux pastry, melt the butter in a large pan, add the water and bring to the boil. As soon as the liquid is boiling, draw the pan away from the heat and beat in the flour all at once, and continue beating until a smooth, glossy paste is formed. Turn the paste into a large mixing bowl and set aside to allow to cool slightly.

2 Beat the eggs into the paste. Season, add the mustard powder and fold in the cheese. Set aside.

3 For the filling, melt the butter and cook the onion. Add the garlic and mushrooms and cook for 3 minutes. Stir in the flour and tomatoes. Bring to the boil, stirring. Season with salt, pepper and sugar. Add the courgettes.

4 Butter a 1.2 litre/2 pint/5 cup ovenproof dish. Spoon the choux pastry in rough mounds around the sides of the dish and turn the filling into the centre. Sprinkle the Parmesan cheese and breadcrumbs on top of the filling. Bake for 35–40 minutes, until the pastry is well risen and golden brown. Sprinkle with chopped parsley and serve hot.

CHEESE, RICE AND VEGETABLE STRUDEL

Based on a traditional Russian recipe called "ulibiac", this dish makes a perfect vegetarian

main course or, for meat-eaters, a welcome accompaniment to cold leftover turkey or sliced ham.

INGREDIENTS

175g/6oz/⅞ cup long grain rice
25g/1oz/2 tbsp butter
1–2 leeks, thinly sliced
350g/12oz/5 cups mushrooms, sliced
225g/8oz Gruyère or Cheddar cheese,
grated
225g/8oz feta cheese, cubed
30ml/2 tbsp currants
50g/2oz/½ cup chopped almonds or
hazelnuts, toasted
30ml/2 tbsp chopped fresh parsley
275g/10oz packet frozen filo pastry,
thawed
30ml/2 tbsp olive oil
salt and freshly ground black pepper

Serves 8

1 Cook the rice in boiling, salted water for 10–12 minutes, until tender but still with a little "bite". Drain, rinse under cold running water and set aside to drain again. Melt the butter and cook the leeks and mushrooms for 5 minutes more. Transfer to a large bowl and set aside until the vegetables have cooled.

2 Add the well-drained rice, the cheeses, currants, toasted almonds or hazelnuts, chopped fresh parsley and season to taste. (You may not need to add very much salt as the feta cheese is very salty.)

3 Preheat the oven to 190°C/375°F/ Gas 5. Unwrap the filo pastry. Cover it with a piece of clear film and a clean damp cloth while you work to stop it drying out. Lay a sheet of filo pastry on a large piece of greaseproof paper and brush it with oil. Lay a second sheet on top, overlapping the first by 2.5cm/1in. Put another sheet with its long side running at right angles to the first two. Lay a fourth sheet in the same way, overlapping by 2.5cm/1in. Continue in this way, alternating the layers of two sheets so that the join between the two sheets runs in the opposite direction for each layer.

4 Place the filling mixture along the centre of the pastry sheet and carefully shape it with your hands into a rectangle that measures approximately 10 x 30cm/4 x 12in.

5 Fold the layers of filo pastry over the filling and carefully roll it over, with the help of the greaseproof paper, so that the join ends up being hidden on the underside of the strudel.

6 Lift the strudel on to a greased baking tray and gently tuck the edges under, so that the filling does not escape during cooking. Brush with oil and bake for 30–40 minutes, until golden-brown and crisp. Allow the strudel to stand for 5 minutes before cutting into thick slices. Serve at once or freeze until needed.

COOK'S TIP

The traditional Koulibiac dish has slices of hard-boiled egg as an ingredient in the filling – you could add it if you like.

VEGETABLE CRUMBLE WITH ANCHOVIES

The anchovies may be left out of this dish so that vegetarians can enjoy it, but they do give the

vegetables a delicious flavour. Serve the dish on its own or as an accompaniment to sliced turkey or ham.

INGREDIENTS

450g/1lb potatoes
225g/8oz leeks
25g/1oz/2 tbsp butter
450g/1lb carrots, chopped
2 garlic cloves, crushed
225g/8oz/3 cups mushrooms, sliced
450g/1lb Brussels sprouts, sliced
40g/1½oz can anchovies, drained
salt and freshly ground black pepper

For the Cheese Crumble
50g/2oz/4 tbsp plain flour
50g/2oz/4 tbsp butter
50g/2oz/1 cup fresh breadcrumbs
50g/2oz Cheddar cheese, grated
30ml/2 tbsp chopped fresh parsley
5ml/1 tsp English mustard powder

Serves 8

2 Melt the butter and cook the leeks and carrots for 2–3 minutes. Add the garlic and sliced mushrooms and cook for a further 3 minutes. Add the Brussels sprouts. Season with pepper only, if using the anchovies, if not, add salt to taste. Transfer to a 2.5 litre/4 pint/ 10 cup ovenproof dish.

4 To make the crumble, sift the flour into a bowl and rub in the butter until the mixture resembles fine breadcrumbs, or process in a food processor. Add the breadcrumbs and fold in the grated cheese, and add the chopped fresh parsley and the mustard powder. Mix together well. Spoon over the vegetables and bake for 20–30 minutes until the crumble topping is golden and crispy.

COOK'S TIP

Anchovies can be too salty for some people's taste – soaking them in milk for about an hour helps to remove some of the excess saltiness.

1 Peel and halve the potatoes and parboil them in salted water until just tender. Drain and cool. Cut the leeks in half lengthways and wash them thoroughly to remove any small pieces of grit or soil. Drain on kitchen paper and slice in 1cm/½in pieces.

3 Preheat the oven to 200°C/400°F/ Gas 6. Chop the anchovies and scatter them over the vegetables. Slice the cooked potatoes and arrange them on top of the anchovies.

CHEESE AND SPINACH FLAN

This flan freezes well and can be reheated. It makes an excellent addition to a festive buffet party.

INGREDIENTS

*115g/4oz/½ cup butter
225g/8oz/2 cups plain flour
2.5ml/½ tsp English mustard powder
2.5ml/½ tsp paprika
large pinch of salt
115g/4oz/1 cup grated Cheddar cheese
45–60ml/3–4 tbsp cold water
1 egg, beaten, to glaze*

For the Filling
*450g/1lb frozen spinach
1 onion, chopped
pinch of grated nutmeg
225g/8oz/1 cup cottage cheese
2 large eggs
50g/2oz Parmesan cheese, grated
150ml/¼ pint/⅔ cup single cream
salt and freshly ground black pepper*

Serves 8

1 Using your fingertips, rub the butter into the flour until it resembles fine breadcrumbs. Rub in the next four ingredients. Alternatively, process in a food processor. Bind to a dough with the cold water. Knead until smooth and pliable, wrap in clear film and chill for about 30 minutes.

2 Put the spinach and onion in a pan, cover, and cook slowly. Increase the heat to drive off any water. Season with salt, pepper and nutmeg. Turn the spinach into a bowl, cool slightly. Add the remaining filling ingredients.

3 Preheat the oven to 200°C/400°F/ Gas 6. Put a baking tray in the oven to preheat. Cut one-third off the pastry for the lid. Roll out the remaining pastry and line a 23cm/9in loose-based flan tin. Press the pastry into the edges and make a lip around the top edge. Remove any excess pastry. Pour the filling into the flan case.

4 Roll out the remaining pastry and cut it with a lattice pastry cutter. Carefully open the lattice. Using a rolling pin, lay it over the flan. Brush the joins with egg glaze. Press the edges together and trim off any excess. Brush the lattice with egg glaze and bake for 40 minutes, until golden brown. Serve hot or cold.

CHESTNUT AND MUSHROOM LOAF

You can prepare this dish ahead, freezing it unbaked. Thaw at room temperature overnight before baking.

INGREDIENTS

*45ml/3 tbsp olive oil, plus extra for
brushing
2 medium onions, chopped
2 cloves garlic, chopped
75g/3oz/1¼ cups chopped button
mushrooms
100ml/4fl oz/½ cup red wine
225g/8oz can unsweetened chestnut purée
50g/2oz/1 cup fresh wholemeal
breadcrumbs
salt and freshly ground black pepper
75g/3oz/¾ cup fresh cranberries, plus
extra to decorate
450g/1lb pastry
flour for dusting
1 small egg, beaten, to glaze*

Serves 8

1 Preheat the oven to 190°C/375°F/
Gas 5. Heat the oil in a pan and fry the
onions over a medium heat until they
are translucent. This will take about
7–8 minutes. Add the chopped garlic
and mushrooms and fry for a further
3 minutes. Pour in the wine, stir well
and simmer over a low heat until it
has evaporated, stirring occasionally.
Remove from the heat, stir in the
chestnut purée and breadcrumbs and
season with salt and pepper. Set aside

2 Simmer the cranberries in a little
water for 5 minutes until they start to
pop then drain and leave to cool.

3 Lightly brush a 600ml/1 pint/2½ cup
loaf tin with oil. On a lightly floured
surface, roll out the pastry to a
thickness of about 3mm/⅛in. Cut
rectangles to fit the base and sides of
the tin and press them in place. Press
the edges together to seal them. Cut
a piece of pastry to fit the top of the
tin and set it aside.

4 Spoon half the chestnut mixture
into the tin and level the surface.
Sprinkle on a layer of the cranberries
and cover with the remaining chestnut
mixture. Cover the filling with the pastry
lid and pinch the edges to join them to
the sides. Dust the work surface with
flour, then cut shapes from the pastry
trimmings to use as decorations.

5 Brush the pastry top and the
decorative shapes with the beaten
egg glaze and arrange the shapes in
a pattern on top.

6 Bake the loaf in the oven for
35 minutes, or until the top is golden
brown. Decorate the top with fresh
cranberries. Serve hot.

Spiced Vegetable Couscous

Couscous, a cereal processed from semolina, is used throughout North Africa, mostly in Morocco.

It is traditionally served with Moroccan vegetable stews or tagines but makes a fabulous alternative

Christmas dish. You can serve it on its own or with roasted meat or poultry.

INGREDIENTS

45ml/3 tbsp vegetable oil
1 large onion, finely chopped
2 garlic cloves, crushed
15ml/1 tbsp tomato purée
2.5ml/½ tsp ground turmeric
2.5ml/½ tsp cayenne pepper
5ml/1 tsp ground coriander
5ml/1 tsp ground cumin
225g/8oz/1½ cups cauliflower florets
225g/8oz baby carrots
1 red pepper, seeded and diced
4 beefsteak tomatoes
225g/8oz/1¼ cups thickly sliced courgettes
400g/14oz can chick-peas, drained and rinsed
45ml/3 tbsp chopped fresh coriander
salt and freshly ground black pepper
coriander sprigs, to garnish

For the Couscous
450g/1lb/2⅔ cups couscous
5ml/1 tsp salt
50g/2oz/2 tbsp butter

Serves 6

1 Heat 30ml/2 tbsp of the oil in a large pan, add the onion and garlic, and cook until soft and translucent. Stir in the tomato purée, turmeric, cayenne, ground coriander and cumin. Cook, stirring, for 2 minutes.

2 Add the cauliflower, carrots and pepper, with enough water to come halfway up the vegetables. Bring to the boil, then lower the heat, cover and simmer for 10 minutes.

3 Plunge the tomatoes into boiling water for 30 seconds, then refresh in cold water. Peel away the skins and chop. Add the sliced courgettes, chick-peas and tomatoes to the other vegetables and cook for a further 10 minutes. Stir in the fresh coriander and season with salt and pepper. Set aside and keep hot.

4 To cook the couscous, bring 475ml/16fl oz/2 cups water to the boil in a large saucepan. Add the remaining oil and the salt. Remove from the heat, and add the couscous, stirring. Allow to swell for 2 minutes, then add the butter, and heat through gently, stirring to separate the grains.

5 Turn the couscous out on to a warm serving dish, and spoon the vegetables on top, pouring over any liquid. Garnish with the coriander sprigs and serve at once.

COOK'S TIP

Beefsteak tomatoes have excellent flavour and are ideal for this recipe, but you can substitute six ordinary tomatoes or two 400g/14oz cans chopped tomatoes, if beefsteak tomatoes are not available.

FILO VEGETABLE PIE

This stunning pie packed with winter vegetables and other goodies makes a delicious main course

for vegetarians. For meat-eaters, it is an excellent accompaniment to

cold sliced turkey or other meat dishes.

INGREDIENTS

225g/8oz leeks
165g/5½oz/11 tbsp butter
225g/8oz carrots, cubed
225g/8oz/3 cups sliced mushrooms
225g/8oz Brussels sprouts, quartered
2 garlic cloves, crushed
115g/4oz/½ cup cream cheese
115g/4oz/½ cup Roquefort or Stilton cheese
150ml/¼ pint/⅔ cup double cream
2 eggs, beaten
225g/8oz cooking apples
225g/8oz/1 cup cashew nuts or pine nuts, toasted
350g/12oz frozen filo pastry, defrosted
salt and freshly ground black pepper

Serves 6–8

3 Whisk the cream cheese and blue cheese, cream, eggs and seasoning together in a bowl. Pour them over the vegetables. Peel and core the apples and cut into 1cm/½in cubes. Stir them into the vegetables. Lastly, add the toasted cashew or pine nuts.

5 Spoon in the vegetable mixture and fold over the excess filo pastry to cover the filling.

6 Brush the remaining filo sheets with butter and cut them into 2.5cm/1in strips. Cover the top of the pie with these strips, arranging them in a rough mound. Bake for 35–45 minutes until golden brown all over. Allow to stand for 5 minutes, and then unclip the spring and gently remove the cake tin. Transfer the pie to a large serving plate.

1 Preheat the oven to 180°C/350°F/ Gas 4. Cut the leeks in half through the root and wash them, separating the layers slightly to check they are clean. Slice into 1cm/½in pieces, drain and dry.

2 Heat 40g/1½oz/3 tbsp of the butter in a large pan and cook the leeks and carrots covered over a medium heat for 5 minutes. Add the mushrooms, sprouts and garlic and cook for another 2 minutes. Turn the vegetables into a bowl and let them cool.

4 Melt the remaining butter. Brush all over the inside of a 23cm/9in loose-based springform cake tin with melted butter. Brush two-thirds of the filo pastry sheets with butter, one sheet at a time, and use them to line the base and sides of the tin, overlapping the layers so that there are no gaps for the filling to fall through.

COOK'S TIP

When working with filo pastry, always keep the sheets you are not using under a clean, damp cloth to prevent them from drying out.

PUMPKIN GNOCCHI

Gnocchi is an Italian pasta dumpling usually made from potatoes; in this special recipe,

pumpkin is added, too. A chanterelle sauce provides both richness and flavour.

INGREDIENTS

450g/1lb floury potatoes, peeled
450g/1lb peeled pumpkin, chopped
2 egg yolks
200g/7oz/1¼ cups plain flour
pinch of ground allspice
1.5ml/¼ tsp ground cinnamon
pinch of grated nutmeg
finely grated rind of ½ orange
salt and freshly ground black pepper

For the Sauce
30ml/2 tbsp olive oil
1 shallot
175g/6oz chanterelles, sliced, or
15g/½oz/¼ cup dried, soaked for
20 minutes in warm water
10ml/2 tsp almond butter
150ml/¼ pint/⅔ cup crème fraîche
a little milk or water
75ml/5 tbsp chopped fresh parsley
50g/2oz/½ cup grated Parmesan cheese

Serves 4

1 Cover the potatoes with cold salted water, bring to the boil and cook for 20 minutes. Drain and set aside. Wrap the pumpkin in foil and bake at 180°C/350°F/Gas 4 for 30 minutes. Drain well, then add to the potato and pass through a vegetable mill into a bowl. Add the egg yolks, flour, spices, orange rind and seasoning and mix well to make a soft dough. Add more flour if necessary.

2 Bring a large pan of salted water to the boil, then dredge a work surface with plain flour. Spoon the gnocchi mixture into a piping bag fitted with a 1cm/½ in plain nozzle. Pipe on to the floured surface to make a 15cm/6in sausage shape. Roll in flour and cut into 2.5cm/1in pieces. Repeat the process, making more sausage shapes, until the dough is used up. Mark each gnocchi lightly with a fork and cook for 3–4 minutes in the boiling water.

3 Meanwhile, make the sauce. Heat the oil in a non-stick frying pan. Add the shallot and fry until soft without colouring. Add the chanterelles and cook briefly, then add the almond butter. Stir to melt, and stir in the crème fraîche. Simmer briefly and adjust the consistency with milk or water. Add the parsley and season to taste.

Right: This Spinach and Ricotta Gnocchi makes a quick variation. Cook 900g/2lb spinach in a saucepan and process in a food processor. Mix with 350g/12oz/1½ cups ricotta cheese, 60ml/4 tbsp freshly grated Parmesan and 3 beaten eggs. Season to taste. Add enough plain flour to make a soft dough and shape into 7.5cm/3in sausages. Cook the gnocchi in salted boiling water for 1–2 minutes. Transfer to a dish, pour over 115g/4oz/½ cup melted butter and sprinkle with grated Parmesan, to serve.

4 Lift the gnocchi out of the water with a slotted spoon, turn into warmed bowls and spoon the chanterelle sauce over the top. Scatter with the grated Parmesan cheese and serve at once.

COOK'S TIP

If you are planning ahead, gnocchi can be shaped and ready for cooking up to 8 hours in advance. Almond butter is available ready-made from health food shops.

FESTIVE BRUSSELS SPROUTS

Be sure to allow plenty of time to peel the chestnuts; they are very fiddly but well worth the effort.

INGREDIENTS

450g/1lb fresh chestnuts
450ml/¾ pint/1⅞ cups vegetable stock
450g/1lb Brussels sprouts
450g/1lb carrots
25g/1oz/2 tbsp butter
salt and freshly ground black pepper

Serves 8

1 Peel the raw chestnuts, leaving the brown papery skins intact. Bringing a small pan of water to the boil, drop the chestnuts into the water for a few minutes, and remove with a slotted spoon. The skins should slip off easily.

2 Put the peeled chestnuts in a pan with the stock. Cover and bring to the boil. Simmer for 10 minutes. Drain.

3 Peel and trim the sprouts. Boil in salted water for 5 minutes. Drain.

4 Cut the carrots in 1cm/½in diagonal slices. Put them in a pan with cold water to cover, bring to the boil and simmer for 6 minutes. Drain. Melt the butter in a clean pan, add the chestnuts, sprouts and carrots and season. Serve hot.

CREAMY SPINACH PURÉE

Crème fraîche, the thick French soured cream, or béchamel sauce usually gives this spinach recipe

its creamy richness, but try this quick, light alternative.

INGREDIENTS

675g/1½lb leaf spinach, stems removed
115g/4oz/1 cup full- or medium-fat soft
cheese
milk (if needed)
freshly grated nutmeg
salt and freshly ground black pepper

Serves 4

1 Rinse the spinach thoroughly under running water. Shake lightly and place in a deep frying pan or wok with just the water clinging to the leaves. Cook, uncovered, over a medium heat for 3–4 minutes until wilted. Drain the spinach in a colander or large sieve, pressing out the excess moisture with the back of a spoon; the spinach doesn't need to be completely dry.

2 In a food processor fitted with a metal blade, purée the spinach and soft cheese until well blended, then transfer the mixture to a large bowl. If the purée is too thick to fall easily from a spoon, add a little of the milk, spoonful by spoonful.

3 Season the spinach with salt, pepper and nutmeg. Transfer to a heavy pan and reheat gently over a low heat. Place in a serving dish and serve hot.

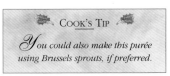
COOK'S TIP
You could also make this purée using Brussels sprouts, if preferred.

LEEK AND ONION TART

This unusual recipe isn't a normal tart with pastry, but an all-in-one savoury slice

that is excellent served as an accompaniment to roast meat.

INGREDIENTS

50g/2oz/4 tbsp unsalted butter
350g/12oz leeks, sliced thinly
350g/12oz onions, sliced thinly
225g/8oz/2 cups self-raising flour
115g/4oz/½ cup hard white fat
150ml/¼ pint/⅔ cup water
salt and freshly ground black pepper

Serves 4

1 Preheat the oven to 200°C/400°F/ Gas 6. Melt the butter in a pan and sauté the leeks and onions until soft. Season well with salt and black pepper.

2 Mix the flour, fat and water together in a large bowl to make a soft but sticky dough. Mix into the leek mixture in the pan. Place the contents of the pan in a greased shallow ovenproof dish and level the surface with a palette knife. Bake in the preheated oven for about 30 minutes, or until brown and crispy. Serve the tart sliced, as a vegetable side dish.

COOK'S TIP

Onions keep very well stored in a cool, dry place. Do not store them in the fridge as they will go soft, and never keep cut onions in the fridge unless you want onion-scented milk and an onion-scented home.

THYME-ROASTED ONIONS

These slow-roasted onions develop a delicious, sweet flavour which is the perfect accompaniment

to roast meat. You could prepare par-boiled new potatoes in the same way.

INGREDIENTS

75ml/5 tbsp olive oil
50g/2oz/4 tbsp unsalted butter
900g/2lb small onions
30ml/2 tbsp chopped fresh thyme
salt and freshly ground black pepper

Serves 4

 COOK'S TIP

Baby yellow or vidalia onions would be perfect for use in this dish as both types are recommended for slow-roasting. Shallots could be used as a very pleasant alternative as they taste excellent cooked in this way.

2 Add the thyme and seasoning and roast for 45 minutes, basting regularly.

1 Preheat the oven to 220°C/425°F/ Gas 7. Heat the oil and butter in a large roasting tin. Remove the outer skin layer from the onions but keep them whole. Add the onions to the roasting tin and toss them in the oil and butter mixture over a medium heat until they are very lightly sautéed.

Sweet and Sour Red Cabbage

This cabbage dish can be cooked the day before and reheated for serving. It is a good

accompaniment to goose, pork or strong-flavoured game dishes.

INGREDIENTS

900g/2lb red cabbage
30ml/2 tbsp olive oil
2 large onions, sliced
2 large cooking apples, peeled, cored and
sliced
30ml/2 tbsp cider vinegar
30ml/2 tbsp soft light brown sugar
225g/8oz rindless streaky bacon, chopped
(optional)
salt and freshly ground black pepper

Serves 8

1 Preheat the oven to 180°C/350°F/ Gas 4. Cut the cabbage into quarters and shred it finely with a sharp knife.

2 Heat the oil in a large ovenproof casserole. Cook the onion over a gentle heat for 2 minutes.

3 Stir the cabbage, apples, vinegar, sugar and seasoning into the casserole. Cover and cook for 1 hour, until tender. Stir halfway through cooking.

4 Fry the bacon, if using, until crisp. Stir it into the cabbage before serving.

PARSNIP AND CHESTNUT CROQUETTES

This is a delightful way to present classic Christmas vegetables.

INGREDIENTS

*450g/1lb parsnips, cut roughly into small
pieces
115g/4oz frozen chestnuts
25g/1oz/2 tbsp butter
1 garlic clove, crushed
15ml/1 tbsp chopped fresh coriander
1 egg, beaten
40–50g/1½–2 oz/½ cup fresh white
breadcrumbs
vegetable oil, for frying
salt and freshly ground black pepper
sprig of coriander, to garnish*

Makes 10–12

1 Place the parsnips in a saucepan with enough water to cover. Bring to the boil, cover and simmer for about 15–20 minutes, until completely tender.

2 Place the frozen chestnuts in a pan of water, bring to the boil and simmer for 8–10 minutes, until very tender. Drain, then place the chestnuts in a mixing bowl and mash roughly.

3 Melt the butter in a small saucepan and cook the garlic for 30 seconds. Drain the parsnips and mash with the garlic butter. Stir in the chestnuts and chopped coriander, then season well.

4 Take about 15ml/1 tbsp of the mixture at a time and form into croquettes, 7.5cm/3in long. Dip into the beaten egg, then roll in breadcrumbs.

5 Heat a little oil in a frying pan and fry the croquettes for 3–4 minutes until golden, turning frequently so they brown evenly. Drain on kitchen paper and then serve at once, garnished with the fresh coriander sprig.

COOK'S TIP

The addition of the chestnuts gives the dish a festive flavour. If you are unable to find frozen chestnuts, you could use unsweetened peeled chestnuts available in cans from supermarkets.

GLAZED CARROTS WITH CIDER

This recipe is extremely simple to make. The carrots are cooked in the minimum of liquid

to bring out the best of their flavour, and the cider adds a pleasant sharpness.

INGREDIENTS

450g/1lb young carrots
25g/1oz/2 tbsp butter
15ml/1 tbsp soft light brown sugar
120ml/4fl oz/½ cup cider
60ml/4 tbsp vegetable stock or water
5ml/1 tsp Dijon mustard
15ml/1 tbsp finely chopped fresh parsley

Serves 4

1 Trim the tops and bottoms off all of the carrots. Peel or scrape them. Using a sharp knife, cut them into julienne strips.

2 Melt the butter in a heavy-based frying pan, add the carrots and sauté for 4–5 minutes, stirring frequently. Sprinkle with the sugar and cook, stirring for 1 minute or until the sugar has dissolved.

3 Add the cider and stock or water to the frying pan. Bring to the boil and stir in the Dijon mustard. Partially cover the pan with the lid and simmer for about 10–12 minutes, until the carrots are just tender. Remove the lid and continue cooking until the liquid has reduced to a thick sauce.

4 Remove the sauce from the heat and stir in the chopped fresh parsley. Spoon the carrots into a warmed serving dish. Serve as an accompaniment to grilled meat or fish or with a vegetarian dish.

> COOK'S TIP
>
> *If the carrots are cooked before the liquid in the saucepan has reduced, transfer the carrots to a serving dish and rapidly boil the liquid until thick. Pour over the carrots and sprinkle with parsley.*

Stir-Fried Brussels Sprouts

Many people are very wary of eating Brussels sprouts because they have had too many

overcooked sprouts served to them in the past. This recipe makes the most of the

vegetable's flavour and has the added interest of an oriental twist.

INGREDIENTS

450g/1lb Brussels sprouts
15ml/1 tbsp sunflower oil
6–8 spring onions, cut into 2.5cm/1in
lengths
2 slices fresh root ginger
40g/1½oz/⅓ cup slivered almonds
150–175ml/4–6fl oz/⅔– ¾ cup vegetable or
chicken stock
salt

Serves 4

1 Remove any large outer leaves and trim the bases of the Brussels sprouts. Cut into slices about 7mm/½in thick.

2 Heat the oil in a wok or heavy-based frying pan, and fry the spring onions and the fresh root ginger for 2–3 minutes, stirring frequently. Add the almonds and stir-fry over a moderate heat until both the onions and almonds begin to brown.

3 Remove and discard the ginger, reduce the heat and stir in the Brussels sprouts. Stir-fry for a few minutes and then pour in the vegetable or chicken stock and cook over a gentle heat for 5–6 minutes, or until the sprouts are nearly tender.

4 Add a little salt to the wok or frying pan, if necessary, and then increase the heat to boil off the excess liquid. Spoon the Brussels sprouts into a warmed serving dish and serve immediately.

COOK'S TIP

If you want to further enhance the oriental flavour of this dish, you could add a couple of dashes of light soy sauce.

PEAS WITH BABY ONIONS AND CREAM

Ideally, use fresh peas and fresh baby onions for this dish. Frozen peas

can be used if fresh ones aren't available, but frozen onions tend to be insipid

and are not worth using. Alternatively, you could use the white part of spring onions.

INGREDIENTS

175g/6oz baby onions
15g/½oz/1 tbsp butter
900g/2lb fresh peas or 350g/12oz/
3 cups shelled or frozen peas
150ml/¼ pint/⅔ cup double cream
15g/½oz/1 tbsp plain flour
10ml/2 tsp chopped fresh parsley
15–30ml/1–2 tbsp lemon juice (optional)
salt and freshly ground black pepper

Serves 4

1 Remove the outer layer of skin from the onions and then halve them, if necessary. Melt the butter in a flameproof casserole and fry the onions for 5–6 minutes over a medium heat, until they just begining to brown and are tender.

2 Add the peas and stir-fry for a few minutes. Add 120ml/4fl oz/½ cup water and bring to the boil. Simmer for about 10 minutes until both are tender. There should be a thin layer of water on the base of the pan.

3 Blend the cream with the flour. Remove the frying pan from the heat and stir in the cream, flour and fresh parsley and season to taste.

4 Cook over a gentle heat for about 3–4 minutes, until the sauce is thick. Add a little lemon juice, if using.

FRENCH BEANS WITH BACON AND CREAM

This baked vegetable accompaniment is rich and full of flavour. It would taste particularly

good served alongside any number of chicken dishes.

INGREDIENTS

350g/12oz French beans
50-75g/2–3oz bacon, chopped
25g/1oz/2 tbsp butter or margarine
15ml/1 tbsp plain flour
350ml/12fl oz/1½ cups milk and single cream, mixed
salt and freshly ground black pepper

Serves 4

1 Preheat the oven to 190°C/375°F/ Gas 5. Trim the beans and cook in lightly salted boiling water for about 5 minutes until just tender. Drain and place them in an ovenproof dish.

2 Dry fry the bacon until crisp, stirring it constantly to make sure that it doesn't stick to the frying pan. Crumble the bacon into very small pieces. Stir into the ovenproof dish with the beans and set aside.

3 Melt the butter or margarine in a large saucepan, stir in the flour and then add the milk and cream to make a smooth sauce, stirring continuously. Season well with plenty of salt and freshly ground black pepper.

4 Pour the sauce over the beans and bacon in the dish and carefully mix it in. Cover the dish lightly with a piece of foil and bake in the preheated oven for 15–20 minutes until hot. Serve immediately.

GRATIN DAUPHINOIS

This dish can be made and baked in advance; reheat it in the oven for 20–30 minutes before serving.

This is a good alternative to roast potatoes and needs no last-minute attention.

INGREDIENTS

butter, for greasing
1.75kg/4lb potatoes
2–3 garlic cloves, crushed
2.5ml/½ tsp grated nutmeg
115g/4oz/1 cup grated Cheddar cheese
600ml/1 pint/2½ cups milk
300ml/½ pint/1¼ cups single cream
2 large eggs, beaten
salt and freshly ground black pepper

Serves 8

❧ COOK'S TIP ❧

The best type of potatoes to use in this dish are Golden Wonder or Kerr's Pink. For the cheese, use a full-flavoured farmhouse Cheddar for the most satisfying taste.

1 Preheat the oven to 180°C/350°F/Gas 4. Butter a 2.4 litre/4 pint/10 cup shallow ovenproof dish. Peel the potatoes, using a potato peeler or a sharp knife, and slice them thinly. If you have a food processor, slice the potatoes in it, using the metal blade.

2 Layer the potato slices in the dish. Add the crushed garlic, nutmeg and two-thirds of the grated Cheddar cheese in alternate layers with the potato. Season well with salt and freshly ground black pepper.

3 Whisk the milk, cream and eggs together and pour them over the potatoes, making sure the liquid goes all the way to the bottom of the dish.

4 Scatter the remaining cheese on top and bake in the preheated oven for 45–50 minutes or until the top layer is golden brown and the cheese is bubbling. Test the potatoes with a sharp knife; they should be very tender. Serve immediately.

Sautéed Potatoes

These rosemary-scented, crisp golden potatoes are an extra-special treat at Christmas time.

INGREDIENTS

1.5kg/3lb baking potatoes
60–90ml/4–6 tbsp oil, bacon dripping or
clarified butter
2 or 3 fresh rosemary sprigs, leaves
removed and chopped
salt and freshly ground black pepper

Serves 6

1 Peel the potatoes and cut into 2.5cm/
1in pieces. Place them in a bowl, cover
with cold water and leave to soak for
10–15 minutes. Drain, rinse and drain
again, then dry thoroughly in a clean
tea towel.

2 In a large, heavy non-stick frying
pan or wok, heat about 60ml/4 tbsp
of the oil, dripping or butter over a
medium-high heat, until very hot,
but not smoking.

COOK'S TIP

*Soaking the potatoes before
cooking removes excess starch,
resulting in a crispier coating to the
cooked potatoes.*

3 Add the potatoes to the frying
pan and cook for 2 minutes, without
stirring, so that they seal completely
and brown on one side.

4 Shake the pan and toss the potatoes
to brown them on the other side, and
continue to stir and shake the pan until
the potatoes are evenly browned all
over. Season with salt and pepper.

5 Add a little more oil, dripping or
butter to the frying pan and continue
cooking the potatoes over a medium-
low to low heat for 20–25, minutes, until
tender when pierced with a knife. Stir
and shake the pan frequently. About
5 minutes before the end of cooking,
sprinkle the potatoes with the chopped
fresh rosemary sprigs.

ℋASSELBACK POTATOES

This is an unusual way to cook with potatoes: each potato half is sliced almost to the base and then

roasted with oil and butter. The crispy potatoes are then coated in an orange glaze and

returned to the oven until deep golden brown and crunchy.

INGREDIENTS

4 large potatoes
25g/1oz/2 tbsp butter, melted
45ml/3 tbsp olive oil

For the Glaze
juice of 1 orange
grated rind of ½ orange
15ml/1 tbsp demerara sugar
freshly ground black pepper

Serves 4–6

1 Preheat the oven to 190°C/375°F/ Gas 5. Cut each potato in half length-ways. If you wish to score the potatoes for decoration, place the flat-side down on the chopping board and then cut down as if making very thin slices, but leaving the bottom 1cm/½in intact.

2 Place the potatoes in a large roasting dish. Using a pastry brush, coat the potatoes generously with the melted butter and pour the olive oil over the base and around the potatoes.

3 Bake the potatoes in the preheated oven for 40–50 minutes, just until they begin to turn brown.

4 Meanwhile, place the orange juice, orange rind and sugar in a small saucepan and heat gently, stirring until the sugar has dissolved. Simmer for 3–4 minutes, until the glaze is fairly thick, and then remove from the heat.

5 When the potatoes begin to brown, brush all over with the orange glaze and return to the oven to roast for a further 15 minutes or until the potatoes are a deep golden brown. Tip onto a warmed serving plate and serve.

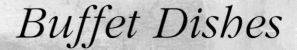

Buffet Dishes

The feasting doesn't end on Christmas Day, but you can serve turkey leftovers for only so long. When the guests come on Boxing Day or New Year's Eve a buffet is the perfect solution. Tarts are one of the easiest dishes to serve and there is a wonderful choice here, including Wild Mushroom Tart, Mini Leek and Onion Tartlets and Turkey and Cranberry Pie. Serve any of these alongside Fillet of Beef with Ratatouille or Classic Whole Salmon, accompanied by Smoked Trout Pilaff or Garden Vegetable Terrine. Provide a little fruit with the tangy Carrot, Apple and Orange Coleslaw and a few nuts with the Celery, Avocado and Walnut Salad, and you're sure to receive a further round of compliments.

Game Terrine

Any game can be used to make this country terrine – hare, rabbit, pheasant or pigeon –

so choose the best meat your butcher has to offer.

INGREDIENTS

225g/8oz rindless, unsmoked streaky bacon
225g/8oz lamb's or pig's liver, minced
450g/1lb minced pork
1 small onion, finely chopped
2 garlic, cloves, crushed
10ml/2 tsp mixed dried herbs
225g/8oz game of your choice
60ml/4 tbsp port or sherry
1 bay leaf
50g/2oz/4 tbsp plain flour
300ml/½ pint/1¼ cups aspic jelly, made up as packet instructions
salt and freshly ground black pepper

Serves 8

2 Mix the minced meats with the chopped onion, garlic and mixed dried herbs. Season well with plenty of salt and ground black pepper.

5 Preheat the oven to 160°C/325°F/ Gas 3. Put the flour into a small bowl and mix it to a firm dough with 30–45ml/2–3 tbsp cold water. Cover the terrine with a lid and seal it with the flour paste. Place the terrine in a roasting tin and pour around enough hot water to come halfway up the sides of the tin. Cook in the preheated oven for about 2 hours.

1 Remove the rind from the bacon and stretch each rasher with the back of a heavy kitchen knife. Use the bacon to line a 1 litre/1¾ pint/4 cup terrine. The terrine should be ovenproof and must have a lid to seal in all the flavours during the long cooking time.

3 Use a heavy kitchen knife to cut the game into thin strips, and put the meat into a large mixing bowl with the port or sherry. Season with salt and freshly ground black pepper.

4 Put one-third of the minced mixture into the terrine. Press the mixture well into the corners. Cover with half the strips of the game and repeat these layers, ending with a minced layer. Level the surface and lay the bay leaf on top.

6 Remove the lid and weight the terrine down with a 2kg/4lb weight. Leave to cool. Remove any fat from the surface and cover with warmed aspic jelly. Leave overnight before turning out onto a serving plate. Serve the terrine cut into thin slices with a mixed salad and some fruit-based chutney.

TURKEY AND CRANBERRY PIE

The cranberries add a tart layer to this turkey pie. Cranberry sauce can be used

if fresh cranberries are not available. The pie freezes well and is an ideal dish to prepare in advance.

INGREDIENTS

450g/1lb pork sausagemeat
450g/1lb lean minced pork
15ml/1 tbsp ground coriander
15ml/1 tbsp mixed dried herbs
finely grated rind of 2 large oranges
10ml/2 tsp grated fresh root ginger or
2.5ml/½ tsp ground ginger
450g/1 lb turkey breast fillets, thinly sliced
115g/4oz/1 cup fresh cranberries
salt and freshly ground black pepper

For the Pastry
450g/1lb/4 cups plain flour
5ml/1 tsp salt
150g/5oz/⅔ cup lard
150ml/¼ pint/⅔ cup mixed milk and water

To Finish
1 egg, beaten
300ml/½ pint/1¼ cups aspic jelly, made up
as packet instructions

Serves 8

1 Preheat the oven to 180°C/350°F/
Gas 4. Place a large baking tray in the
oven to preheat. In a large bowl, mix
together the sausagemeat, minced pork,
coriander, mixed dried herbs, orange
rind and ginger with plenty of salt and
freshly ground black pepper.

2 To make the pastry, put the flour into
a large bowl with the salt. Heat the lard
in a small pan with the milk and water
until just beginning to boil. Draw the
pan aside and allow to cool slightly.

3 Using a wooden spoon, quickly stir
the liquid into the flour until a very
stiff dough is formed. Turn on to a work
surface and knead until smooth. Cut
one-third off the dough for the lid, wrap
it in clear film and keep it in a warm
place.

4 Roll out the large piece of dough
on a floured surface and line the base
and sides of a well-greased 20cm/8in
loose-based, springform cake tin.
Work with the dough while it is still
warm, as it will start to crack and
break if it is left to get cold.

5 Put the turkey breast fillets between
two pieces of clear film and flatten with
a rolling pin to a 3mm/⅛in thickness.
Spoon half the pork mixture into the
base of the tin, pressing it well into the
edges. Cover with half of the turkey
slices and then the cranberries, followed
by the remaining turkey and finally the
rest of the pork mixture.

6 Roll out the rest of the dough and
cover the filling, trimming any excess
and sealing the edges with beaten egg.
Make a steam hole in the lid and
decorate with pastry trimmings. Brush
with beaten egg. Bake for 2 hours.
Cover the pie with foil if it gets too
brown. Place the pie on a wire rack to
cool. When cold, use a funnel to fill the
pie with aspic jelly. Allow to set
overnight before unmoulding the pie.

FILLET OF BEEF WITH RATATOUILLE

This succulent rare beef is served cold with a colourful garlicky ratatouille.

INGREDIENTS

700–900g/1½–2lb fillet of beef
45ml/3 tbsp olive oil
300ml/½ pint/1¼ cups aspic jelly, made up
as packet instructions

For the Marinade
30ml/2 tbsp sherry
30ml/2 tbsp olive oil
30ml/2 tbsp soy sauce
10ml/2 tsp grated fresh root ginger or
5ml/1 tsp ground ginger
2 garlic cloves, crushed

For the Ratatouille
60ml/4 tbsp olive oil
1 onion, sliced
2–3 garlic cloves, crushed
1 large aubergine, cubed
1 small red pepper, seeded and sliced
1 small green pepper, seeded and sliced
1 small yellow pepper, seeded and sliced
225g/8oz courgettes, sliced
450g/1lb tomatoes, skinned and quartered
15ml/1 tbsp chopped mixed fresh herbs
30ml/2 tbsp French dressing
salt and freshly ground black pepper

Serves 8

1 Mix all the marinade ingredients together in a shallow dish, put the beef in and turn it over to coat it. Cover the dish with clear film and leave for 30 minutes, to allow the flavours to penetrate.

2 Preheat the oven to 220°C/425°F/ Gas 7. Using a large slotted spoon, lift the fillet out of the marinade and pat it dry with kitchen paper. Heat the oil in a frying pan until smoking hot and then brown the beef all over to seal it. Transfer to a roasting tin and roast for 10–15 minutes, basting it occasionally with the marinade. Lift the beef on to a large plate and leave it to cool.

3 Meanwhile, for the ratatouille, heat the oil in a large casserole and cook the onion and garlic over a low heat, until tender, without letting the onions become brown. Add the aubergine cubes to the casserole and cook for a further 5 minutes, until soft. Add the sliced peppers and courgettes and cook for 2 minutes more. Then add the tomatoes, chopped herbs and season well with salt and pepper. Cook for a few minutes longer.

4 Turn the ratatouille into a dish and set aside to cool. Drizzle the ratatouille with a little French dressing. Slice the beef and arrange overlapping slices on a serving platter. Brush the slices with cold aspic jelly that is on the point of setting.

5 Leave the jelly to set completely, then brush with a second coat. Spoon the ratatouille around the beef slices on the platter and serve immediately.

COOK'S TIP

Ratatouille is a traditional French recipe that is at its best when made with the choicest fresh ingredients. It makes a wonderful side dish for a buffet or can be eaten as a snack, as a vegetarian filling for jacket potatoes.

WILD MUSHROOM TART

The flavour of wild mushrooms makes this tart really rich: use as wide a variety of

mushrooms as you can get hold of, for added flavour.

INGREDIENTS

For the Pastry
225g/8oz/2 cups plain flour
2.5ml/½ tsp salt
*50g/2oz/4 tbsp hard white
vegetable fat*
10ml/2 tsp lemon juice
*about 150ml/¼ pint/⅔ cup
ice-cold water*
115g/4oz/½ cup butter, chilled, cubed
1 egg, beaten

For the Filling
150g/5oz/10 tbsp butter
2 shallots, finely chopped
2 garlic cloves, crushed
450g/1lb mixed wild mushrooms, sliced
45ml/3 tbsp chopped fresh parsley
30ml/2 tbsp double cream
salt and freshly ground black pepper

Serves 6

1 To make the pastry, sieve the flour and salt together into a large mixing bowl. Add the white fat and rub into the mixture until it resembles fine breadcrumbs.

2 Add the lemon juice and enough iced water to make a soft but not too sticky dough. Cover and set aside to chill for 20 minutes.

3 Roll the pastry out into a rectangle on a lightly floured surface. Mark the dough into three equal strips and arrange half the butter cubes over two-thirds of the dough.

4 Fold the outer two-thirds over, folding over the uncovered third last. Seal the edges with a rolling pin. Give the dough a quarter turn and roll it out again. Mark it into thirds and dot with the remaining butter in the same way.

5 Chill the pastry for 20 minutes. Repeat the process of marking into thirds, folding over, giving a quarter turn and rolling out three times, chilling for 20 minutes in between each time. To make the filling, melt 50g/2oz/ 4 tbsp butter and fry the shallots and garlic until soft, but not browned. Add the remaining butter and the mushrooms and cook for 35–40 minutes. Drain off any excess liquid and stir in the remaining ingredients. Leave to cool. Preheat the oven to 220°C/425°F/Gas 7.

6 Divide the pastry in two. Roll out one half into a 23cm/9in round, cutting around a plate to make a neat shape. Pile the filling into the centre. Roll out the remaining pastry large enough to cover the base. Brush the edges of the base with water and then lay the second pastry circle on top. Press the edges together to seal and brush the top with a little beaten egg to glaze. Bake for 45 minutes, or until the pastry is risen, golden and flaky.

GARDEN VEGETABLE TERRINE

Perfect for a Christmas buffet menu, this is a softly set, creamy terrine of colourful vegetables

wrapped in glossy spinach leaves. Select large spinach leaves for the best results.

INGREDIENTS

225g/8oz fresh leaf spinach
3 carrots, cut in sticks
3–4 long, thin leeks
about 115g/4oz long green beans, topped and tailed
1 red pepper, cut in strips
2 courgettes, cut in sticks
115g/4oz broccoli florets

For the Sauce
1 egg and 2 yolks
300ml/½ pint/1¼ cups single cream
fresh nutmeg, grated
5ml/1 tsp salt
50g/2oz/½ cup grated Cheddar cheese
oil, for greasing
freshly ground black pepper

Serves 6

1 Preheat oven to 180°C/350°F/Gas 4. Blanch the spinach quickly in boiling water, then drain, refresh in cold water and carefully pat dry.

2 Grease a 1kg/2lb loaf tin and line the base with a sheet of greaseproof paper. Line with the spinach leaves, allowing them to overhang the tin.

3 Blanch the rest of the vegetables in boiling, salted water until just tender. Drain and refresh in cold water then, when cool, pat dry with pieces of kitchen paper.

4 Place the vegetables into the loaf tin in a colourful mixture, making sure the sticks of vegetables lie lengthways.

5 Beat the sauce ingredients together and slowly pour over the vegetables. Tap the loaf tin to ensure the sauce seeps into the gaps. Fold over the spinach leaves at the top of the terrine to make a neat surface.

6 Cover the terrine with a sheet of greased foil, then bake in a roasting tin half full of boiling water for about 1–1¼ hours until set.

7 Cool the terrine in the tin, then chill. To serve, loosen the sides and shake out gently. Serve cut in thick slices.

CHICKEN ROLL

This roll can be prepared and cooked the day before it is needed and will freeze well, too.

Remove from the refrigerator about an hour before serving.

INGREDIENTS

2 kg/4lb chicken

For the Stuffing
*1 medium onion, finely chopped
50g/2oz/4 tbsp melted butter
350g/12oz lean minced pork
115g/4oz streaky bacon, chopped
15ml/1 tbsp chopped fresh parsley
10ml/2 tsp chopped fresh thyme
115g/4oz/2 cups fresh white breadcrumbs
30ml/2 tbsp sherry
1 large egg, beaten
25g/1oz/¼ cup shelled pistachio nuts
25g/1oz/¼ cup stoned black olives
(about 12)
salt and freshly ground black pepper*

Serves 8

3 Cut the flesh away from the carcass, scraping the bones clean. Carefully cut through the sinew around the leg and wing joints and scrape down the bones to free them. Remove the carcass, taking care not to cut through the skin along the breastbone so that the stuffing will not escape during cooking.

4 To stuff the chicken, lay it flat, skin side down, and level the flesh as much as possible. Shape the stuffing down the centre and fold the sides over.

5 Sew the flesh together, using dark thread (this will be easier to see when the roll is cooked). Tie the flesh with string to form a roll.

6 Preheat the oven to 180°C/350°F/ Gas 4. Place the roll, with the join underneath, on a roasting rack in a roasting tin and brush with the remaining butter. Bake uncovered for about 1¼ hours or until cooked. Baste the chicken often. Leave to cool completely before removing the string and thread. Wrap in foil and chill until ready for serving or freezing.

1 To make the stuffing, cook the chopped onion gently in a frying pan with 25g/1oz/2 tbsp butter until soft. Turn into a bowl and allow to cool. Add the remaining ingredients, mix thoroughly and season well with salt and freshly ground black pepper.

2 Set the chicken on a clean chopping board and bone it. To start, use a small, sharp knife to remove the wing tips Turn the chicken over on to its breast and cut a deep line down the backbone.

Mini Leek and Onion Tartlets

The savoury filling in these tartlets is traditional to France where many types of quiche are popular.

Baking in individual tins makes for easier serving and looks attractive on the buffet table.

Ingredients

25g/1oz/2 tbsp butter, cut into 8 pieces
1 onion, thinly sliced
2.5ml/½ tsp dried thyme
450g/1lb leeks, thinly sliced
50g/2oz/5 tbsp grated Gruyère or
Emmenthal cheese
3 eggs
300ml/½ pint/1¼ cups single cream
pinch of freshly grated nutmeg
salt and freshly ground black pepper
lettuce leaves, parsley leaves and cherry
tomatoes, to serve

For the Pastry
175g/6oz/1½ cup plain flour
85g/3oz/6 tbsp cold butter
1 egg yolk
30–45ml/2–3 tbsp cold water
2.5ml/½ tsp salt

Serves 6

1 To make the pastry, sift the flour into a bowl and add the butter. Using your fingertips or a pastry blender, rub or cut the butter into the flour until the mixture resembles fine breadcrumbs.

2 Make a well in the flour mixture. In a small bowl, beat together the egg yolk, water and salt. Pour into the well and, using a fork, lightly combine the flour and liquid until the dough begins to stick together. Form into a flattened ball. Wrap and chill for 30 minutes.

3 Lightly butter six 10cm/4in tartlet tins. On a lightly floured surface, roll out the dough until about 3mm/⅛in thick, then using a 13cm/5in fluted cutter, cut out as many rounds as possible. Gently ease the pastry rounds firmly into the base and sides of each tin. Re-roll the trimmings and use to line the remaining tins. Prick the bases all over with a fork and chill for about 30 minutes.

4 Preheat the oven to 190°C/375°F/Gas 5. Line the pastry cases with foil and fill each one with baking beans or a heaping handful of dried pulses. Place them on a baking sheet and bake for 6–8 minutes until the pastry edges are golden. Lift out the foil and beans and bake the pastry cases for a further 2 minutes until the bases appear dry. Transfer to a wire rack and leave to cool. Reduce the oven temperature to 180°C/350°F/Gas 4.

5 In a large frying pan, melt the butter over a medium heat, then add the onion and thyme and cook for 3–5 minutes until the onion is just softened, stirring frequently. Add the leeks and cook for 10–12 minutes more until they are soft and tender. Divide the mixture among the cooled pastry cases and sprinkle the top of each tartlet with cheese, dividing it evenly between them.

6 In a medium-size bowl, beat together the eggs, cream, nutmeg and salt and pepper. Place the pastry cases on a baking sheet and slowly pour in the egg mixture, being careful not to let them overflow. Bake for 15–20 minutes until set and golden. Transfer the tartlets to a wire rack to cool slightly, then remove them from the tins and serve warm or at room temperature, with a mixture of lettuce and parsley leaves and cherry tomatoes.

Classic Whole Salmon

Serving a boneless whole salmon is a delight. If you own a fish kettle the method is slightly different:

cover the salmon with water and a dash of white wine, add a bay leaf, sliced lemon and black

peppercorns and bring to the boil for 6 minutes. Leave to cool completely in the water until cold.

Drain, pat dry, and continue as instructed in the recipe.

INGREDIENTS

1 whole salmon
3 bay leaves
1 lemon, sliced
12 black peppercorns
300ml/½ pint/1¼ cups water
150ml/¼ pint/⅔ cup white wine
2 cucumbers, thinly sliced
large bunches of mixed fresh herbs such
as parsley, chervil and chives, to
garnish
mayonnaise, to serve

Serves 8

1 Preheat the oven to 180°C/350°F/ Gas 4. Clean the inside of the salmon. Make sure all the gut has been removed and the inside cavity has been well rinsed in several changes of cold water and then wiped out with kitchen paper. Cut the tail into a neat "V" shape with a sharp pair of kitchen scissors. Place the fish on a large piece of double thickness foil. Lay the bay leaves, sliced lemon and black peppercorns inside the cavity. Wrap the foil around the fish and up the sides, and pour on the water and wine. Seal the parcel tightly and place in a large roasting tin.

2 Bake in the preheated oven, allowing 15 minutes per pound plus 15 minutes extra. Remove from the oven, and, being careful not to scald yourself on the steam, open up the parcel. Leave to cool. Don't be tempted to leave the salmon to chill overnight as the skin will be impossible to remove the next day.

3 Using a sharp knife or a sharp pair of kitchen scissors, cut off the head and tail, reserving them if you want to display the fish later. Turn the fish upside-down on to a board so the flattest side is uppermost. Carefully peel off the base foil and the skin. Using a sharp knife, gently scrape away any excess brown flesh from the pink salmon flesh.

4 Make an incision down the back fillet, drawing the flesh away from the central bone. Take one fillet and place on the serving dish. Remove the second fillet and place it beside the first to form the base of the fish.

5 Then carefully remove the central backbone from the salmon. Place the other half of the fish with the skin still intact, flesh-side down, on top of the base fish. Peel off the upper skin and any brown bits. Replace the head and tail if required. Using the cucumber slices, lay them on top of the fish, working from the tail end until all the flesh is covered and the cucumber resembles scales. Garnish the serving plate with the fresh herbs of your choice. Serve with mayonnaise.

Layered Salmon Terrine

This elegant fish mousse is perfect for a Christmas buffet table or as a starter course.

INGREDIENTS

*200ml/7fl oz/⅞ cup milk
50g/2oz/4 tbsp butter
65g/2½oz/⅔ cup plain flour
450g/1lb fresh haddock fillet, boned and
skinned
450g/1lb fresh salmon fillet, boned and
skinned
2 eggs, beaten
60ml/4 tbsp double cream
115g/4oz smoked salmon or trout, cut in
strips
salt and freshly ground black pepper*

Serves 8

1 Heat the milk and butter in a saucepan until the milk is boiling. Draw the saucepan aside and beat in the flour until a thick, smooth paste forms. Season well with salt and freshly ground black pepper, and turn the flour paste out on to a plate and leave to cool.

2 Put the haddock into a food processor and process it until smooth. Put it into a bowl. Process the salmon fillet in the same way and put it into a separate bowl. Add an egg and half the cream to each of the fish mixtures. Then beat in half the milk and flour paste to each mixture.

3 Preheat the oven to 180°C/350°F/Gas 4. Butter a 900g/2lb loaf tin and line it with a piece of greaseproof paper. Lay strips of smoked salmon or trout diagonally over the base and up the side of the lined tin.

4 Spoon the haddock mixture into the tin and level the surface. Cover with the salmon mixture and level the surface.

5 Cover the tin with a layer of buttered greaseproof paper and a layer of foil. Place it in a roasting tin and half fill the tin with hot water. Cook for 40 minutes.

6 Remove the terrine from the oven and let stand for 10 minutes. Turn the terrine out of the loaf tin and serve it warm or leave it to cool, as preferred.

SMOKED TROUT PILAFF

Smoked trout might seem an unusual partner for rice, but this is a winning combination with an original

Indian-influenced flavour that will be well appreciated at Christmas time.

INGREDIENTS

225g/8oz/1¼ cups white basmati rice
40g/1½oz/3 tbsp butter
2 onions, sliced into rings
1 garlic clove, crushed
2 bay leaves
2 whole cloves
2 green cardamom pods
2 cinnamon sticks
5ml/1 tsp cumin seeds
4 smoked trout fillets, skinned
50g/2oz/½ cup slivered almonds, toasted
50g/2oz/⅓ cup seedless raisins
30ml/2 tbsp chopped fresh parsley
mango chutney and poppadums, to serve

Serves 4

COOK'S TIP

The use of the mango chutney and poppadums as a serving suggestion with this dish really rings the changes and shows that alternative fare at Christmas can be no less festive. Ready-made poppadums can easily be found in specialist shops and supermarkets. They can be heated in the oven or a microwave in just a few minutes.

1 Wash the rice thoroughly in several changes of water and drain well. Set aside. Melt the butter in a large frying pan and fry the onions until well browned, stirring frequently.

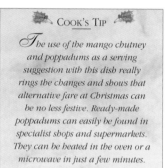

2 Add the garlic, bay leaves, cloves, cardamom pods, cinnamon sticks and cumin seeds and stir-fry for 1 minute.

3 Stir in the rice, then add 600ml/ 1 pint/2½ cups boiling water. Bring to the boil. Cover the pan tightly, reduce the heat and cook very gently for 20–25 minutes, until the water has been absorbed and the rice is tender.

4 Flake the smoked trout and add to the pan with the almonds and raisins. Fork through gently. Re-cover the pan and allow the smoked trout to warm in the rice for a few minutes. Remove the spices and bay leaves. Scatter over the parsley and serve with mango chutney and poppadums.

Tomato and Basil Tart

This mouthwatering savoury tart will be very popular at buffet parties, and vegetarians will love it, too.

It is a very simple tart to make, with rich shortcrust pastry, topped with slices of mozzarella cheese

and tomatoes and enriched with olive oil and basil leaves.

INGREDIENTS

150g/5oz mozzarella, thinly sliced
4 large tomatoes, thickly sliced
about 10 basil leaves
30ml/2 tbsp olive oil
2 garlic cloves, thinly sliced
sea salt and freshly ground black pepper

For the Pastry
115g/4oz/1 cup plain flour
pinch of salt
50g/2oz/4 tbsp butter or margarine
1 egg yolk

Serves 4

1 To prepare the pastry, mix together the flour and salt, then rub in the butter and egg yolk. Add enough cold water to make a smooth dough and knead lightly on a floured surface. Place in a plastic bag and chill for about 1 hour.

2 Preheat the oven to 190°C/375°F/Gas 5. Remove the pastry from the fridge, and allow about 10 minutes for it to return to room temperature and then roll out into a 20cm/8in round. Press into the base of a 20cm/8in flan dish or tin. Prick the case all over with a fork and then bake in the oven for about 10 minutes until firm but not brown. Allow to cool slightly. Reduce the oven temperature to 180°C/350°F/Gas 4.

3 Arrange the mozzarella slices over the pastry base. On top, arrange a single layer of the sliced tomatoes, overlapping them slightly. Dip the basil leaves in olive oil and arrange them on the tomatoes.

4 Scatter the garlic on top, drizzle with the remaining olive oil and season with a little salt and a good sprinkling of black pepper. Bake for 40–45 minutes, until the tomatoes are well cooked. Serve hot or at room temperature.

COOK'S TIP

Pricking the base or sides of the pastry before it goes into the oven ensures the tart does not puff up during the cooking time, making it easier to fill. If the cheese exudes a lot of liquid during baking, tilt the flan dish and spoon it off to keep the pastry from becoming soggy.

Turkey Rice Salad

A delicious, crunchy salad to use up leftover turkey during the holiday festivities.

INGREDIENTS

225g/8oz/1¼ cups brown rice
50g/2oz/⅓ cup wild rice
2 red dessert apples, quartered, cored and chopped
2 celery sticks, coarsely sliced
115g/4oz seedless grapes
45ml/3 tbsp lemon or orange juice
150ml/¼ pint/⅔ cup thick mayonnaise
350g/12oz cooked turkey, chopped
salt and freshly ground black pepper
frilly lettuce leaves, to serve

Serves 8

1 Cook the brown and wild rice in boiling salted water for 25 minutes or until tender. Rinse under cold running water and drain.

2 Turn the well-drained rice into a large bowl and add the apples, celery and grapes. Beat the lemon or orange juice into the mayonnaise, season with salt and pepper and pour over the rice.

3 Add the turkey and mix well to coat with the lemon or orange mayonnaise.

4 Arrange the frilly lettuce leaves over the base and around the sides of a warmed serving dish and spoon the rice on top.

128

HAM AND BULGUR WHEAT SALAD

This flavoursome, nutty salad is ideal for using up leftover cooked ham for a quick and

simple addition to a Christmas buffet menu.

INGREDIENTS

225g/8oz/1⅓ cup bulgur wheat
45ml/3 tbsp olive oil
30ml/2 tbsp lemon juice
1 red pepper
225g/8oz cooked ham, diced
30ml/2 tbsp chopped fresh mint
30ml/2 tbsp currants
salt and freshly ground black pepper
sprigs of fresh mint and lemon slices, to garnish

Serves 8

3 Quarter the pepper, removing the stalk and seeds. Rinse under running water. Using a sharp knife, cut the pepper quarters cut into wide strips and then into diamonds.

4 Add the pepper, ham, chopped fresh mint and currants to the wheat in the bowl. Mix with a spoon to ensure the ingredients are well distributed, then transfer the salad to a serving dish, garnish with the fresh mint sprigs and lemon slices and serve.

1 Put the bulgur wheat into a bowl, pour over enough boiling water to cover and leave to stand until all the water has been absorbed and the grains look as if they have swelled up.

2 Add the oil, lemon juice, and seasoning to taste. Toss to separate the grains using two forks.

Celery, Avocado and Walnut Salad

The crunchiness of the celery and walnuts contrasts perfectly with the smooth avocado.

Serve it with a soured cream dressing as suggested or simply dressed with a little

extra-virgin olive oil and freshly squeezed lemon juice.

INGREDIENTS

3 bacon rashers (optional)
8 tender white or green celery sticks, very
thinly sliced
3 spring onions, finely chopped
50g/2oz/½ cup chopped walnuts
1 ripe avocado
lemon juice

For the Dressing
120ml/4fl oz/½ cup soured cream
15ml/1 tbsp extra-virgin olive oil
pinch of cayenne pepper

Serves 4

1 Dry fry the bacon, if using, until golden and then chop into small pieces and place in a salad bowl with the celery, spring onions and walnuts.

2 Halve the avocado and, using a very sharp knife, cut into thin slices. Peel away the skin from each slice and sprinkle generously with lemon juice and add to the celery mixture.

3 Lightly beat the soured cream, olive oil and cayenne pepper together in a jug or small bowl. Either fold carefully into the salad or serve separately.

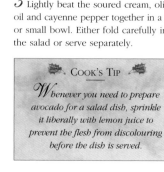

COOK'S TIP

Whenever you need to prepare avocado for a salad dish, sprinkle it liberally with lemon juice to prevent the flesh from discolouring before the dish is served.

CARROT, APPLE AND ORANGE COLESLAW

This dish is as delicious as it is easy to make. The garlic and herb dressing adds the

necessary contrast to the sweetness of the salad.

INGREDIENTS

350g/12oz young carrots, finely grated
2 eating apples
15ml/1 tbsp lemon juice
1 large orange

For the Dressing
45ml/3 tbsp olive oil
60ml/4 tbsp sunflower oil
45ml/3 tbsp lemon juice
1 garlic clove, crushed
60ml/4 tbsp natural yogurt
15ml/1 tbsp chopped mixed fresh herbs
such as tarragon, parsley or chives
salt and freshly ground black pepper

Serves 4

1 Place the carrots in a large serving bowl. Quarter the apples, remove the core and then slice thinly. Sprinkle them with the lemone juice, to prevent them from discolouring, and then add to the carrots.

2 Using a sharp knife, remove the peel and pith from the orange and then separate it into segments. Add to the carrots and apples.

3 To make the dressing, place both the oils with the lemon juice, crushed garlic, natural yogurt, mixed fresh herbs and seasoning in a jar with a lid and shake to blend.

4 Just before serving, pour the dressing over the salad and toss well together to mix.

COOK'S TIP

You can prepare the dressing in advance and keep it in the fridge for up to a week.

Party Foods

*G*one are the days of an uninspiring bowl of peanuts or
a mediocre choice of cheeses and canapés. The tremendous
range of ingredients available in the shops today means
that there are endless possibilities for lavish festive party
foods. Try mixing a few of these fabulous dishes for a truly
international taste: Tapas of Almonds, Olives and Cheese,
Prawn Toasts and Hot Salt Beef on a Stick would always
go together well. For vegetarians, try Mini Filled Jacket
Potatoes and Spicy Sun-dried Tomato Pizza Wedges.
Spoil your guests with mincemeat-filled Filo Crackers,
or provide a Rich Chocolate and Fruit Fondue and see
them welcome in the New Year around the cooking pot.

CHEESELETS

These crispy cheese biscuits are irresistible, and will disappear in moments.

INGREDIENTS

115g/4oz/1 cup plain flour
2.5ml/½ tsp salt
2.5ml/½ tsp cayenne pepper
2.5ml/1½ tsp dry mustard
115g/4oz/½ cup butter
50g/2oz/½ cup grated Cheddar cheese
50g/2oz/½ cup grated Gruyère cheese
1 egg white, beaten
15g/1 tbsp sesame seeds

Makes about 80

1 Preheat the oven to 220°C/425°F/ Gas 7. Line several baking sheets with non-stick baking paper. Sift the flour, salt, cayenne pepper and mustard into a mixing bowl. Cut the butter into pieces and rub into the flour mixture.

2 Divide the mixture in half, add the Cheddar to one half and the Gruyère to the other. Using a fork or your fingertips, work each mixture into a soft dough and knead on a floured surface until smooth.

3 Roll out both pieces of dough very thinly and cut into 2.5cm/1in squares. Transfer to the lined baking sheets. Brush the squares with beaten egg white, sprinkle with sesame seeds and bake for 5–6 minutes or until slightly puffed up and pale gold in colour. Cool on the baking sheets, then carefully remove with a palette knife. Repeat the process until you have used up all the biscuit dough. Pack the biscuits in airtight tins or present as a gift, packed in boxes tied with ribbon.

VARIATION

Try using different cheeses sprinkled with a variety of seeds to give alternative flavours.

COCKTAIL BISCUITS

Tiny savoury biscuits are always a welcome treat.

Experiment with different flavours and shapes and make a batch of biscuits to give as gifts.

INGREDIENTS

350g/12oz/3 cups plain flour
2.5ml/½ tsp salt
2.5ml/½ tsp black pepper
5ml/1 tsp wholegrain mustard
175g/6oz/¾ cup butter
115g/4oz/½ cup grated Cheddar
1 egg, beaten

Flavourings
5ml/1 tsp chopped nuts
10ml/2 tsp dill seeds
10ml/2 tsp curry paste
10ml/2 tsp chilli sauce

Makes about 80

1 Preheat the oven to 200°C/400°F/ Gas 6. Line several baking sheets with non-stick baking paper. Sift the flour into a mixing bowl and add the salt, pepper and mustard. Cut the butter into pieces and rub into the flour mixture until it resembles fine breadcrumbs. Use a fork to stir in the cheese and egg, and mix together to form a soft dough. Knead lightly on a floured surface and cut into 4 equal pieces.

2 Knead chopped nuts into one piece, dill seeds into another piece and curry paste and chilli sauce into each of the remaining pieces. Wrap each piece of flavoured dough in clear film and leave to chill in the fridge for at least an hour. Remove from the clear film and roll out one piece at a time.

3 Using different shaped cutters, stamp out about 20 shapes from each piece. Arrange the shapes on the baking sheets and bake in the oven for 6–8 minutes or until slightly puffed up and pale gold in colour. Cool on wire racks, then remove the biscuits from the baking sheets, using a palette knife.

TAPAS OF ALMONDS, OLIVES AND CHEESE

These three simple ingredients are lightly flavoured to create a delicious Spanish tapas medley

that is perfect for a casual starter or nibbles to serve with pre-dinner drinks.

INGREDIENTS

2.5ml/½ tsp coriander seeds
2.5ml/½ tsp fennel seeds
5ml/1 tsp chopped fresh rosemary
10ml/2 tsp chopped fresh parsley
2 garlic cloves, crushed
15ml/1 tbsp sherry vinegar
30ml/2 tbsp olive oil
115g/4oz/¾ cup black olives
115g/4oz/¾ cup green olives

For the Marinated Cheese
150g/5oz goat's cheese
90ml/6 tbsp olive oil
15ml/1 tbsp white wine vinegar
5ml/1 tsp black peppercorns
1 garlic clove, sliced1
3 fresh tarragon or thyme sprigs
tarragon sprigs, to garnish

For the Salted Almonds
1.5ml/¼ tsp cayenne pepper
30ml/2 tbsp sea salt
25g/1oz/2 tbsp butter
60ml/4 tbsp olive oil
200g/7oz/1¼ cups blanched almonds
extra sea salt for sprinkling (optional)

Serves 6–8

🌿 COOK'S TIP 🌿

If serving with pre-dinner drinks, provide cocktail sticks for spearing the olives and cheese.

1 To make the marinated olives, crush the coriander and fennel seeds with a pestle and mortar. Or, put them into a strong plastic bag and crush them with a rolling pin. Mix together with the rosemary, parsley, garlic, vinegar and oil and pour over the olives in a small bowl. Cover with clear film and chill for up to 1 week.

2 To make the marinated cheese, cut the cheese into bite-size pieces, leaving the rind on. Mix together the oil, vinegar, peppercorns, garlic and herb sprigs and pour over the cheese in a small bowl. Cover with clear film and chill for up to 3 days.

3 To make the salted almonds, mix together the cayenne pepper and salt in a large mixing bowl. Melt the butter with the olive oil in a frying pan. Add the almonds to the frying pan and stir-fry for about 5 minutes, until the almonds are golden.

4 Tip the almonds out of the frying pan, into the salt mixture, and toss together until the almonds are coated. Leave to cool, then remove with a slotted spoon and store them in a jar or airtight container for up to 1 week.

5 To serve the tapas, arrange in small, shallow serving dishes. Use fresh sprigs of tarragon to garnish the cheese and scatter the almonds with a little more salt, if desired.

GUACAMOLE

This fiery version of a popular Mexican dish always proves a favourite at parties. The dip can be

served with any number of accompaniments, including tortilla chips, crudités or breadsticks.

INGREDIENTS

2 ripe avocados, peeled and stoned
2 tomatoes, peeled, seeded and finely
chopped
6 spring onions, finely chopped
1–2 chillies, seeded and finely chopped
30ml/2 tbsp fresh lime or lemon juice
15ml/1 tbsp chopped fresh coriander
salt and freshly ground black pepper
coriander sprigs, to garnish

Serves 4

1 Put the avocado halves into a large mixing bowl and mash them roughly with a large fork.

2 Add the remaining ingredients. Mix well and season according to taste. Serve garnished with fresh coriander.

COOK'S TIP

When preparing chillies, always
be sure to wash your hands
immediately after slicing them.
The oils released can burn if
you accidentally touch your face
or eyes. If you have sensitive skin,
it is a good idea to wear
a pair of plastic gloves.

ᏢRAWN ᏭOASTS

These crunchy sesame-topped toasts are simple to prepare using a food processor for the prawn paste.

INGREDIENTS

*225g/8oz/2 cups cooked, shelled prawns,
well drained and dried
1 egg white
2 spring onions, chopped
5ml/1 tsp chopped fresh root ginger
1 garlic clove, chopped
5ml/1 tsp cornflour
2.5ml/½ tsp salt
2.5ml/½ tsp sugar
2–3 dashes hot pepper sauce
8 slices firm textured white bread
60–75ml/4–5 tbsp sesame seeds
vegetable oil, for frying
spring onion pompom, to garnish*

Makes 64

2 Spread the prawn paste evenly over the bread slices, then sprinkle on the sesame seeds, pressing to make them stick. Remove the crusts, then cut each slice diagonally into 4 triangles, then cut each in half again to make 64.

3 Heat 5cm/2in vegetable oil in a heavy saucepan or wok, until hot but not smoking. Fry the triangles for 30–60 seconds, turning once. Drain well and serve hot, garnished with the spring onion pompom.

⇜ COOK'S TIP ⇝

You can prepare these toasts in advance and heat them up in a hot oven before serving. Make sure they are crisp and properly heated through – they won't be nearly as enjoyable if there's no crunch.

1 Put the first 9 ingredients in the bowl of a food processor and process until the mixture forms a smooth paste, scraping down the side of the bowl occasionally.

PASTRY-WRAPPED CHORIZO PUFFS

These flaky pastry puffs, filled with spicy chorizo sausage and grated cheese, make a perfect

accompaniment to a glass of sherry or cold beer at an informal Christmas party.

INGREDIENTS

225g/8oz puff pastry, thawed if frozen
115g/4oz cured chorizo sausage,
chopped
50g/2oz/½ cup grated hard cheese
1 small egg, beaten
5 ml/1 tsp paprika

Serves 8

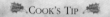

COOK'S TIP

To prepare the chorizo puffs ahead, chill them without the glaze wrapped in a plastic bag, until ready to bake, then allow them to come back to room temperature while you preheat the oven. Glaze before baking.

1 Roll out the pastry thinly on a floured surface. Using a 7.5cm/3in cutter, stamp out as many rounds as possible, then re-roll the trimmings, and stamp out more rounds to make 16 in all.

2 Preheat the oven to 220°C/425°F/ Gas 7. Toss the chopped chorizo sausage and grated cheese together.

3 Lay one of the pastry rounds on the palm of your hand and place a little of the chorizo mixture across the centre.

4 Using your other hand, carefully pinch the edges of the pastry together along the top to seal, as when making a miniature pastie. Repeat the process with the remaining rounds to make 16 puffs in all. Place the pastries on a non-stick baking sheet as you work.

5 Lightly brush each of the pastries with the beaten egg to glaze. Using a small sieve or tea strainer, dust the tops lightly with a little of the paprika.

6 Bake the pastries in the preheated oven for 10–12 minutes, until they are puffed and golden brown. Transfer the pastries to a wire rack and leave them to cool for about 5 minutes, then serve them warm, dusted with the rest of the paprika.

Hot Salt Beef on a Stick

Because this nibble-on-a-stick is so quick to make, it makes an excellent choice for a party.

Ingredients

vegetable oil, for frying
unsliced rye bread with caraway seeds,
cut into 24 x 1 cm/½in cubes
225g/8oz salt beef or pastrami, in one
piece
mild mustard, for spreading
2 pickled cucumbers, cut into small pieces
24 cocktail onions

Makes 24

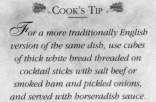

🌿 Cook's Tip 🌿

For a more traditionally English version of the same dish, use cubes of thick white bread threaded on cocktail sticks with salt beef or smoked ham and pickled onions, and served with horseradish sauce.

1 In a heavy medium-sized frying pan, heat 1cm/½in of oil. When very hot, but not smoking, add half the bread cubes and fry for about 1 minute until just golden, turning occasionally. Remove the cubes with a slotted spoon and drain them on kitchen paper. Repeat with the remaining cubes.

2 Cut the salt beef or pastrami into 1cm/½in cubes on a chopping board, and spread one side of each cube with a little of the mustard.

3 Thread a bread cube on to a cocktail stick, then a piece of meat with the mustard side against the bread, then a piece of pickled cucumber, and finally an onion. Arrange the cocktail sticks on a plate or tray, and serve immediately.

*L*AMB *T*IKKA

Creamy yogurt and nuts go wonderfully with the spices in these little Indian meatballs.

INGREDIENTS

450g/1lb lamb fillet
2 spring onions, chopped

For the Marinade
350ml/12fl oz/1½ cups natural yogurt
15ml/1 tbsp ground almonds, cashews or peanuts
15ml/1 tbsp vegetable oil
2–3 garlic cloves, finely chopped
juice of 1 lemon
5ml/1 tsp garam masala or curry powder
2.5ml/½ tsp ground cardamom
1.5ml/¼ tsp cayenne pepper
15–30ml/1–2 tbsp chopped fresh mint

Makes about 20

1 Prepare the marinade. In a medium-size bowl, stir together all the ingredients. In a separate small bowl, reserve about 120ml/4fl oz/½ cup of the mixture to use as a dipping sauce.

2 Cut the lamb into small pieces and put in a food processor with the spring onions. Process until the meat is finely chopped. Add 30–45ml/2–3 tbsp of the marinade and process again.

3 Test to see if the mixture holds together by pinching a little between your fingertips. Add a little more marinade if necessary, but do not make the mixture too wet and soft.

4 With moistened palms, form the meat mixture into slightly oval-shaped balls about 4cm/1½in long and arrange in a shallow baking dish. Spoon over the remaining marinade and refrigerate the meat balls for 8–10 hours or overnight.

5 Preheat the grill and line a baking sheet with foil. Thread each meatball on to a skewer and arrange on the baking sheet. Grill for 4–5 minutes, turning occasionally, until crisp and golden on all sides. Serve with the reserved marinade/dipping sauce.

Chicken Satay with Peanut Sauce

These skewers of marinated chicken can be prepared in advance and served at room temperature.

Beef, pork or even lamb fillet can be used instead of chicken, if you prefer.

Ingredients

450g/1lb boneless, skinless chicken breasts
sesame seeds, for sprinkling
red pepper, to garnish

For the Marinade
90ml/6 tbsp vegetable oil
60ml/4 tbsp tamari or light soy sauce
60ml/4 tbsp fresh lime juice
2.5cm/1in piece fresh root ginger, peeled and chopped
3–4 garlic cloves
30ml/2 tbsp soft light brown sugar
5ml/1 tsp Chinese-style chilli sauce or 1 small red chilli pepper, seeded and chopped
30ml/2 tbsp chopped fresh coriander

For the Peanut Sauce
30ml/2 tbsp smooth peanut butter
30ml/2 tbsp soy sauce
15ml/1 tbsp sesame or vegetable oil
2 spring onions, chopped
2 garlic cloves
15–30ml/1–2 tbsp fresh lime or lemon juice
15ml/1 tbsp soft light brown sugar

Makes about 24

1 Prepare the marinade. Place all the marinade ingredients in the bowl of a food processor or blender and process until smooth and well blended, scraping down sides of the bowl once. Pour into a shallow dish and set aside.

2 Into the same food processor or blender, put all the peanut sauce ingredients and process until well blended. If the sauce is too thick, add a little water and process again. Pour the sauce into a small bowl and cover until ready to serve.

3 Put the chicken breasts in the freezer for about 5 minutes to firm. On a chopping board, slice the chicken breasts in half horizontally, then cut them into thin strips. Cut the strips into 2cm/¾in pieces.

4 Add the chicken pieces to the marinade in the dish. Toss the chicken well to coat, cover with clear film and marinate for 3–4 hours in a cool place, or overnight in a refrigerator.

5 Preheat the grill. Line a baking sheet with foil and brush lightly with oil. Thread 2–3 pieces of marinated chicken on to skewers and sprinkle with the sesame seeds. Grill for 4–5 minutes until golden, turning once. Serve with the peanut sauce and a garnish of red pepper strips.

Spicy Sun-dried Tomato Pizza Wedges

These spicy pizza wedges can be made with or without the pepperoni or sausage.

INGREDIENTS

45–60ml/3–4 tbsp olive oil
2 onions, thinly sliced
2 garlic cloves, chopped
225g/8oz mushrooms, sliced
225g/8oz can chopped tomatoes
225g/8oz pepperoni or cooked Italian-style
spicy sausage, chopped
5ml/1 tsp chilli flakes
5ml/1 tsp dried oregano
115g/4oz sun-dried tomatoes, packed in oil,
drained and sliced
450g/1lb bottled marinated artichoke
hearts, well drained and cut into quarters
225g/8oz mozzarella cheese, shredded
60ml/4 tbsp freshly grated Parmesan cheese
fresh basil leaves, stoned black olives and
sliced fresh red pepper, to garnish

For the Dough
1 packet pizza dough mix
cornmeal, for dusting
virgin olive oil, for brushing and drizzling

Makes 32

1 Prepare the pizza dough according to the manufacturer's instructions on the packet. Set the prepared dough aside to rise for the required amount of time.

2 Prepare the tomato sauce. In a large deep frying pan, heat the oil over medium-high heat. Add the sliced onions and cook for 3–5 minutes until softened. Add the chopped garlic and mushrooms and cook for 3–4 minutes more, until the mushrooms begin to change colour.

3 Stir in the chopped tomatoes, pepperoni or sausage, chilli flakes and oregano and simmer for 20–30 minutes, stirring frequently, until the sauce is thickened and reduced. Stir in the sun-dried tomatoes and set the sauce aside to cool slightly.

4 Preheat the oven to 240°C/475°F/ Gas 9. Line 1 large or 2 small baking sheets with foil, shiny side up. Sprinkle generously with cornmeal. Cut the dough in half and roll out each half to a 30cm/ 12in round. Transfer to the baking sheet and brush the dough with oil.

5 Divide the spicy tomato sauce between the dough rounds, spreading to within 1 cm/½in of the edge. Bake in the preheated oven for 5 minutes, on the lowest shelf of the oven. Arrange half the artichoke hearts over each dough round, sprinkle evenly with the mozzarella and a little Parmesan. Bake each one in the oven on the bottom shelf for 12–15 minutes longer, until the edge of the crust is crisp and brown and the topping is golden and bubbling. Transfer the pizza rounds on to a wire rack, using a palette knife, and allow to cool slightly.

6 Slide the pizzas on to a chopping board and cut each into 16 thin wedges. Garnish each pizza wedge with a basil leaf, one black olive and a slice of pepper and serve immediately.

BLINIS WITH SMOKED SALMON AND DILL CREAM

This recipe is perfect for New Year's Eve celebrations. The blinis go well with a glass of sparkling wine.

INGREDIENTS

115g/4oz/scant cup buckwheat flour
115g/4oz/1 cup plain flour
pinch of salt
15ml/1 tbsp easy-blend dried yeast
2 eggs
350ml/12fl oz/1½ cups warm milk
15g/½oz/1 tbsp melted butter,
150ml/¼ pint/⅔ cup crème fraîche
45ml/3 tbsp chopped fresh dill
225g/8oz smoked salmon, thinly sliced
fresh dill sprigs, to garnish

Serves 4

1 Mix together the flours in a large bowl with salt. Sprinkle in the yeast and mix. Separate one egg. Whisk together the whole egg and the yolk, the warmed milk and the melted butter.

2 Pour the egg mixture on to the flour mixture. Beat well to form a smooth batter. Cover with clear film and leave to rise for 1–2 hours.

3 Whisk the remaining egg white until it holds stiff peaks, and fold into the batter.

4 Preheat a heavy-based frying pan or griddle and brush with melted butter. Drop tablespoons of the batter on to the pan, spacing them well apart. Cook for about 40 seconds, until bubbles appear on the surface.

5 Flip over the blinis and cook for 30 seconds on the other side. Wrap in foil and keep warm in a low oven. Repeat with the remaining mixture, buttering the pan each time.

6 Mix together the crème fraîche and the chopped fresh dill. Serve the blinis topped with the slices of smoked salmon and the dill cream. Garnish each of the blinis with sprigs of fresh dill before serving.

PARMESAN FILO TRIANGLES

You can whip up these light and crunchy triangles at the last minute, using fresh or frozen sheets of filo pastry.

INGREDIENTS

3 large sheets filo pastry
olive oil, for brushing
45–60ml/3–4 tbsp freshly grated
Parmesan cheese
2.5ml/½ tsp crumbled dried thyme or sage

Makes about 24

1 Preheat the oven to 180°C/350°F/ Gas 4. Line a large baking sheet with foil and brush lightly with oil. Lay one sheet of filo pastry on a work surface and brush lightly with a little olive oil. Sprinkle lightly with half the Parmesan cheese and a little of the crumbled dried thyme or sage.

2 Cover with a second sheet of filo, brush with a little more oil and sprinkle with the remaining cheese and thyme or sage. Top with the remaining sheet of filo and brush very lightly with a little more oil. With a sharp knife, cut the filo pastry stack in half lengthways and then into squares. Cut each square into triangles.

COOK'S TIP

These will keep in an airtight container for up to three days, but handle carefully as they are very fragile. Reheat the triangles in a moderate oven to crisp them up when you are ready to serve them.

3 Arrange the triangles on the baking sheet, scrunching them up slightly. Do not allow them to touch. Bake for 6–8 minutes until crisp and golden. Cool slightly and serve immediately.

MINI FILLED JACKET POTATOES

Jacket potatoes are always delicious, and the toppings can easily be varied: choose from luxurious

and extravagant ingredients, such as caviar and smoked salmon, to equally satisfying,

but more everyday fare, such as cheese and baked beans.

INGREDIENTS

36 potatoes, about 4cm/1½ in in diameter,
well scrubbed
250ml/8fl oz/1 cup thick soured cream
45–60ml/3–4 tbsp snipped fresh chives
coarse salt, for sprinkling

Makes 36

🌿 COOK'S TIP 🌿

The potatoes can be baked in advance in the oven, then reheated in the microwave on high (100%) for 3–4 minutes.

1 Preheat the oven to 180°C/350°F/ Gas 4. Place the potatoes on a baking sheet and bake in the oven for 30– 35 minutes, or until the potatoes are tender when pierced with the tip of a sharp kitchen knife.

2 To serve, make a cross in the top of each potato and squeeze gently to open. Make a hole in the centre of each potato. Fill each one with soured cream, then sprinkle with the salt and the snipped chives. Serve immediately.

🌿 VARIATION 🌿

If your guests are likely to be hungry, use medium-size potatoes. When cooked, cut in half, scoop out the flesh, mash with the other ingredients and spoon the mixture back into the skin. Serve warm.

FILO CRACKERS

These festive-shaped sweet treats will make any party go with a bang! The crackers can be prepared a day in advance, brushed with melted butter and kept covered with clear film in the fridge or freezer before baking.

INGREDIENTS

2 x 275g/10oz packet frozen filo pastry, thawed
115g/4oz/½ cup butter, melted
thin foil ribbon, to decorate
sifted icing sugar, to decorate

For the Filling
450g/1lb eating apples, peeled, cored and finely chopped
5ml/1 tsp ground cinnamon
25g/1oz/2 tbsp soft light brown sugar
50g/2oz/½ cup chopped pecan nuts
50g/2oz/1 cup fresh white breadcrumbs
25g/1oz/3 tbsp sultanas
25g/1oz/3 heaped tbsp currants

For the Lemon Sauce
115g/4oz/⅔ cup caster sugar
finely grated rind of 1 lemon
juice of 2 lemons

Makes about 24

1 Unwrap the filo pastry and cover it with clear film and a damp cloth, to prevent it from drying out. Put the chopped apples in a large bowl and mix in the remaining filling ingredients.

2 Take one sheet of pastry at a time and cut it into 15 x 30cm/6 x 12in strips. Brush with butter. Place a spoonful of the filling at one end and fold in the sides, so the pastry measures 13cm/5in across. Brush the edges with the melted butter and roll up. Pinch the "frill" tightly at either end of the cracker. Brush once again with melted butter.

3 Place the crackers on baking trays, cover and chill for 10 minutes. Preheat the oven to 190°C/375°F/Gas 5. Brush each cracker with melted butter. Bake the crackers for 30–35 minutes, or until they are golden brown. Let them cool slightly on the baking trays and then transfer them to a wire rack to allow them to cool completely.

4 To make the lemon sauce, put all the ingredients in a small saucepan and heat gently until all of the ingredients are dissolved, stirring occasionally. Pour the warm sauce into a sauce boat and serve with the filo crackers.

COOK'S TIP
Make sure people know they will be eating a sweet-filled cracker by dredging the serving plate with icing sugar.

Sablés with Goat's Cheese and Strawberries

Sablés are little French biscuits. They contrast well with the cheese and fruit in this recipe

and taste great served with a glass of chilled white wine.

Ingredients

75g/3oz/6 tbsp butter, at room
temperature
140g/5oz/1 generous cup plain flour
75g/3oz/6 tbsp blanched hazelnuts, lightly
toasted and ground
30ml/2 tbsp caster sugar
2 egg yolks beaten with 30–45ml/
2–3 tbsp water
115g/4oz goat's cheese
4–6 large strawberries, cut into small
pieces
chopped hazelnuts, to decorate

Makes about 24

1 Make the pastry. Put the butter, flour, ground hazelnuts, sugar and beaten egg yolks into a food processor and process to make a smooth dough.

2 Put the dough on to clear film and use the film to shape it into a log 4cm/1½in in diameter. Wrap and refrigerate overnight until very firm.

3 Preheat the oven to 200°C/400°F/Gas 6 and line a large baking sheet with non-stick baking paper. Slice the dough into 5mm/¼in thick rounds and arrange on the baking sheet. Bake for 7–10 minutes until golden brown. Remove to a wire rack to cool.

4 Crumble the cheese into pieces and mound a little on each sablé. Top with strawberry and sprinkle with hazelnuts. Serve warm.

Variation

*B*eat 75g/3oz cream cheese with 15ml/1 tbsp icing sugar and a little lemon zest. Spread on top of the sablé and top with any sliced fruits.

Rich Chocolate and Fruit Fondue

This sumptuous fruit fondue, with its rich, delicious sauce, makes a lavish finale to a party menu.

Ingredients

*a selection of mixed fruit, such as
kumquats, apples, peaches and pears,
bananas, clementines, seedless grapes,
cherries, lychees, mango and papaya,
figs, plums and strawberries
lemon juice*

For the Chocolate
*225g/8oz good quality plain chocolate,
chopped
30ml/2 tbsp golden syrup
120ml/4fl oz/½ cup whipping cream
30–45ml/2–3 tbsp brandy or
orange liqueur*

Makes 350ml/12fl oz/1½ cups

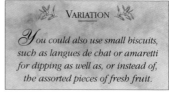

Variation

*You could also use small biscuits,
such as langues de chat or amaretti
for dipping as well as, or instead of,
the assorted pieces of fresh fruit.*

2 In a pan over a low heat, combine the chocolate, golden syrup and cream. Stir until the chocolate is melted and smooth. Remove from the heat and stir in the brandy or liqueur. Pour into a serving bowl and serve with the fruit.

1 On a chopping board, cut the kumquats, apples, peaches, pears and bananas into slices. Break the clementines into segments and peel the lychees, cube the mango and papaya and then cut the figs and plums into wedges. Leave the strawberries whole. Arrange the fruits in an attractive pattern on a large serving dish. Brush any cut-up fruit such as apples, pears or bananas with lemon juice to prevent the pieces from discolouring. Cover the dish with clear film and refrigerate until ready to serve.

Stuffings, Sauces & Preserves

Stuffings and sauces make up an essential part

of the Christmas fare but they often require plenty

of preparation time. This causes many cooks, if they

don't forget about them altogether amid the hustle and

bustle of the main events, to decide against them as

an optional extra. It is a good idea to tackle as much

as possible in advance. Many of the recipes here improve

with keeping and most can be stored in the fridge or

freezer until they are needed. In the weeks leading up

to Christmas, make the best use of the seasonal produce

available by bottling and preserving it in jars for use

throughout the festive weeks.

APRICOT AND RAISIN STUFFING

INGREDIENTS

40 g/1½oz/3 tbsp butter
1 large onion, sliced
100g/4oz/1 cup dried apricot pieces,
soaked and drained
100g/4oz/⅔ cup seedless raisins
juice and grated rind of 1 orange
1 cooking apple, peeled, cored and
chopped
100g/4oz/2 cups fresh white
breadcrumbs
1.5ml/¼ tsp ground ginger
salt and freshly ground black pepper

Makes about 400g/14oz

1 Heat the butter in a small pan and fry the onion over a moderate heat until it is translucent.

2 Turn the onion into a large mixing bowl and stir in the dried apricots, raisins, orange juice and rind, chopped apple, breadcrumbs and ground ginger.

3 Season with salt and black pepper. Mix well with a wooden spoon, then allow to cool. Use the stuffing to pack the neck end of the bird.

CHESTNUT STUFFING

INGREDIENTS

40g/1½oz/3 tbsp butter
1 large onion, chopped
450g/1lb can unsweetened chestnut purée
50g/2oz/1 cup fresh white breadcrumbs
45ml/3 tbsp orange juice
grated nutmeg
½ tsp caster sugar
salt and freshly ground black pepper

Makes about 400g/14oz

1 Heat the butter in a saucepan and fry the onion over a moderate heat for about 3 minutes until it is translucent.

2 Remove the saucepan from the heat and mix the onion with the chestnut purée, breadcrumbs, orange juice, grated nutmeg and sugar.

3 Season with salt and ground black pepper. Allow to cool. Use the stuffing to pack the neck end of the turkey.

CRANBERRY AND RICE STUFFING

INGREDIENTS

225g/8oz/1¼ cups long grain rice, washed
and drained
600ml/1 pint/2½ cups meat or poultry
stock
50g/2oz/4 tbsp butter
1 large onion, chopped
150g/6oz/1 cup cranberries
60ml/4 tbsp orange juice
15ml/1 tbsp chopped parsley
10ml/2 tsp chopped thyme
grated nutmeg
salt and freshly ground black pepper

Makes about 450g/1lb

1 Boil the rice and stock in a small pan. Cover and simmer for 15 minutes. Tip the rice into a bowl and set aside. Heat the butter in a small pan and fry the onion. Add it to the rice.

2 Put the cranberries and orange juice in the cleaned pan and simmer until the fruit is tender. Tip the fruit and any remaining juice into the rice.

3 Add the herbs and season. Allow to cool. Use to pack the turkey neck.

Clockwise from top: Chestnut Stuffing, Cranberry and Rice Stuffing, Apricot and Raisin Stuffing.

Apricot and Orange Stuffing

INGREDIENTS

15g/½oz/1 tbsp butter
1 small onion, finely chopped
115g/4oz/2 cups fresh breadcrumbs
50g/2oz/¼ cup finely chopped dried apricots
grated rind of ½ orange
1 small egg, beaten
15ml/1 tbsp chopped fresh parsley
salt and freshly ground black pepper

Makes about 400g/14oz

1 Heat the butter in a frying pan and cook the onion gently until tender.

2 Allow to cool slightly, and add the onion to the rest of the ingredients.

3 Mix until thoroughly combined and season with plenty of salt and pepper.

Parsley, Lemon and Thyme Stuffing

INGREDIENTS

115g/4oz/2 cups fresh breadcrumbs
25g/1oz/2 tbsp butter
25g/1 tbsp chopped fresh parsley
2.5ml/½ tsp dried thyme
grated rind of ¼ lemon
1 rasher streaky bacon, chopped
1 small egg, beaten
salt and freshly ground black pepper

Makes about 400g/14oz

1 Mix all the ingredients together in a large bowl and stir to combine them thoroughly.

Raisin and Nut Stuffing

INGREDIENTS

115g/4oz/2 cups fresh breadcrumbs
50g/2oz/⅓ cup raisins
50g/2oz/½ cup walnuts, almonds, pistachios or pine nuts
15ml/1 tbsp chopped fresh parsley
5ml/1 tsp chopped mixed herbs
1 small egg, beaten
25g/1oz/2 tbsp melted butter
salt and freshly ground black pepper

Makes about 400g/14oz

1 Mix all the ingredients together thoroughly. Season well with plenty of salt and ground black pepper.

Prune, Orange and Nut Stuffing

You could also finely chop the reserved turkey liver and mix it into this stuffing.

Ingredients

115g/4oz/1 cup stoned prunes
60ml/4 tbsp red wine or sherry
1 onion, finely chopped
25g/1oz/2 tbsp butter
225g/8oz/5 cups fresh white breadcrumbs
finely grated rind of 1 orange
2 eggs, beaten
30ml/2 tbsp chopped fresh parsley
15ml/1 tbsp mixed dried herbs
large pinch of ground allspice
large pinch of grated nutmeg
115g/4oz/1 cup chopped walnuts or
pecans
2 celery sticks, finely chopped
salt and freshly ground black pepper

Serves 12
(enough to stuff a 4.5kg/10lb turkey)

1 Put the prunes and red wine or sherry in a small pan, cover and simmer gently until tender. Set aside to cool.

2 Cook the onion gently in the butter until tender, about 10 minutes.

3 Cut each prune into four pieces. Mix all the ingredients in a large bowl and season well with salt and pepper.

Rice, Mushroom and Leek Stuffing

The rice gives this stuffing a crumbly, light texture.

Ingredients

115g/4oz/1/2 cup rice
25g/1oz/2 tbsp butter
225g/8oz leeks, washed and sliced
225g/8oz mushrooms, chopped
2 celery sticks, finely chopped
50g/2oz/1/2 cup chopped walnuts
1 egg, beaten
60ml/4 tbsp chopped fresh parsley
10ml/2 tsp dried thyme
finely grated rind of 1 lemon
225g/8oz apple, cored and diced
salt and freshly ground black pepper

Serves 12
(enough to stuff a 4.5kg/10lb turkey)

1 Cook the rice in plenty of boiling, salted water for 12 minutes until tender. Drain thoroughly and let it cool. Melt the butter in a frying pan and cook the leeks and mushrooms until tender. Increase the heat and cook to evaporate any remaining moisture in the pan. Set aside to cool.

2 Mix all the remaining ingredients together thoroughly in a large bowl and season with salt and pepper.

3 Add the rice and the leek and mushroom mixture to the bowl and mix together thoroughly.

BREAD SAUCE

Smooth and surprisingly delicate, this old-fashioned sauce is traditionally served with roast

chicken, turkey and game birds. If you'd prefer a less strong flavour, reduce the number

of cloves and add a little freshly grated nutmeg instead.

INGREDIENTS

1 small onion
4 cloves
bay leaf
300ml/½ pint/1¼ cup milk
115g/4oz/2 cups fresh white breadcrumbs
15ml/1 tbsp butter
15ml/1 tbsp light cream
salt and freshly ground black pepper

Serves 6

1 Peel the onion and stick the cloves into it. Put it into a saucepan with the bay leaf and pour in the milk.

2 Bring to the boil then remove from the heat and steep for 15–20 minutes. Remove the bay leaf and onion.

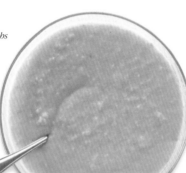

3 Return to the heat and stir in the crumbs. Simmer for 4–5 minutes or until thick and creamy.

4 Stir in the butter and cream. Season with salt and pepper and serve.

CRANBERRY SAUCE

This is the sauce for roast turkey, but don't just keep it for festive occasions. The vibrant colour and tart taste

are perfect partners for any white roast meat, and it makes a great addition to a chicken sandwich.

INGREDIENTS

1 orange
225g/8oz/2 cups cranberries
250g/9oz/1¼ cups sugar

Serves 6

1 Pare the rind thinly from the orange, taking care not to remove any white pith. Squeeze the juice.

2 Place the orange rind in a saucepan with the cranberries, sugar and 150 ml/¼ pint/⅔ cup water.

3 Bring to the boil, stirring until the sugar has dissolved, then simmer for 10–15 minutes or until the berries burst.

4 Remove the rind. Cool before serving.

Tartare Sauce

This is an authentic tartare sauce to serve with all kinds of fish, but for a simpler version

you could always stir the flavourings into mayonnaise.

INGREDIENTS

2 hard-boiled eggs
1 egg yolk from a large egg
10ml/2 tsp lemon juice
175ml/6fl oz/¾ cup olive oil
5ml/1 tsp chopped capers
5ml/1 tsp chopped gherkins
5ml/1 tsp chopped fresh chives
5ml/1 tsp chopped fresh parsley
salt and white pepper

Serves 6

1 Halve the hard-boiled eggs, remove the yolks and press them through a strainer into a mixing bowl.

2 Using a spatula, blend in the raw yolk and mix thoroughly until smooth. Stir in the lemon juice.

3 Add the oil very slowly, a little at a time, whisking constantly. When it begins to thicken, add the oil more quickly to form a thick emulsion. Use a hand blender (mixer) if you prefer.

4 Finely chop one egg white and stir into the sauce with the capers, gherkins and herbs. Season to taste. Serve as an accompaniment to fried or grilled fish.

Mousseline Sauce

This truly luscious sauce is subtly flavoured, rich and creamy. Serve it as a dip with prepared

artichokes or artichoke hearts, or with fish or poultry goujons.

INGREDIENTS

1 quantity Hollandaise sauce
or for a less rich sauce:
2 egg yolks
15ml/1 tbsp lemon juice
75g/3oz/6 tbsp softened butter
90ml/6 tbsp double cream
salt and freshly ground black pepper

Serves 4

3 Using a large balloon whisk, whisk the double cream in a bowl. Continue to whisk the mixture until stiff peaks form.

4 Fold into the warm Hollandaise or prepared sauce and adjust the seasoning. You can add a little more lemon juice for extra tang.

1 If you are not using prepared Hollandaise, make the sauce: whisk the yolks and lemon juice in a bowl over a pan of barely simmering water until very thick and fluffy.

2 Whisk in the softened butter, adding only a very little at a time; whisk well until it is thoroughly absorbed and the sauce has the consistency of mayonnaise.

CRÈME ANGLAIS

Here is the classic English custard; it is light and creamy without the harsh flavours

or gaudy colouring of its poorer package relations. Serve hot or cold.

INGREDIENTS

1 vanilla pod
450ml/15fl oz/1⅛ cups milk
40g/1½oz/3 tbsp icing sugar
4 egg yolks

Serves 4

✲ VARIATION ✲

Steep a few strips of thinly pared lemon or orange rind with the milk, instead of the vanilla pod.

1 Put the vanilla pod in a saucepan with the milk. Bring slowly to the boil. Remove from the heat and steep for 10 minutes before removing the pod.

2 Beat together the sugar and egg yolk until thick, light and creamy.

3 Slowly pour the warm milk on to the egg mixture, stirring constantly.

4 Place the bowl over a saucepan of hot water. Stir over a low heat for 10 minutes or until the mixture coats the back of the spoon. Remove from the heat immediately as curdling will occur if the custard is allowed to simmer.

5 Strain the custard into a jug if serving hot or, if serving cold, strain into a bowl and cover the surface with buttered paper or clear film.

Brandy Butter

The traditional accompaniment to Christmas pudding or mince pies.

Ingredients

75g/3oz/6 tbsp unsalted butter
75g/3oz/6 tbsp caster sugar
finely grated rind of 1 small orange
45ml/3 tbsp brandy

Makes about 175g/6oz

1 Whisk the butter, sugar and orange rind together until soft and fluffy.

2 Gradually whisk in the brandy. Chill until ready to serve.

Whisky Sauce

This is another delicious way to serve Christmas pudding or mince pies.

Ingredients

30ml/2 tbsp cornflour
600ml/1 pint/2½ cups milk
25g/1oz/2 tbsp caster sugar
60ml/4 tbsp whisky
grated nutmeg

Makes about 600ml/1 pint

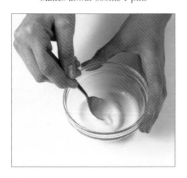

1 In a small bowl, mix the cornflour with 15ml/1 tbsp of the milk to make a smooth paste.

2 Bring the remaining milk to the boil. Remove from the heat and pour a little on to the cornflour mixture, then mix the cornflour into the pan.

3 Return to the heat, stirring constantly until thickened. Simmer for 2 minutes. Turn off the heat and add the sugar and whisky. Pour into a serving jug and sprinkle with grated nutmeg.

CUMBERLAND RUM BUTTER

No Christmas Dinner would be complete without a traditional Christmas pudding to round it off.

This rich and luscious rum butter is the perfect accompaniment.

INGREDIENTS

225g/8oz/1 cup unsalted butter at room temperature
225g/8oz/1 cup soft light brown sugar
90ml/6 tbsp dark rum, or to taste

Makes about 450g/1lb

1 Beat the butter and sugar until the mixture is soft, creamy and pale in colour. Gradually add the rum, almost drop by drop, beating to incorporate each addition before adding more. If you are too hasty in adding the rum, the mixture may curdle.

2 When all the rum has been added, spoon the mixture into a covered container and chill for at least 1 hour. The butter will keep well in the fridge for about 4 weeks.

VARIATION

A variety of liqueurs can be added to the butter and sugar to make delicious alternative accompaniments. Try the recipe with brandy or an orange-flavoured liqueur.

Savoury Butters

This selection of 8 tiny pots of unusual flavoured butters can be used as garnishes for meat,

fish and vegetables, as a topping for canapés or as a tasty addition to sauces.

INGREDIENTS

450g/1lb/2 cups unsalted butter
25g/1oz/2 tbsp Stilton
3 anchovy fillets
5ml/1 tsp curry paste
1 garlic clove, crushed
10g/2 tsp finely chopped fresh tarragon
15ml/1 tbsp creamed horseradish
15ml/1 tbsp chopped fresh parsley
5ml/1 tsp grated lime rind
1.5ml/¼ tsp chilli sauce

Makes about 50g/2oz/¼ cup
of each flavour

1 Place the butter in a food processor. Process until light and fluffy. Divide the butter into 8 portions.

2 Crumble the Stilton and mix together with a portion of butter. Pound the anchovies to a paste with a mortar and pestle and mix with the second portion of butter. Stir the curry paste into the third and the crushed garlic into the fourth portion.

3 Stir the tarragon into the fifth portion and the creamed horseradish into the sixth portion. Into the seventh portion add the parsley and the lime rind, and to the last portion add the chilli sauce. Pack each flavoured butter into a tiny sterilized jar with a lid and label clearly. Store in the fridge.

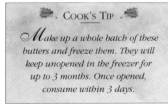

COOK'S TIP

Make up a whole batch of these butters and freeze them. They will keep unopened in the freezer for up to 3 months. Once opened, consume within 3 days.

Anchovy Spread

This delicious spread has an intense concentrated flavour and is best served with plain toast.

INGREDIENTS

*2 x 50g/2oz cans anchovy
fillets in olive oil
4 garlic cloves, crushed
2 egg yolks
30m/2 tbsp red wine vinegar
300ml/½ pint/1¼ cups olive oil
1.5ml/¼ tsp freshly ground black pepper
30ml/2 tbsp chopped fresh basil or thyme*

Makes 600ml/1 pint/2½ cups

1 Drain the oil from the anchovies and reserve. Place the anchovies and garlic in a food processor. Process until smooth. Add the egg yolks and vinegar, and process until the egg and vinegar have been absorbed by the anchovies.

2 Measure out the oil into a measuring jug and add the reserved anchovy oil. Set the food processor to a low speed and gradually add the oil, drop by drop, to the anchovy mixture until it is thick and smooth.

3 Add some freshly ground black pepper and the chopped fresh herbs, and blend well until the mixture is smooth. Spoon the mixture into small sterilized jars with lids, seal with a wax paper disc, cover with the lid, and label with the name of the spread and the date it was made. Store the unopened jars of spread in the fridge until it is needed.

CHRISTMAS CHUTNEY

This chutney makes the perfect accompaniment to cold meats, pâtés and cheese. It has a sweet

but spicy flavour. The fruits may be changed for quince, greengage or rhubarb.

INGREDIENTS

450g/1lb/9 plums, stoned
450g/1lb/6 pears, peeled and cored
225g/8oz/2 cooking apples, peeled and cored
225g/8oz/4 sticks celery
450g/1lb onions, sliced
450g/1 lb tomatoes, skinned
115g/4oz/½ cup raisins
15ml/1 tbsp grated fresh root ginger
30ml/2 tbsp pickling spice
850ml/1½ pints/3¾ cups cider vinegar
450g/1lb/2 cups granulated sugar

Makes 1.75kg/4½lb

1 Chop the plums, pears, apples, celery and onions and cut the tomatoes into quarters. Place all these ingredients with the raisins and ginger into a very large saucepan.

2 Place the pickling spice into a square of clean, fine muslin and tie with string to secure. Add to the saucepan of fruit and vegetables with half the vinegar and bring to the boil, stirring. Cook for 2 hours.

3 Meanwhile, sterilize the jars and lids you will need to fill. When all the ingredients are tender, stir in the remaining vinegar and the sugar. Boil until thick, remove the bag of spices and fill each jar with chutney. Cover with a wax paper disc and plastic lid, and label when cold.

COOK'S TIP

Once opened, this chutney will keep for up to one week in a resealable jar. If you wish, add attractive ribbons, tags and labels and give it to a friend as a special Christmas gift.

Piccalilli

The piquancy of this relish partners well with sausages, as well as with most bacon or ham dishes.

INGREDIENTS

675g/1½lb cauliflower
450g/1lb small onions
350g/12oz French beans
5ml/1 tsp ground turmeric
5ml/1 tsp dry mustard powder
10ml/2 tsp cornflour
600ml/1 pint/2½ cups vinegar

Makes 3 x 450g/1lb jars

1 Cut the cauliflower into tiny florets.

2 Peel the onions and top and tail the French beans.

3 In a small saucepan, measure in the turmeric, mustard powder and cornflour. Pour the vinegar into the saucepan. Stir well and simmer for 10 minutes over a gentle heat.

4 Pour the vinegar mixture over the vegetables in a large saucepan, mix well and simmer for 45 minutes.

5 Pour into sterilized jars. Seal each jar with a wax disc and a tightly fitting cellophane top. Store in a cool, dark place. The piccalilli will keep well, unopened, for up to a year. Once opened, store in the fridge and consume within a week.

Tomato Chutney

This spicy chutney is delicious with a selection of cheeses and biscuits, or with cold meats.

INGREDIENTS

900g/2lb tomatoes
225g/8oz/1⅓ cups raisins
225g/8oz onions, chopped
225g/8oz/1⅛ cups caster sugar
600ml/1 pint/2½ cups malt vinegar

Makes 3 x 450g/1lb jars

1 Put the tomatoes in a bowl and pour over boiling water. Leave the tomatoes immersed in the water for 30 seconds, then remove with a slotted spoon and plunge them into cold water. Peel the tomatoes and chop roughly. Put in a preserving pan.

2 Add the raisins, chopped onions and caster sugar.

3 Pour over the vinegar. Bring to the boil and let it simmer for 2 hours, uncovered. Pot into sterilized jars. Seal with a wax disc and cover with a tightly fitting cellophane top. Store in a cool, dark place. The chutney will keep well, unopened, for up to a year. Once opened, store in the fridge and consume within a week.

QUINCE PASTE

This paste is known in Spain as pasta de membrillo. *It is decorated with icing sugar and sometimes cloves, and served after meals or to decorate desserts. If you find quinces difficult to get hold of, try using fresh apricots or even cranberries.*

INGREDIENTS

1kg/2¼ lb quinces
1 litre/1¾ pints/4 cups water
1kg/2¼lb/4¼ cups caster sugar
vegetable oil, for brushing
icing sugar, for dusting
whole cloves, to decorate

Makes about 1.25kg/2½lb

🌿 COOK'S TIP 🌿

If you would like to pack this tangy paste as a gift, layer it in a box between sheets of non-stick baking paper.

---

1 Wash and slice the quinces and put them into a large pan with the water. Bring to the boil, then simmer for about 45 minutes, until the fruit is soft.

2 Mash the fruit against the sides of the pan, then spoon it and the liquid into a jelly bag suspended over a large bowl. Leave to drain for at least 2 hours, without squeezing the bag.

3 Pour the strained juice into the cleaned pan, add the sugar and stir over a low heat to dissolve. Cook over a low heat for about 2 hours, stirring frequently, until a spoon drawn through the paste parts it into 2 sections.

4 Lightly brush a Swiss roll tin with oil, pour in the preserve and leave to set. When it is cool, cut it into diamonds or other shapes, dust with icing sugar and stud each piece with a clove. Store between layers of non-stick baking paper in an airtight container.

CRAB-APPLE AND LAVENDER JELLY

This fragrant, clear jelly can be made in the months before Christmas and stored until needed.

INGREDIENTS

*900g/2lb/5 cups crab-apples
1.75 litres/3 pints/7½ cups water
lavender stems
900g/2lb/4 cups granulated sugar*

Makes about 900g/2lb

1 Cut the crab-apples into chunks and place in a large pan with the water and 2 stems of lavender. Bring to the boil then cover the pan and simmer very gently for 1 hour, stirring occasionally until the fruit is pulpy.

2 Suspend a jelly bag and place a large bowl underneath. Sterilize the jelly bag by pouring through some boiling water. When the bowl is full of water, discard the water and replace the bowl to sit underneath the bag.

3 Pour the pulped fruit mixture from the saucepan slowly into the jelly bag. Allow the juice from the mixture to drip slowly through for several hours. Do not try to speed up the straining process by squeezing the bag or the jelly will become cloudy.

4 Discard the pulp and measure the quantity of juice in the bowl. To each 600ml/1 pint/2½ cups of juice add 450g/1lb/2 cups of sugar and pour into a clean pan. Sterilize the jars and lids required.

5 Heat the juice gently, stirring occasionally, until the sugar has dissolved. Bring to the boil and boil rapidly for about 8–10 minutes until setting point has been reached. When tested, the temperature should be 105°C/221°F. If you don't have a sugar thermometer, put a small amount of jelly on a cold plate and allow to cool. The surface should wrinkle when you push the jelly. If not yet set, continue to boil and then re-test.

6 Remove from the heat and remove any froth from the surface. Pour the jelly into the warm sterilized jars. Dip the lavender into boiling water and insert a stem into each jar. Cover with a disc of wax paper and then with cellophane paper and a rubber band.

Apple and Mint Jelly

This jelly tastes delicious served with freshly cooked vegetables.

It also makes a traditional accompaniment to rich roasted meat such as lamb.

INGREDIENTS

900g/2lb Bramley apples
granulated sugar
45ml/3 tbsp chopped fresh mint

Makes 3 x 450g/1lb jars

1 Chop the apples roughly and put them in a preserving pan.

2 Add enough water to cover the apples. Simmer until the fruit is soft.

3 Suspend a jelly bag and place a bowl underneath. Pour the mixture through the bag, allowing it to drip overnight. Do not squeeze the bag.

4 Measure the amount of juice that drains from the jelly bag. To every 600ml/1 pint/2½ cups of juice, add 500g/1¼ lb/2¾ cups granulated sugar. Stir the sugar into the juice.

5 Place the juice and sugar in a large saucepan and warm over a gentle heat, stirring continuously. Dissolve the sugar in the juice and then increase the heat and bring the liquid to the boil. Test for setting by pouring about 15ml/1 tbsp onto a cold plate and allowing it to cool. If a wrinkle forms on the surface when pushed with a fingertip, the jelly is almost set. When a set is reached, leave the jelly to cool.

6 Stir in the chopped mint and pot into sterilized jars. Seal each jar with a wax disc and a tightly fitting cellophane top. Store in a cool, dark place. The jelly will keep unopened for up to a year. Once opened, keep in the fridge and consume within a week.

POACHED SPICED PLUMS IN BRANDY

Bottling spiced fruit is a great way to preserve summer flavours for eating in winter.

Serve these spiced plums as a dessert, with freshly whipped cream, if liked.

INGREDIENTS

600ml/1 pint/2½ cups brandy
rind of 1 lemon, peeled in a long strip
350g/12oz/1⅔ cups caster sugar
1 cinnamon stick
900g/2lb fresh plums

Makes 900g/2lb

VARIATION

Other fruits that can be preserved successfully in this way include fresh pears and peaches.

1 Put the brandy, sugar and cinnamon stick in a large pan and heat gently to dissolve the sugar. Add the plums and lemon rind. Poach for 15 minutes, or until soft. Remove with a slotted spoon.

2 Reduce the syrup by a third by rapid boiling. Strain it over the plums. Bottle the plums in large sterilized jars. Seal tightly and store for up to 6 months in a cool, dark place.

Spiced Pickled Pears

These delicious pears are the perfect accompaniment for cooked ham or cold meat salads.

INGREDIENTS

900g/2lb pears
600ml/1 pint/2½ cups white wine vinegar
225g/8oz/1 cup caster sugar
1 cinnamon stick
5 star anise
10 whole cloves

Makes 900g/2lb

COOK'S TIP

The pears will keep for up to a year unopened. Once opened, store in the fridge and consume within one week.

1 Use a sharp knife to peel the pears, keeping them whole and leaving the flesh on the stalks. Heat the white wine vinegar and caster sugar together in a saucepan, stirring continuously, until the sugar has melted. Pour over the pears and poach for 15 minutes.

2 Add the cinnamon stick, star anise and cloves and simmer for 10 minutes. Remove the pears and pack tightly into sterilized jars. Simmer the syrup for a further 15 minutes and strain it over the pears. Seal the jars tightly and store in a cool, dark place.

Puddings & Desserts

Christmas is a time to indulge in puddings and desserts. At Christmas Dinner, most guests will expect Traditional Christmas Pudding, but other variations on the festive theme such as Chocolate and Chestnut Yule Log or Christmas Cranberry Bombe will be just as welcome. After a heavy meal, a fruit-based dessert like Ruby Fruit Salad or Spiced Pears in Red Wine will always be appreciated, and, for successful entertaining, try individual desserts such as sinful Frozen Grand Marnier Soufflés laced with alcohol. Specialities for chocaholics include Amaretto Mousses with Chocolate Sauce, while Chocolate Crêpes with Plums and Port will provide a sophisticated end to any main course dish.

GINGER TRIFLE

This is a good way to use up leftover cake, whether plain, chocolate or gingerbread. You can substitute

runny honey for the ginger and syrup, if you prefer. This pudding can be made the day before.

INGREDIENTS

225g/8oz gingerbread or other cake
60ml/4 tbsp Grand Marnier or sherry
2 ripe dessert pears, peeled, cored and cubed
2 bananas, thickly sliced
2 oranges, segmented
1–2 pieces stem ginger, finely chopped, plus 30ml/2 tbsp syrup

For the Custard
2 eggs
50g/2oz/4 tbsp caster sugar
15ml/1 tbsp cornflour
450ml/¾ pint/1⅞ cups milk
few drops vanilla essence

To Decorate
150ml/¼ pint/⅔ cup double cream, lightly whipped
25g/1oz/¼ cup chopped almonds, toasted
4 glacé cherries
8 small pieces angelica

Serves 8

1 Cut the gingerbread into 4cm/1½in cubes. Put them in the bottom of a 1.75 litre/3 pint/7½ cup glass bowl. Sprinkle over the liqueur and set aside.

2 For the custard, whisk the eggs, sugar and cornflour into a pan with a little milk. Heat the remaining milk until almost boiling. Pour it on to the egg mixture, whisking. Heat, stirring, until thickened. Simmer for 2 minutes. Add the vanilla essence and leave to cool.

3 Mix all the prepared fruit with the ginger and syrup. Spoon into the bowl on top of the gingerbread. Spoon over the custard to cover and chill until set.

4 Cover the top with whipped cream and scatter on the toasted almonds. Arrange the glacé cherries and angelica around the edge.

RUBY FRUIT SALAD

After a rich main course, this port-flavoured fruit salad is light and refreshing.

You can use any fruit that is available.

INGREDIENTS

300ml/½ pint/1¼ cups water
115g/4oz/8 tbsp caster sugar
1 cinnamon stick
4 cloves
pared rind of 1 orange
300ml/½ pint/1¼ cups port
2 oranges
1 small ripe Ogen, Charentais or
Honeydew melon
4 small bananas
2 dessert apples
225g/8oz seedless grapes

Serves 8

3 On a chopping board, cut the melon in half, remove the seeds and scoop out the flesh with a melon baller, or cut it into small cubes. Add it to the syrup. Peel the bananas and cut them in 1cm/½ in slices.

4 Quarter and core the apples and cut them in small cubes. (Leave the skin on or peel if the skin is tough.) Halve the grapes if large, or leave them whole. Stir all the fruit into the syrup, cover and chill for an hour before serving.

1 Put the water, sugar, spices and pared orange rind into a saucepan and stir, over a gentle heat, to dissolve the sugar. Then bring the liquid to the boil, cover the pan with a lid and allow to simmer gently for 10 minutes. Remove the pan from the heat and set aside to cool, then add the port.

2 Strain the liquid through a sieve into a mixing bowl, to remove the spices and orange rind. With a sharp knife, cut off all the skin and pith from the oranges. Then, holding each orange over the bowl to catch the juice, cut away the segments, by slicing between the membrane that divides each segment and allowing the segments to drop into the syrup. Squeeze the remaining pith to release as much of the remaining juice as possible.

Golden Ginger Compote

Warm, spicy and full of sun-ripened ingredients – this is the perfect Christmas dessert.

INGREDIENTS

2 cups kumquats
150g/5oz/1¼ cups dried apricots
25g/1oz/2 tbsp raisins
400ml/14fl oz/1⅔ cups water
1 orange
2.5cm/1in piece fresh root ginger, peeled and grated
4 cardamom pods, crushed
4 cloves
30ml/2 tbsp honey
15g/½oz/1 tbsp slivered almonds, toasted

Serves 4

1 Wash the kumquats, and, if they are large, cut them in half. Place them in a pan with the apricots, raisins and water. Bring to the boil.

2 Pare the rind from the orange and add to the pan. Add the ginger, the cardamom pods and the cloves.

3 Reduce the heat, cover and simmer for about 30 minutes or until the fruit is tender, stirring occasionally.

4 Squeeze the orange juice and add to the pan with honey to sweeten. Sprinkle with almonds and serve.

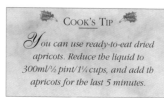

COOK'S TIP

You can use ready-to-eat dried apricots. Reduce the liquid to 300ml/½ pint/1¼ cups, and add th apricots for the last 5 minutes.

Spiced Pears in Red Wine

Serve these pears hot or cold, with lightly whipped cream. The flavours improve with

keeping, so you can make this several days before you want to serve it.

Ingredients

600ml/1 pint/2½ cups red wine
225g/8oz/1 cup caster sugar
cinnamon stick
6 cloves
finely grated rind of 1 orange
10ml/2 tsp grated root ginger
8 even-sized firm pears, with stalks
15ml/1 tbsp brandy
25g/1oz/2 tbsp almonds or hazelnuts,
toasted, to decorate

Serves 8

3 Remove the pears from the syrup, using a slotted spoon, being careful not to pull out the stalks. Put the pears in one large serving bowl or into 8 individual bowls.

4 Bring the syrup to the boil and boil it rapidly until it thickens and reduces. Allow to cool slightly, add the brandy and strain over the pears. Scatter on the toasted nuts, to decorate.

1 Choose a pan large enough to hold all the pears upright in one layer. Put all the ingredients except the pears, brandy and almonds into the pan and heat slowly until the sugar has dissolved. Simmer for 5 minutes.

2 Peel the pears, leaving the stalks on, and cut away the flower end. Arrange them upright in the pan. Cover with a lid and simmer until they are tender. The cooking time will depend on their size, but will be about 45–50 minutes.

Stuffed Peaches with Mascarpone Cream

Mascarpone is a thick, velvety Italian cream cheese, made from cow's milk.

Although it can be used as a thickening agent in savoury recipes, it is often used

in desserts or eaten with a variety of fresh fruit.

INGREDIENTS

4 large peaches, halved and stoned
40g/1½oz amaretti biscuits, crumbled
30ml/2 tbsp ground almonds
45ml/3 tbsp sugar
15ml/1 tbsp cocoa powder
150ml/¼ pint/⅔ cup sweet white wine
25g/1oz/2 tbsp butter

For the Mascarpone Cream
30ml/2 tbsp caster sugar
3 egg yolks
15ml/1 tbsp sweet white wine
225g/8oz/1 cup mascarpone cheese
150ml/¼ pint/⅔ cup double cream

Serves 4

1 Preheat the oven to 200°C/400°F/ Gas 6. Using a teaspoon, scoop some of the flesh from the cavities in the peaches, to make a reasonable space for stuffing. Chop up the scooped-out flesh with a knife.

2 Mix together the amaretti, ground almonds, sugar, cocoa and peach flesh. Add enough wine to make the mixture into a thick paste.

3 Place the halved peaches in a buttered ovenproof dish and fill them with the stuffing. Dot each peach with the butter, then pour the remaining wine into the dish. Bake for 35 minutes.

4 To make the mascarpone cream, beat the sugar and egg yolks until thick and pale. Stir in the wine, then fold in the mascarpone. Whip the double cream to form soft peaks and fold into the mixture. Remove the peaches from the oven and leave to cool. Serve the peaches at room temperature, with the mascarpone.

VARIATION

As a low-fat alternative to mascarpone cream, mix ½ cup ricotta cheese or fromage frais with 1 tbsp light brown sugar. Spoon the cheese mixture into the hollow of each peach half, using a teaspoon, and sprinkle with a little ground star anise or allspice. Grill for 6–8 minutes and serve.

CRÊPES WITH ORANGE SAUCE

This is a sophisticated dessert that is easy to make at home. You can make

the crêpes in advance; you will be able to put the dish together quickly at the last minute.

INGREDIENTS

115g/4oz/¾ cup plain flour
1.5ml/¼ tsp salt
25g/1oz/2 tbsp caster sugar
2 eggs, lightly beaten
250ml/8fl oz/1 cup milk
60ml/4 tbsp water
30ml/2 tbsp orange flower water or orange
liqueur (optional)
25g/1oz/2 tbsp unsalted butter, melted,
plus more for frying

For the Orange Sauce
75g/3oz/6 tbsp unsalted butter
55g/2oz/¼ cup caster sugar
grated rind and juice of 1 large unwaxed
orange
grated rind and juice of 1 unwaxed
lemon
150ml/¼ pint/⅔ cup fresh orange juice
60ml/4 tbsp orange liqueur
brandy and orange liqueur, for flaming
(optional)
orange segments, to decorate

Serves 6

2 Heat an 18–20cm/7–8in crêpe pan (preferably non-stick) over a medium heat. Stir the melted butter into the crêpe batter. Brush the hot pan with a little extra melted butter and pour in about 30ml/2 tbsp of batter. Quickly tilt and rotate the pan to cover the base with a thin layer of batter. Cook for about 1 minute until the top is set and the base is golden. With a palette knife, lift the edge to check the colour, then carefully turn over the crêpe and cook for 20–30 seconds, just to set. Tip out on to a plate.

4 To make the sauce, melt the butter in a large frying pan over a medium-low heat, then stir in the sugar, orange and lemon rind and juice, the additional orange juice and the orange liqueur, if using.

5 Place a crêpe in the pan browned-side down, swirling gently to coat with the sauce. Fold it in half, then in half again to form a triangle and push to the side of the pan. Continue heating and folding the crêpes until all are warm and covered with the sauce.

1 Sift together the flour, salt and sugar. Make a well in the centre and pour in the eggs. Beat the eggs, whisking in the flour until it is all incorporated. Whisk in the milk and water until smooth. Whisk in the orange flower water or liqueur. Then strain the batter into a jug and set aside.

3 Continue cooking the crêpes, stirring the batter occasionally and brushing the pan with a little melted butter as and when necessary. Place a sheet of clear film between each crêpe as they are stacked to prevent sticking. (Crêpes can be prepared ahead to this point – wrap and chill until ready to use.)

6 If you want to flame the crêpes, heat 30–45ml/2–3tbsp each of orange liqueur and brandy in a small saucepan over a medium heat. Remove the pan from the heat, carefully ignite the liquid with a match then gently pour over the crêpes. Scatter over the orange segments and serve at once.

$\mathscr{M}$INI $\mathscr{M}$ILLEFEUILLE

This pâtisserie *classic is a delectable combination of tender puff pastry sandwiched with luscious*

pastry cream. It is difficult to cut, making individual servings a brilliant solution.

INGREDIENTS

450g/1lb rough-puff or puff pastry
6 egg yolks
70g/2½oz/⅓ cup caster sugar
45ml/3 tbsp plain flour
350ml/12fl oz/1½ cups milk
30ml/2 tbsp Kirsch or cherry liqueur
(optional)
450g/1lb/2⅔ cups raspberries
icing sugar, for dusting
strawberry or raspberry coulis, to serve

Serves 8

1 Lightly butter two large baking sheets and then sprinkle them very lightly with cold water.

2 On a lightly floured surface, roll out the pastry to a 3mm/⅛in thickness. Using a 10cm/4in cutter, cut out 12 rounds. Place on the baking sheets and prick with a fork. Chill for 30 minutes. Preheat the oven to 200°C/400°F/Gas 6.

3 Bake the pastry rounds for about 15–20 minutes until golden, then transfer to wire racks to cool.

4 Whisk the egg yolks and sugar until light and creamy, then whisk in the flour until blended. Bring the milk to the boil and pour it over the egg mixture, whisking. Return to the saucepan, bring to the boil and boil for 2 minutes, whisking. Remove the pan from the heat and whisk in the Kirsch or liqueur. Pour into a bowl and press clear film on to the surface to prevent a skin forming. Set aside to cool.

5 To assemble, split the pastry rounds in half. Spread one round at a time with a little pastry cream. Arrange a layer of raspberries over the cream and top with a second pastry round. Spread with a little more cream and a few more raspberries. Top with a third pastry round flat side up. Dust with icing sugar and serve with the coulis.

RED FRUIT FILO BASKETS

This elegant dessert looks very festive. It is also low in fat and needs only a fine brushing of oil

before use: a light oil such as sunflower is the best choice for this recipe.

INGREDIENTS

3 sheets filo pastry (about 90g/3½oz)
15ml/1 tbsp sunflower oil
175g/6oz/1½ cups redcurrants
250ml/8fl oz/1 cup strained plain yogurt
5ml/1 tsp icing sugar
115 g/4 oz/1 cup whole strawberries and
raspberries, to decorate

Serves 6

1 Preheat the oven to 200°C/400°F/ Gas 6. Using a sharp kitchen knife, cut the sheets of filo pastry into 18 squares with sides about 10cm/4in long.

2 Brush each filo square thinly with oil, then arrange the squares to overlap in six small tartlet pans, layering them in threes. Bake for 6–8 minutes, until crisp and golden. Remove the baskets from the tartlet pans, using a palette knife, and allow them to cool.

3 Reserve a few sprigs of redcurrants to add to the decoration and string the rest through the tines of a fork. Stir the currants into the yogurt.

4 Spoon the yogurt into the filo baskets. Decorate the baskets with the red fruits and sprinkle them lightly with icing sugar.

CRUNCHY APPLE AND ALMOND FLAN

Do not be tempted to put any sugar with the apples, as this makes them produce too

much liquid. All the sweetness you'll need is in the pastry and topping.

INGREDIENTS

75g/3oz/6 tbsp butter
175g/6oz/1½ cups plain flour
25g/1oz/scant ¼ cup ground almonds
25g/1oz/2 tbsp caster sugar
1 egg yolk
15ml/1 tbsp cold water
1.5ml/¼ tsp almond essence
sifted icing sugar, to decorate

For the Crunchy Topping
115g/4oz/1 cup plain flour
1.5ml/¼ tsp mixed spice
50g/2oz/4 tbsp butter, cut in small cubes
50g/2oz/4 tbsp demerara sugar
50g/2oz/½ cup flaked almonds

For the filling
675g/1½lb cooking apples
25g/1oz/2 tbsp raisins or sultanas

Serves 8

2 Meanwhile, make the crunchy topping. Sift the flour and mixed spice into a bowl and rub in the butter. Stir in the sugar and almonds.

3 Roll out the pastry on a lightly floured surface and use it to line a 23cm/9in loose-based flan tin, taking care to press it neatly into the edges and to make a lip around the top edge.

4 Roll off the excess pastry to neaten the edge. Allow to chill in the fridge for about 15 minutes.

5 Preheat the oven to 190°C/375°F/ Gas 5. Place a baking sheet in the oven to preheat. Peel, core and slice the apples thinly. Arrange the slices in the flan in overlapping, concentric circles, doming the centre. Scatter over the raisins or sultanas. The flan will seem too full at this stage, but as the apples cook the filling will drop slightly.

6 Cover the apples with the crunchy topping mixture, pressing it on lightly. Bake on the hot baking sheet for 25– 30 minutes, or until the top is golden brown and the apples are tender (test them with a fine skewer). Leave the flan to cool in the tin for 10 minutes before turning out. The flan can be served either warm or cool, dusted with sifted icing sugar.

1 To make the pastry, rub the butter into the flour, either with your fingertips in a large mixing bowl or in a food processor, until it resembles fine breadcrumbs. Stir in the ground almonds and sugar. Whisk the egg yolk, water and almond essence together and mix them into the dry ingredients to form a soft, pliable dough. Knead the dough lightly until smooth, wrap in clear film and leave in a cool place or in the fridge to rest for about 20 minutes.

MANGO AND AMARETTI STRUDEL

Fresh mango and crushed amaretti wrapped in wafer-thin filo pastry make a

seasonal treat that is equally delicious made with apricots or plums.

INGREDIENTS

1 large mango
grated rind of 1 lemon
2 amaretti biscuits
25g/1oz/3 tbsp demerara sugar
60ml/4 tbsp wholemeal breadcrumbs
2 sheets of filo pastry, each
48 x 28cm/19 x 11in
20g/¾oz/4 tsp soft margarine, melted
15ml/1 tbsp chopped almonds
icing sugar, for dusting

Serves 4

1 Preheat the oven to 190°C/375°F/ Gas 5. Lightly grease a large baking sheet. Halve, stone and peel the mango. Cut the flesh into cubes, then place them in a bowl and sprinkle with the grated lemon rind.

2 Crush the amaretti biscuits with a rolling pin and mix them with the demerara sugar and the wholemeal breadcrumbs.

3 Lay one sheet of filo on a flat surface and brush with a quarter of the melted margarine. Top with the second sheet, brush with one-third of the remaining margarine, then fold both sheets over, if necessary, to make a rectangle measuring 28 x 24cm/11 x 9½in. Brush the rectangle with half the remaining margarine.

4 Sprinkle the filo with the amaretti mixture, leaving a 5cm/2in border on each long side. Arrange the mango cubes over the top.

5 Roll up the filo from one of the long sides, Swiss roll fashion. Lift the strudel on to the baking sheet with the join underneath. Brush with the remaining melted margarine and sprinkle with the chopped almonds.

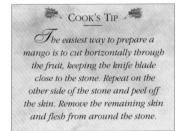

6 Bake the strudel for 20–25 minutes until golden brown, then carefully transfer it to a board. Dust the strudel with the icing sugar, slice diagonally and serve warm.

COOK'S TIP

The easiest way to prepare a mango is to cut horizontally through the fruit, keeping the knife blade close to the stone. Repeat on the other side of the stone and peel off the skin. Remove the remaining skin and flesh from around the stone.

Traditional Christmas Pudding

This recipe makes enough to fill one 1.2 litre/2 pint/5 cup basin or two 600ml/1 pint/2½ cup basins.

It can be made up to a month before Christmas and stored in a cool, dry place.

Steam the pudding for 2 hours before serving. Serve topped with a decorative sprig of holly.

INGREDIENTS

115g/4oz/½ cup butter
*225g/8oz/1 heaped cup soft dark
brown sugar*
50g/2oz/½ cup self-raising flour
5ml/1 tsp mixed spice
1.5ml/¼ tsp nutmeg
2.5ml/½ tsp ground cinnamon
2 eggs
115g/4oz/2 cups fresh white breadcrumbs
175g/6oz/1 cup sultanas
175g/6oz/1 cup raisins
115g/4oz/½ cup currants
25g/1oz/3 tbsp chopped mixed peel
25g/1oz/¼ cup chopped almonds
*1 small cooking apple, peeled, cored and
coarsely grated*
finely grated rind of 1 orange or lemon
*juice of 1 orange or lemon, made up to
150ml/¼ pint/⅔ cup with brandy, rum
or sherry*

Serves 8

3 Turn the mixture into the greased basin(s) and level the top.

4 Cover with another disc of buttered greaseproof paper.

5 Make a pleat across the centre of a large piece of greaseproof paper and cover the basin(s), tying it with string. Pleat a piece of foil in the same way and cover the basin(s), tucking it under the greaseproof frill.

1 Cut a disc of greaseproof paper to fit the base of the basin(s) and butter the disc and basin(s).

2 Whisk the butter and sugar together until soft. Beat in the flour, spices and eggs. Stir in the remaining ingredients thoroughly. The mixture should have a soft dropping consistency.

6 Tie another piece of string around the basin(s) and across the top, as a handle. Place the basin(s) in a steamer over a pan of simmering water and steam for 6 hours. Alternatively, put the basin(s) into a large pan and pour round enough boiling water to come halfway up the basin(s) and cover the pan with a tight-fitting lid. Check the water is simmering and top it up with boiling water as it evaporates. When the pudding(s) have cooked, leave to cool completely. Then remove the foil and greaseproof paper. Wipe the basin(s) clean and replace the greaseproof paper and foil with clean pieces, ready for reheating.

❧ To Serve ❧

*Steam for 2 hours. Turn on to a
plate and leave to stand for
5 minutes before removing the
pudding basin (the steam will rise to
the top of the basin and help to
loosen the pudding).*

CHOCOLATE AND CHESTNUT YULE LOG

This chocolate log is traditionally served at Christmas. Make it the day before it is needed

or some time in advance and freeze it. It makes an excellent dessert for a party.

INGREDIENTS

25g/1oz/2 tbsp plain flour
30ml/2 tbsp cocoa powder
pinch of salt
3 large eggs, separated
large pinch of cream of tartar
115g/4oz/8 tbsp caster sugar
2–3 drops almond essence
sifted cocoa powder and holly sprigs,
to decorate

For the Filling
15ml/1 tbsp rum or brandy
5ml/1 tsp powdered gelatine
115g/4oz plain chocolate, broken into
squares
50g/2oz/4 tbsp caster sugar
250g/8oz can chestnut purée
225ml/½ pint/1¼ cups double cream

Serves 8

1 Preheat the oven to 180°C/350°F/
Gas 4. Grease and line a 23 x 33cm/
9 x 13in Swiss roll tin and line the
base with non-stick baking paper.
Sift the flour, cocoa and salt together
on to a piece of greaseproof paper.

2 Put the egg whites into a large clean
bowl and whisk them until frothy. Add
the cream of tartar and whisk until stiff.
Gradually whisk in half the sugar, until
the mixture will stand in stiff peaks.

3 Put the egg yolks and the remaining
sugar into another bowl and whisk
until thick and pale. Add the almond
essence. Stir in the sifted flour and
cocoa mixture. Lastly, fold in the
egg whites, using a metal spoon,
until everything is evenly blended.
Be careful not to over-mix.

4 Turn the mixture into the prepared
Swiss roll tin and level the top. Bake
for 15–20 minutes, or until springy
to the touch. Have ready a large piece
of greaseproof paper dusted liberally
with caster sugar. Turn the Swiss roll
on to the paper, remove the baking
lining paper, and roll it up with the
greaseproof paper still inside. Leave
to cool completely on a wire rack.

5 Put the rum or brandy in a cup and
sprinkle over the gelatine; leave to
become spongy. Melt the chocolate
in a 600ml/1 pint/2½ cup basin over
a pan of hot water. Melt the gelatine
over barely simmering water and add
to the chocolate. With an electric
beater, whisk in the sugar and chestnut
purée. Remove from the heat and leave
to cool. Whisk the cream until it holds
soft peaks. Fold the two mixtures
together evenly.

6 Unroll the Swiss roll carefully,
spread it with half the filling and roll
it up again. Place it on a serving dish
and spread over the rest of the
chocolate cream to cover it. Mark it
with a fork to resemble a log. Chill
until firm. Dust the cake with sifted
cocoa powder and decorate around the
edges of the plate with sprigs of holly.

Frozen Grand Marnier Soufflés

These luxurious puddings are always appreciated and make a wonderful end to any Christmas-time meal.

INGREDIENTS

200g/7oz/1 cup caster sugar
6 large eggs, separated
250ml/8fl oz/1 cup milk
15g/½oz powdered gelatine, soaked in
45ml/3 tbsp cold water
450ml/¾ pint/1⅞ cups double cream
60ml/4 tbsp Grand Marnier

Serves 8

1 Fold a double collar of greaseproof paper around eight ramekin dishes and tie with string. (You could make one large pudding, if you prefer.) Put 75g/3oz/6 tbsp of the caster sugar in a large mixing bowl with the egg yolks and whisk until the yolks are pale. This will take about 5 minutes by hand and about 3 minutes if you use an electric hand mixer.

2 Heat the milk until almost boiling and pour it on to the yolks, whisking all the time. Return to the pan and stir it over a gentle heat until it is thick enough to coat the back of the spoon. Remove the pan from the heat. Stir the soaked gelatine into the custard. Pour into a bowl and leave to cool. Whisk occasionally, until the custard is on the point of setting.

3 Put the remaining sugar in a pan with the water and dissolve it over a low heat. Bring to the boil and boil rapidly until it reaches the soft ball stage or 119°C/238°F on a sugar thermometer. Remove from the heat. In a clean bowl, whisk the egg whites until they are stiff. Pour the hot syrup on to the whites, whisking all the time. Leave to cool.

4 Whisk the cream until it holds soft peaks. Add the Grand Marnier to the cold custard and fold into the cold meringue, with the cream. Pour into the prepared ramekin dishes. Freeze overnight. Remove the paper collars. Leave at room temperature for 30 minutes before serving.

COOK'S TIP

The soft ball stage of a syrup is when a teaspoon of the mixture dropped into a glass of cold water clumps into a ball.

TIRAMISU IN CHOCOLATE CUPS

Give in to the temptation of tiramisu, with its magical mocha flavour.

INGREDIENTS

1 egg yolk
30ml/2 tbsp caster sugar
2.5ml/½ tsp vanilla essence
250g/9oz/generous cup mascarpone cheese
120ml/4fl oz/½ cup strong black coffee
15ml/1 tbsp cocoa powder
30ml/2 tbsp coffee liqueur
16 amaretti biscuits
cocoa powder, for dusting

For the Chocolate Cups
175g/6oz good quality plain chocolate, broken into squares
25g/1oz/2 tbsp unsalted butter

Serves 6

COOK'S TIP

When spreading the chocolate for the cups, don't aim for perfectly regular edges; uneven edges will give a prettier frilled effect.

1 Make the chocolate cups. Cut out six 15cm/6 in rounds of non-stick baking paper. Melt the chocolate with the butter in a heatproof bowl over barely simmering water. Stir until smooth, then spread a spoonful of the chocolate mixture over each circle, to within 2cm/¾in of the edge.

2 Carefully lift each paper round and drape it over an upturned teacup or ramekin so that the edges curve into frills. Leave until completely set, then carefully lift off and peel away the paper to reveal the chocolate cups.

3 To make the filling, beat the egg yolk and sugar in a bowl until smooth, then stir in the vanilla essence and mascarpone. Mix until a smooth, creamy consistency is achieved.

4 In a separate bowl, mix the coffee, cocoa and liqueur. Break up the biscuits and stir into the mixture.

5 Divide half the biscuit mixture among the chocolate cups, then spoon over half the mascarpone mixture.

6 Spoon over the remaining biscuit mixture, top with the rest of the mascarpone mixture and dust with cocoa. Serve as soon as possible.

Iced Praline Torte

Make this elaborate torte several days ahead, decorate it and return it to the freezer until you

are nearly ready to serve it. Allow the torte to stand at room temperature for an hour before

serving, or leave it in the refrigerator overnight to soften.

INGREDIENTS

115g/4oz/1 cup almonds or hazelnuts
115g/4oz/8 tbsp caster sugar
115g/4oz/⅔ cup raisins
90ml/6 tbsp rum or brandy
115g/4oz plain chocolate, broken into
squares
30ml/2 tbsp milk
450ml/¾ pint/1⅞ cups double cream
30ml/2 tbsp strong black coffee
16 sponge-finger biscuits

To Finish
150ml/¼ pint/⅔ cup double cream
50g/2oz/½ cup flaked almonds, toasted
15g/½oz plain chocolate, melted

Serves 8

1 To make the praline, have ready an oiled cake tin or baking sheet. Put the nuts into a heavy-based saucepan with the sugar and heat gently until the sugar melts. Swirl the pan to coat the nuts in the hot sugar. Cook slowly until the nuts brown and the sugar caramelizes. Watch all the time, as this will only take a few minutes. Turn the nuts quickly into the cake tin or on to the baking sheet and leave them to cool completely. When cool, break the praline up and grind it to a fine powder in a food processor.

2 Soak the raisins in 45ml/3 tbsp of the rum or brandy for an hour (or better still overnight), so they soften and absorb the full flavour of the alcohol. Melt the chocolate with the milk in a bowl over a pan of barely simmering water. Remove and allow to cool. Lightly grease a 1.2 litre/ 2 pint/5 cup loaf tin and line it with greaseproof paper.

3 Whisk the cream in a bowl until it holds soft peaks. Whisk in the cold chocolate. Then fold in the praline and the soaked raisins, with any liquid.

4 Mix the coffee and remaining rum or brandy in a shallow dish. Dip in each of the sponge-finger biscuits and arrange half in a layer over the base of the prepared loaf tin.

5 Cover the sponge biscuits with the chocolate mixture and add another layer of soaked sponge fingers. Freeze overnight.

6 Dip the cake tin briefly into warm water to loosen it and turn the torte out on to a serving plate. Cover with whipped cream. Sprinkle the top with toasted flaked almonds and drizzle the melted chocolate over the top. Return the torte to the freezer until it is needed.

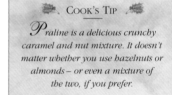

COOK'S TIP

Praline is a delicious crunchy caramel and nut mixture. It doesn't matter whether you use hazelnuts or almonds – or even a mixture of the two, if you prefer.

Baked Custard with Burnt Sugar

You can add a little liqueur to this dessert if you like, but it is equally delicious without it.

Ingredients

2 vanilla pods
1 litre/1¾ pints/4 cups double cream
6 egg yolks
100g/3½oz/½ cup caster sugar
30ml/2 tbsp almond or orange liqueur
75g/3oz/⅓ cup soft light brown sugar

Serves 6

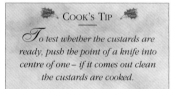

Cook's Tip

To test whether the custards are ready, push the point of a knife into centre of one – if it comes out clean the custards are cooked.

1 Preheat the oven to 150°C/300°F/ Gas 2. Place six 120ml/4fl oz/½ cup ramekins in a roasting tin or ovenproof dish and set aside.

2 With a sharp knife, split the vanilla pods lengthways. Scrape the black seeds into a medium saucepan and add the pods. Add the cream and bring just to the boil over a medium-high heat, stirring frequently. Remove from the heat and cover. Set aside to stand for 15–20 minutes. This will allow the vanilla to infuse the cream.

3 In a bowl, whisk the egg yolks, caster sugar and liqueur until well blended. Whisk in the hot cream and strain into a large jug. Divide the custard equally among the ramekins.

4 Pour enough boiling water into the roasting tin to come halfway up the sides of the ramekins. Cover the tin with foil and bake in the preheated oven for about 30 minutes until the custards are just set. Remove the ramekins from the tin and leave to cool. Return to the dry roasting tin and allow to chill in the fridge for at least 2 hours or overnight.

5 Preheat the grill. Sprinkle the sugar evenly over the surface of each custard and grill for 30–60 seconds until the sugar melts and caramelizes. (Do not let the sugar burn or the custard curdle.) Place in the fridge again to set the crust and chill completely before serving.

CHRISTMAS CRANBERRY BOMBE

This is a light alternative to Christmas pudding that is still very festive.

INGREDIENTS

For the Sorbet Centre
*225g/8oz/2 cups fresh or frozen
cranberries
150ml/¼ pint/⅔ cup orange juice
finely grated rind of ½ orange
2.5ml/½ tsp allspice
60ml/4 tbsp raw sugar*

For the Outer Layer
*600ml/1 pint/2½ cups vanilla ice cream
30ml/2 tbsp chopped angelica
30ml/2 tbsp candied citrus rind
15ml/1 tbsp slivered almonds, toasted*

Serves 6

3 Pack the mixture into a 5 cup pudding mould and, using a metal spoon, hollow out the centre. Freeze the mould until firm to the touch. This will take at least 3 hours.

4 Fill the hollowed-out centre of the bombe with cranberry mixture, smooth over and freeze until firm. To serve, allow to soften slightly at room temperature, turn out and slice.

1 Put the cranberries, orange juice, rind and spice in a pan and cook gently until the cranberries are soft. Add the sugar, then purée in a food processor until almost smooth, but still with some texture. Leave to cool.

2 Allow the vanilla ice cream to soften slightly then stir in the chopped angelica, mixed peel and almonds.

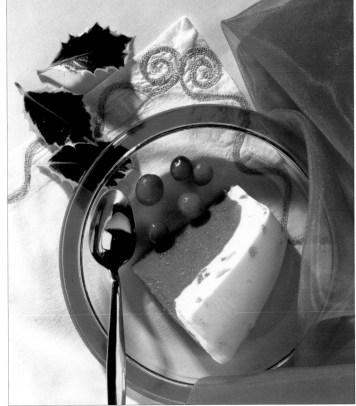

CHOCOLATE SORBET WITH RED FRUITS

This velvety smooth sorbet has long been a favourite. Bitter chocolate gives by far the

richest flavour, but if you can't track this down, then use 250g/9oz of the very best quality

dark Continental plain chocolate that you can find. If not the sorbet will be too sweet.

INGREDIENTS

150g/5oz bitter chocolate, roughly chopped
115g/4oz plain chocolate, roughly chopped
200g/7oz/1 cup caster sugar
475ml/16fl oz/2 cups water
chocolate curls, to decorate
sprigs of fresh berries, to decorate

Serves 6

1 Put the chopped bitter and plain chocolate in a food processor fitted with a metal blade, and process for 20–30 seconds until the chunks of chocolate are finely chopped.

2 In a large heavy-based saucepan over a medium-high heat, bring the sugar and water to the boil, stirring continuously, until the sugar dissolves. Boil for about 2 minutes, then remove the saucepan from the heat.

3 With the food processor running, pour the hot syrup over the chocolate. Allow the machine to continue running for 1–2 minutes until the chocolate is completely melted and the mixture is smooth, scraping down the bowl once.

4 Strain the chocolate mixture into a large measuring jug or bowl, and leave to cool, then chill, stirring occasionally. Freeze the mixture in an ice cream machine, following the manufacturer's instructions or see Cook's Tip (below). Allow the sorbet to soften for 5–10 minutes at room temperature and serve in scoops, decorated with chocolate curls and the sprigs of fresh berries.

COOK'S TIP

If you don't have an ice cream machine, freeze the sorbet until it is firm around the edges. Process the mixture until smooth, then freeze again.

Amaretto Mousses with Chocolate Sauce

These little desserts are extremely rich and derive their flavour from Amaretto, an

almond-flavoured liqueur, and amaretti, little almond-flavoured biscuits.

INGREDIENTS

*115g/4oz amaretti, ratafia or macaroon
biscuits
60ml/4 tbsp Amaretto di sarono liqueur
350g/12oz white chocolate, broken into
squares
15g/½oz powdered gelatine, soaked in
45ml/3 tdsp cold water
450ml/¾ pint/1⅞ cups double cream*

For the Choocolate Sauce
*225g/8oz dark chocolate, broken into
squares
300ml/½ pint/1¼ cups single cream
50g/2oz/4 tdsp caster sugar*

Serves 8

1 Lightly oil eight individual 120ml/
4fl oz/½ cup moulds and line the base
of each mould with a small disc of
oiled greaseproof paper. Put the
biscuits into a large bowl and crush
them finely with a rolling pin.

2 Melt the Amaretto and white
chocolate together gently in a bowl
over a pan of hot but not boiling
water (be very careful not to overheat
the chocolate or it will begin to
separate and go unpleasantly grainy).
Stir well until smooth; remove from
the pan and leave to cool.

3 Melt the gelatine over hot water
and blend it into the chocolate
mixture. Whisk the cream until it
holds soft peaks. Gently fold in the
chocolate mixture, with 60ml/4 tbsp
of the crushed biscuits.

4 Put a teaspoonful of the crushed
biscuits into the bottom of each mould
and spoon in the chocolate mixture.
Tap each mould to disperse any air
bubbles. Level the tops and sprinkle
the remaining crushed biscuits on top.
Press down gently and chill for 4 hours.

5 To make the chocolate sauce, put
all the ingredients in a small saucepan
and heat gently to melt the chocolate
and dissolve the sugar. Simmer for
2–3 minutes. Leave to cool completely.

6 Slip a knife around the sides of each
mould, and turn out on to individual
plates. Remove the greaseproof paper
from the bottom and pour round a little
dark chocolate sauce.

COOK'S TIP

*When melting chocolate, always
set the bowl over a half-full pan of
barely simmering water; chocolate
reacts badly to splashes of water
and overheating.*

CHOCOLATE CRÊPES WITH PLUMS AND PORT

A good dinner party dessert, this dish can be made in advance and always looks impressive.

INGREDIENTS

50g/2oz plain chocolate, broken into
squares
200ml/7fl oz/scant 1 cup milk
120ml/4fl oz/½ cup single cream
30ml/2 tbsp cocoa powder
115g/4oz/1 cup plain flour
2 eggs
oil, for frying

For the Filling
500g/1¼ lb red or golden plums
50g/2oz/¼ cup caster sugar
30ml/2 tbsp water
30ml/2 tbsp port
175g/6oz/¾ cup crème fraîche

For the Sauce
150g/5oz plain chocolate, broken into
squares
175ml/6fl oz/¾ cup double cream
30ml/2 tbsp port

Serves 6

1 Place the chocolate in a saucepan with the milk. Heat gently until the chocolate has dissolved. Pour into a blender or food processor and add the cream, cocoa powder, flour and eggs. Process until smooth, then tip into a jug and chill for 30 minutes.

2 Meanwhile, make the filling. Halve and stone the plums. Place them in a saucepan and add the sugar and water. Bring to the boil, then cover and simmer for about 10 minutes. Stir in the port; simmer for a further 30 seconds. Remove from the heat and keep warm.

3 Have ready a sheet of non-stick baking paper. Heat a crêpe pan, grease it lightly with a little oil, then pour in just enough batter to cover the base of the pan, swirling to coat evenly. Cook until the crêpe has set, then flip it over to cook the other side. Slide the crêpe out on to the sheet of paper, then cook 9–11 more crêpes in the same way.

4 Make the chocolate sauce. Combine the chocolate and cream in a saucepan. Heat gently, stirring until smooth. Add the port and heat gently for 1 minute.

5 Divide the plum filling between the crêpes, add a generous spoonful of crème fraîche to each and roll them up. Serve with the chocolate sauce.

CHOCOLATE, DATE AND ALMOND FILO COIL

Experience the allure of the Middle East with this delectable dessert. Crisp filo pastry conceals

a chocolate and rose water filling studded with dates and almonds.

INGREDIENTS

275g/10oz packet filo pastry, thawed if frozen
50g/2oz/4 tbsp unsalted butter, melted
icing sugar, cocoa powder and ground cinnamon, for dusting

For the Filling
75g/3oz/6 tbsp unsalted butter
115g/4oz plain chocolate, broken into squares
115g/4oz/1 cup ground almonds
115g/4oz/⅔ cup chopped dates
75g/3oz/⅔ cup icing sugar
10ml/2 tsp rose water
2.5ml/½ tsp ground cinnamon

Serves 6

1 Preheat the oven to 180°C/350°F/ Gas 4. Grease a 22cm/8½in round cake tin. Make the chocolate, date and almond filling. Melt the butter with the chocolate in a heatproof bowl over a saucepan of barely simmering water, then remove the saucepan from the heat and stir in all of the remaining ingredients to make a thick paste. Set the pan aside to cool.

2 Lay one sheet of the filo pastry on a clean work surface. Brush the filo with melted butter, then lay a second sheet of filo on top and brush again with butter.

3 Roll a handful of the chocolate almond mixture into a long sausage shape and place along one edge of the filo. Roll the pastry tightly around.

4 Place the roll around the outside of the tin. Make enough rolls to fill the tin.

5 Brush the coil with the remaining melted butter. Bake for 30–35 minutes until the pastry is golden brown and crisp. Remove the coil from the tin; place it on a plate. Serve warm, dusted with icing sugar, cocoa and cinnamon.

Raspberry and White Chocolate Cheesecake

Raspberries and white chocolate are an irresistible combination, especially when

teamed with smooth, rich mascarpone cheese on a crunchy ginger and pecan nut base.

INGREDIENTS

50g/2oz/4 tbsp unsalted butter
225g/8oz ginger nut biscuits, crushed
50g/2oz/½ cup chopped pecan nuts or walnuts

For the Filling
275g/10oz/1¼ cups mascarpone cheese
175g/6oz/¾ cup fromage frais
2 eggs, beaten
45ml/3 tbsp caster sugar
250g/9oz white chocolate, broken into squares
225g/8oz/1½ cups fresh or frozen raspberries

For the Topping
115g/4 oz/½ cups mascarpone cheese
75g/3oz/⅓ cup fromage frais
white chocolate curls and raspberries, to decorate

Serves 8

1 Preheat the oven to 150°C/300°F/ Gas 2. Melt the butter in a large saucepan, then stir in the crushed biscuits and nuts. Press the mixture into the base of a 23cm/9in springform cake tin.

2 To make the filling, beat the mascarpone cheese and fromage frais in a bowl, then beat in the eggs and caster sugar until evenly mixed.

3 Melt the white chocolate gently in a heatproof bowl over hot water, then stir into the cheese mixture with the fresh or frozen raspberries.

4 Tip into the prepared tin and spread evenly, then bake for about 1 hour or until just set. Switch off the oven, but do not remove the cheesecake. Leave it until cold and completely set.

5 Remove the sides of the tin and carefully lift the cheesecake on to a serving plate. Make the topping by mixing together the mascarpone and fromage frais in a bowl and spreading the mixture over the cheesecake. Decorate with white chocolate curls and the fresh raspberries.

COOK'S TIP

The biscuits for the base should be crushed quite finely. This can easily be done in a food processor. Alternatively, place the biscuits in a stout plastic bag and crush them with a rolling pin.

CHOCOLATE ROULADE WITH COCONUT CREAM

This sinfully rich roulade is the ultimate in Christmas treats.

It makes the perfect dessert for a New Year's Eve dinner party.

INGREDIENTS

50g/5oz/¾ cup caster sugar
5 eggs, separated
50g/2oz/½ cup cocoa powder

For the Filling
300ml/½ pint/1¼ cups double cream
45ml/3 tbsp whisky
50g/2oz piece solid creamed coconut
30ml/2 tbsp caster sugar

For the Topping
coarsely grated curls of fresh coconut
chocolate curls

Serves 8

1 Preheat the oven to 180°C/350°F/
Gas 4. Grease a 33 x 23cm/13 x 9in
Swiss roll tin. Dust a large sheet of
greaseproof paper with 30ml/2 tbsp
of caster sugar.

2 Place the egg yolks in a heatproof
bowl. Add the remaining caster sugar
and whisk with a hand-held electric
mixer until the mixture is thick enough
to leave a trail. Sift the cocoa over, then
fold in carefully and evenly with a
metal spoon.

3 Whisk the egg whites in a clean,
grease-free bowl until they form soft
peaks. Fold about 15ml/1 tbsp of the
whites into the chocolate mixture to
lighten it, then fold in the rest evenly.

4 Scrape the mixture into the prepared
tin, taking it right into the corners.
Smooth the surface with a palette knife,
then bake for 20–25 minutes or until
well risen and springy to the touch.

5 Turn the cooked sponge out on to
the sugar-dusted greaseproof paper
and carefully peel off the lining paper.
Cover with a damp, clean dish towel
and leave to cool.

> ### COOK'S TIP
>
> *Either Irish or Scotch Whisky can
> be used to make the cream filling for
> this dessert. If whisky is not
> available, you can use white rum or
> a rum-based spirit, such as Malibu,
> as a suitable alternative.*

6 To make the filling, whisk the cream
with the whisky in a bowl until the
mixture just holds its shape, then finely
grate the creamed coconut and stir it in
with the sugar.

7 Remove the dish towel to uncover
the sponge. Spread about three-quarters
of the cream mixture to the edges of
the sponge. Roll up carefully from a
long side. Transfer the roulade to a
plate and pipe or spoon the remaining
cream mixture on top. Then grate the
fresh coconut to make the curls and
place them on top, along with the
chocolate curls.

Christmas Baking

Nuts and spices, dried fruit and mincemeat all
mean Christmas and the delicious cakes and biscuits baked
during this time. Some, like the Moist and Rich Christmas
Cake, need advance preparation, while others, like the
Christmas Biscuits, are simple enough to make with
the children. Gingerbread is essential to Christmas and there
are recipes here to double as pretty tree decorations and a table
centrepiece. There is the traditional Italian Panettone and
Austrian Stollen, Hogmanay Shortbread and Middle Eastern
Date-filled Pastries. Finally, there are three lovely recipes with
mincemeat – the all-time favourite – to ensure that
everyone finishes the festive meal feeling satisfied.

Lining a Deep Cake Tin

For a rich or light fruit cake, use a good-quality fixed-base deep cake tin.

Ensure that you have the correct size of tin for the quantity of cake mixture.

1 Place the tin on a piece of double-thickness greaseproof paper or non-stick baking paper and draw around the base following the tin shape. Cut out the marked shape with a pair of scissors.

2 Measure and cut a strip of double-thickness greaseproof paper or non-stick baking paper long enough to wrap around the outside of the tin with a small overlap and to stand 2.5cm/1in above the top of the tin.

3 Brush the base and sides of the tin with oil. Place the cut-out paper shape in the base of the tin and press flat. Fit the double strip of greaseproof paper or non-stick baking paper inside the tin, pressing well against the sides and making sharp creases where the paper fits into the corners of the tin. Ensure that the paper strip is level and fits neatly without any creases. Brush the base and sides well with oil.

4 Measure and fit a double thickness strip of brown paper around the outside of the tin. Tie securely with string.

5 Line a baking sheet with several layers of brown paper and stand your prepared cake tin in the centre.

COOK'S TIP

To line a round tin, measure the circumference of the tin and cut a double strip of greaseproof paper 2.5cm/1in longer, to allow for overlap, and 2.5cm/1in deeper, to allow for turning. Draw around the base with a pencil and cut out.

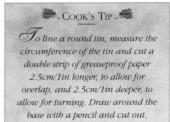

TESTING CAKES

It is very important to check that cakes are properly cooked,

otherwise they may sink in the middle and be too moist.

TESTING A FRUIT CAKE

TESTING A SPONGE CAKE

1 To test if a fruit cake is ready, push a skewer or cake tester into it; if it comes out clean, the cake is cooked.

2 Fruit cakes are generally left to cool in the tin for 30 minutes. Then turn the cake out carefully, peel away the paper and place on a wire rack or board.

1 To test if a sponge cake is ready, press down lightly on the centre of the cake with your fingertips – if the cake springs back, it is cooked.

2 To remove the cooked sponge cake from the tin, loosen around the edge by carefully running round the inside of the tin with a palette knife. Invert the cake on to a wire rack, cover with a second rack, then invert again. Remove the top rack and leave to cool.

STORING CHRISTMAS CAKE

A rich fruit Christmas cake can be made well ahead, provided you store it properly.

1 To store a fruit cake, leave the lining paper on. Wrap in a double layer of foil and keep in a cool place. Never seal a fruit cake in an airtight container for long periods of time as this may encourage mould.

2 Rich, heavy fruit cakes can be happily stored for up to 3 months. If you are going to keep a fruit cake for several months before marzipanning or icing it, pour over alcohol such as brandy a little at a time at monthly intervals, turning the cake each time. This procedure is known as "feeding".

3 Light fruit cakes are at their best when first made, or eaten within 1 month of making.

4 For long-term storage, fruit cakes can be frozen in their double wrapping of foil.

5 Once a cake has been marzipanned and iced it will keep longer, but iced cakes must be stored in cardboard cake boxes in a warm, dry atmosphere. Damp and cold are the worst conditions, causing the icing to stain and the colourings to run.

6 You can freeze a decorated celebration cake in the cake box, ensuring the lid is sealed with tape. Take the cake out of its box and thaw it slowly in a cool, dry place. When the cake has thawed, transfer it to a warm, dry place so that the icing dries completely.

Fondant Icing

This icing can be used for modelling decorations and for covering a Christmas cake.

INGREDIENTS

60ml/4 tbsp water
15g/½ oz/1 tbsp powdered gelatine
10ml/2 tsp liquid glucose
500g/1¼lb/5 cups icing sugar

Makes enough to cover a
20cm/8in round cake

1 Put the water in a small bowl and sprinkle over the gelatine. Leave to soak for 2 minutes. Place the bowl in a pan of hot water and leave to dissolve over a very gentle heat.

2 Remove the bowl from the hot water and add the liquid glucose to the dissolved gelatine.

3 Sift the icing sugar into a bowl and add the gelatine mixture. Mix thoroughly, then knead into a smooth paste. Wrap in clear film until ready to use.

Apricot Glaze

Cover the cake with this delicious fruit glaze. The stickiness of the jam helps

marzipan adhere to your Christmas cake.

INGREDIENTS

450g/1lb/2 cups apricot jam
30ml/2 tbsp water

Makes 450g/1lb

2 Boil the jam rapidly for 1 minute, then strain through a sieve. Rub through as much fruit as possible, using a spoon. Discard any skins left in the sieve.

3 Pour the glaze into a clear, hot jar, seal with a clean lid and cool. Store in the fridge, where it will keep well for up to 2 months.

1 Place the jam and water in a saucepan. Heat gently, stirring occasionally, until melted.

ALMOND PASTE

Use this rich paste as a base for royal or fondant icing. It will help to keep the cake moist.

INGREDIENTS

350g/12oz/4 cups ground almonds
175g/6oz/⅞ cup caster sugar
175g/6oz/1½ cups icing sugar
5ml/1 tsp lemon juice
1.5ml/¼ tsp almond essence
1 egg

Makes enough to cover a
20cm/8in round cake

1 Sift the ground almonds, caster sugar and icing sugar together into a bowl.

2 With a fork, beat the lemon juice, almond essence and egg together in a small bowl. Stir them into the dry ingredients and mix well.

3 Knead together until smooth and wrap in clear film until needed.

ROYAL ICING

This icing will dry very hard and is the traditional covering for a Christmas cake.

INGREDIENTS

2 egg whites
5ml/1 tsp lemon juice
5ml/1 tsp glycerine (optional)
450g/1lb icing sugar

Makes enough to cover a
20cm/8in round cake

1 In a large bowl, beat the egg whites, lemon juice and glycerine (if using) together with a fork.

2 Gradually sift in enough icing sugar to make a thick paste.

3 Using a wooden spoon, beat in the remaining icing sugar until the icing forms stiff peaks. Cover with clear film until ready to use.

COOK'S TIP

Never add more than the stated amount of glycerine. Too much will make the icing crumbly and too fragile to use. The lemon juice will prevent the icing from discolouring, but too much will make the icing become hard.

FESTIVE GINGERBREAD

In all its forms, gingerbread has been part of the Christmas tradition for generations.

It is particularly well-loved in Germany, from where many present-day baking traditions originate.

INGREDIENTS

30ml/2 tbsp golden syrup
15ml/1 tbsp black treacle
50g/2oz/¼ cup soft light brown sugar
25g/1oz/2 tbsp butter
175g/6oz/1½ cups plain flour
3.5ml/¾ tsp bicarbonate of soda
2.5ml/½ tsp mixed spice
7.5ml/1½ tsp ground ginger
1 egg yolk

Icing and Decoration
½ quantity royal icing
red, yellow and green food colourings
brightly coloured ribbons

Makes 20

1 Preheat the oven to 190°C/375°F/
Gas 5. Line several baking sheets
with non-stick baking paper. Place
the syrup, treacle, sugar and butter
in a saucepan. Heat gently, stirring
occasionally, until the butter has
melted into the syrup.

2 Sift the flour, bicarbonate of soda,
mixed spice and ginger together in a
mixing bowl. Using a wooden spoon,
stir in the treacle mixture and the egg
yolk and mix to form a soft dough.
Remove the dough from the bowl
and knead on a lightly floured surface
until smooth.

3 Roll out the dough thinly, and using a
selection of festive cutters such as stars
and Christmas trees, stamp out as many
shapes as possible, kneading and re-
rolling the dough as necessary. Arrange
the shapes, well spaced apart, on the
baking sheets. Make a hole in the top of
each shape, using a drinking straw, if
you wish to use the biscuits
as hanging decorations.

4 Bake in the oven for 15–20 minutes
or until risen and golden and leave
to cool on the baking sheets before
transferring to a wire rack using a
palette knife.

5 Divide the royal icing into 4 and
colour ¼ red, ¼ yellow and ¼ green
using the food colourings. Make
4 greaseproof paper piping bags and fill
each one with the different coloured
icings. Fold down the tops and snip off
the points.

6 Pipe lines, dots, and zigzags on the
gingerbread biscuits using the coloured
icings. Leave to dry. If you intend
to hang the biscuits, thread ribbons
through the holes made in the biscuits.

COOK'S TIP

These brightly decorated
gingerbread biscuits are fun to make
and may be used as edible
Christmas tree decorations.

GINGERBREAD HEART RING

This table centrepiece is inspired by traditional Polish Christmas decorations. You could make the

centrepiece with other cut-out shapes, such as gingerbread men and women, teddy bears or stars.

EQUIPMENT

stiff cardboard
pencil and scissors
glacé icing made with 115g/4oz/1 cup
sifted icing sugar and, if you wish,
coloured red
palette knife
7 heart-shaped gingerbread biscuits,
baked and decorated
5cm/2in-wide ribbon
Victorian-style paper scraps (optional)

1 On a piece of stiff cardboard, draw a ring shape with an outer diameter of 25cm/10in and an inner diameter of 15cm/6in. Cut out the ring with a pair of scissors. Cover the cardboard ring with the glacé icing, using a palette knife, and quickly – before it sets – press on the heart-shaped gingerbread biscuits to cover it. Set the ring aside until the glacé icing has dried and the gingerbread biscuits are fixed in place.

2 Tie the ribbon into a bow, trim the ends and fix it to the ring with a generous dab of glacé icing to ensure it stays securely in place throughout the season. To preserve the ring as a decoration throughout the Christmas holidays, it may be as well to make extra heart-shaped biscuits for young gingerbread enthusiasts to eat!

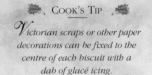

COOK'S TIP

Victorian scraps or other paper decorations can be fixed to the centre of each biscuit with a dab of glacé icing.

GLACÉ ICING

To make glacé icing, sift the required amount of icing sugar into a bowl. Add a few drops of water at a time, and beat into the icing sugar. Keep adding water, a little at a time, until the desired consistency has been achieved.

Nut and Glacé Fruit Ring

The cake can be made two or three weeks before Christmas. Store it in a tin in a cool place until needed.

INGREDIENTS

60ml/4 tbsp rum, brandy or sherry
115g/4oz/½ cup glacé cherries, quartered
115g/4oz/¾ cup raisins or sultanas
115g/4oz dried apricots, quartered
115g/4oz/1 cup prunes, stoned and quartered
115g/4oz/½ cup stoned and chopped dates
115g/4oz/½ cup butter
115g/4oz/½ cup soft dark brown sugar
2.5ml/½ tsp ground cinnamon
2.5ml/½ tsp mixed spice
2 eggs, beaten
50g/2oz/⅔ cup ground almonds
115g/4oz/1 cup coarsely chopped walnuts
225g/8oz/2 cups self-raising flour

To Finish
30ml/2 tbsp rum, brandy or sherry
60ml/4 tbsp apricot jam
whole blanched almonds, split
3 glacé cherries, halved
few strips angelica

Makes 1 ring

1 The day before you want to bake the cake, put the rum, brandy or sherry in a large mixing bowl and add all the dried fruit. Cover the bowl with clear film and leave overnight in a cool place so that the fruit is well soaked. Meanwhile, grease a 23cm/ 9in ring mould, with a 1.5 litre/ 2½ pint/6¼ cup capacity.

2 The next day, preheat the oven to 160°C/325°F/Gas 3. In a large mixing bowl, whisk the butter, sugar and spices together until they are light and fluffy. Whisk in the eggs, and then fold in the soaked fruits, with any of the remaining liquid. Mix the ground almonds and chopped walnuts into the bowl and sift in the flour.

3 Spoon the mixture into the prepared cake tin. Level the top of the mixture with the back of a spoon and bake in the preheated oven for 1½–2 hours. Leave the cake to cool in the tin for 30 minutes, then turn out on to a wire rack and allow to cool completely. Brush the cake with the rum, brandy or sherry.

4 Put the apricot jam in a small pan and heat it gently to melt it. Sieve the jam. Brush the hot glaze over the top of the cake. Arrange the nuts and fruit in a flower design on top of the cake and brush them liberally with more apricot glaze. The glaze must be used very hot, or the decoration will lift while you are brushing the jam over it.

ᏢANETTONE

This popular Italian cake is perfect for the festive season.

INGREDIENTS

150ml/¼ pint/⅔ cup lukewarm milk
1 packet easy-blend dried yeast
400g/12–14oz/3–3½ cups flour
60g/2½oz/⅓ cup sugar
10ml/2 tsp salt
2 eggs
5 egg yolks
175g/6oz/¾ cup unsalted butter, at room temperature
115g/4oz/¾ cup raisins
grated rind of 1 lemon
75g/3oz/½ cup candied citrus peel, chopped

Makes 1 loaf

1 Combine the milk and yeast in a large, warmed mixing bowl and leave for 10 minutes to dissolve the yeast.

2 Sift in 115g/4oz/1 cup of the flour, stir in and cover loosely, and leave in a warm place for 30 minutes.

3 Sift over the remaining flour. Make a well in the centre and add the sugar, salt, eggs and egg yolks.

4 Stir the dough mixture with a wooden spoon until it becomes too stiff, then continue to stir the mixture with your hands to obtain a very elastic and sticky dough. Add a little more of the flour, if necessary, blending it in well, to keep the dough as soft as possible.

5 Smear the butter into the dough, then work it in with your hands. When evenly distributed, cover and leave to rise in a warm place until doubled in volume, 3–4 hours.

6 Line the bottom of a 2 litre/3½ pint/ 8 cup charlotte mould or 2 pound coffee can with greaseproof paper, then grease the bottom and sides.

7 Punch down the dough and transfer to a floured surface. Knead in the raisins, lemon rind, and citrus peel.

8 Transfer the dough to the mould. Cover with a plastic bag and leave to rise until the dough is well above the top of the container, about 2 hours.

9 Preheat the oven to 200°C/400°F/ Gas 6. Bake for 15 minutes, cover with foil, and lower the heat to 180°C/350°F/ Gas 4. Bake for 30 minutes. Cool in the mould then transfer the cake to a rack.

Stollen

Stollen is a fruity yeast bread traditionally served in Austria and Germany at

Christmas-time. It may be served at breakfast with coffee or tea.

INGREDIENTS

150ml/¼ pint/⅔ cup lukewarm milk
40g/1½oz/3 tbsp caster sugar
10ml/2 tsp easy-blend dried yeast
350g/12oz/3 cups plain flour, plus extra
for dusting
1.5ml/¼ tsp salt
100g/4oz/½ cup butter, softened
1 egg, beaten
50g/2oz/⅓ cup seedless raisins
25g/1oz/⅛ cup sultanas
40g/1½oz/⅓ cup candied orange peel,
chopped
25g/1oz/½ cup blanched almonds,
chopped
5ml/1 tbsp rum
40g/1½oz/3 tbsp butter, melted
about 50g/2oz/½ cup icing sugar

Makes 1 loaf

1 Mix together the warm milk, sugar and yeast and leave it in a warm place until it is frothy.

2 Sift together the flour and salt, make a well in the centre and pour on the yeast mixture. Add the softened butter and egg and mix to form a soft dough. Mix in the raisins, sultanas, peel and almonds and sprinkle on the rum. Knead the dough on a lightly floured board until it is pliable.

3 Place the dough in a large, greased mixing bowl, cover it with non-stick baking paper and set it aside in a warm place for about 2 hours, until it has doubled in size.

4 Turn the dough out on to a floured board and knead it lightly until it is smooth and elastic again. Shape the dough to a rectangle about 25 x 20cm/10 x 8in. Fold the dough over along one of the long sides and press the 2 layers together. Cover the loaf and leave it to stand for 20 minutes.

5 Heat the oven to 200°C/400°F/Gas 6. Bake the loaf in the oven for 25–30 minutes, until it is well risen. Allow it to cool slightly on the baking sheet, then brush it with melted butter. Sift the sugar over the top and transfer the loaf to a wire rack to cool. Serve the stollen in thin slices.

LIGHT JEWELLED FRUIT CAKE

This cake can be made up to two weeks before eating it. For serving, brush the top

with hot apricot jam and tie a pretty ribbon around the sides.

INGREDIENTS

115g/4oz/½ cup currants
115g/4oz/⅔ cup sultanas
225g/8oz/1 cup quartered glacé cherries
50g/2oz/⅓ cup finely chopped mixed candied peel
30ml/2 tbsp rum, brandy or sherry
225g/8oz/1 cup butter
225g/8oz/1 cup caster sugar
finely grated rind of 1 orange
finely grated rind of 1 lemon
4 eggs
50g/2oz/½ cup chopped almonds
50g/2oz/⅔ cup ground almonds
225g/8oz/2 cups plain flour

To Finish
50g/2oz whole blanched almonds

Makes 1 cake

1 The day before you want to bake the cake, soak the currants, sultanas, glacé cherries and the mixed peel in the rum, brandy or sherry. Cover with clear film and leave overnight. The day you bake the cake, grease and line a 20cm/8in round cake tin or an 18cm/7in square cake tin with a double thickness of greaseproof paper.

2 Preheat the oven to 160°C/325°F/Gas 3. In a large bowl, whisk the butter, sugar and orange and lemon rinds together until they are light and fluffy. Beat in the eggs, one at a time.

3 Mix in the chopped almonds, ground almonds, soaked fruits (with their liquid) and the flour, to make a soft dropping consistency. Spoon into the cake tin. Bake for 30 minutes.

4 Gently place the whole almonds in a pattern on top of the cake. Do not press them into the cake or they will sink during cooking. Return the cake to the oven and cook for a further 1½ –2 hours, or until the centre is firm to the touch. Let the cake cool in the tin for 30 minutes. Then remove it and cool completely on a wire rack, but leave the paper on; this helps to keep the cake moist while stored.

Spiced Christmas Cake

This light cake mixture is flavoured with spices and fruit. It can be served with

a dusting of icing sugar and decorated with holly leaves.

INGREDIENTS

225g/8oz/1 cup butter, plus extra for greasing
15g/½oz/1 tbsp fresh white breadcrumbs
225g/8oz/1 cup caster sugar
50ml/2fl oz/¼ cup water
3 eggs, separated
225g/8oz/2 cups self-raising flour
7.5g/1½ tsp mixed spice
25g/1oz/2 tbsp chopped angelica
25g/1oz/2 tbsp mixed peel
50g/2oz/¼ cup chopped glacé cherries
50g/2oz/½ cup chopped walnuts
icing sugar, to dust

Makes 1 cake

1 Preheat the oven to 180°C/350°F/ Gas 4. Brush a 20cm/8in x 1.5 litre/ 2½ pint fluted ring mould with melted butter and coat with breadcrumbs, shaking out any excess.

2 Place the butter, sugar and water into a saucepan. Heat gently, stirring occasionally, until melted. Boil for 3 minutes until syrupy, then allow to cool. Place the egg whites in a clean bowl, whisk until stiff. Sift the flour and spice into a bowl, add the angelica, mixed peel, cherries and walnuts and stir well to mix. Add the egg yolks.

3 Pour the cooled mixture into the bowl and beat to form a soft batter. Gradually fold in the egg whites, until the mixture is evenly blended. Pour into the prepared mould and bake for 50–60 minutes or until the cake springs back when pressed in the centre. Turn out and allow to cool on a wire rack. Dust with icing sugar to serve.

Moist and Rich Christmas Cake

The cake can be made 4–6 weeks before Christmas. During this time, pierce the cake with a

fine needle and spoon over 30–45ml/2–3 tbsp brandy.

INGREDIENTS

225g/8oz/1⅓ cups sultanas
225g/8oz/1 cup currants
225g/8oz/1⅓ cups raisins
115g/4oz/1 cup stoned and chopped prunes
50g/2oz/¼ cup halved glacé cherries
50g/2oz/⅓ cup chopped mixed peel
45ml/3 tbsp brandy or sherry
225g/8oz/2 cups plain flour
pinch of salt
2.5ml/½ tsp ground cinnamon
2.5ml/½ tsp grated nutmeg
15ml/1 tbsp cocoa powder
225g/8oz/1 cup butter
225g/8oz/1 generous cup soft dark brown sugar
4 large eggs
finely grated rind of 1 orange or lemon
50g/2oz/⅔ cup ground almonds
50g/2oz/½ cup chopped almonds

To Decorate
60ml/4 tbsp apricot jam
450g/1lb almond paste
450g/1lb fondant icing
225g/8oz royal icing

Makes 1 cake

1 The day before you want to bake the cake, soak the dried fruit in the brandy or sherry, cover and leave overnight. The next day, grease a 20cm/8in round cake tin and line it with greaseproof paper.

2 Preheat the oven to 160°C/325°F/Gas 3. Sift together the flour, salt, spices and cocoa powder. Whisk the butter and sugar together until light and fluffy and beat in the eggs gradually. Finally, mix in the orange or lemon rind, the ground and chopped almonds, dried fruits (with any liquid) and the flour mixture.

3 Spoon into the cake tin, level the top and give the cake tin a gentle tap on the work surface to disperse any air bubbles. Bake for 3 hours, or until a fine skewer inserted into the middle comes out clean. Transfer the cake tin to a wire rack and let the cake cool in the tin for an hour. Then turn the cake out on to the wire rack, but leave the paper on, as it will help to keep the cake moist during storage. When the cake is cold, wrap it in foil and store it in a cool place.

4 Warm, then sieve the apricot jam to make a glaze. Remove the paper from the cake, place it in the centre of the cake board and brush it with hot apricot glaze. Cover the cake with a layer of almond paste and then a layer of fondant icing. Pipe a border around the base of the cake with royal cing. Tie a ribbon around the sides.

5 Roll out any trimmings from the fondant icing and stamp out 12 small holly leaves with a cutter. Make one bell motif with a biscuit mould, dusted first with sifted icing sugar. Roll 36 small balls for the holly berries. Leave the decorations on greaseproof paper to dry for 24 hours. Decorate the cake with the fondant icing leaves, berries and bell, attaching them to the cake with a dab of royal icing. Allow the icing to dry, then cover the cake and pack in an airtight tin until needed.

ORANGE SHORTBREAD FINGERS

These are a real tea-time treat. The fingers will keep in an airtight tin for up to two weeks.

INGREDIENTS

115g/4oz/½ cup unsalted butter, softened
50g/2oz/4 tbsp caster sugar, plus a little
extra for sprinkling
finely grated rind of 2 oranges
175g/6oz/1½ cups plain flour

Makes 18

🍂 COOK'S TIP 🍂

*This recipe is the ideal
life-saver for busy cooks. It is a
good idea to make extra dough and
store it, well wrapped, in the freezer.
When guests arrive unexpectedly,
you will be able to make up
freshly-baked fingers in minutes.*

1 Preheat the oven to 190°C/375°F/
Gas 5. Beat the butter and sugar
together until they are soft and creamy.
Beat in the orange rind. Gradually add
the flour and gently pull the dough
together to form a soft ball.

2 Roll the dough out on a lightly
floured surface until about 1cm/½in
thick. Cut it into fingers, sprinkle over
a little extra sugar, prick with a fork and
bake for about 20 minutes, or until the
fingers are a light golden colour.

Hogmanay Shortbread

Light, crisp shortbread looks so professional when shaped in a mould,

although you could also shape it by hand.

INGREDIENTS

175g/6oz/¾ cup plain flour
50g/2oz/¼ cup cornflour
50g/2oz/¼ cup caster sugar
115g/4oz/½ cup unsalted butter

Makes 2 large or 8 individual
shortbreads

COOK'S TIP

*The secret of successful
shortbread baking is to have cool
hands when working the butter and
sugar together.*

---

1 Preheat the oven to 160°C/325°F/
Gas 3. Lightly flour the mould and
line a baking sheet with non-stick
baking paper. Sift the flour, cornflour
and sugar into a large mixing bowl.
Cut the butter into pieces and rub into
the flour mixture, using your fingertips
or in a food processor. When the
mixture begins to bind together,
you can knead it into a soft dough,
using your hands.

2 Place the dough into the mould
and press to fit neatly. Invert the
mould on to the baking sheet and tap
firmly to release the dough shape.
Bake in the preheated oven for about
35–40 minutes or until the shortbread
is pale golden in colour.

3 Sprinkle the top of the shortbread
with a little caster sugar and set aside
to cool on the baking sheet. Wrap the
shortbread in cellophane paper and
pack in an airtight tin, or place in a
box tied with ribbons, to give as a gift.

CHRISTMAS BISCUITS

These biscuits are great fun for children to make as presents. Any shape of biscuit cutter can be used.

Store the biscuits in an airtight tin, and for a change, omit the lemon rind and add 25g/1oz/⅓ cup

of ground almonds and a few drops of almond essence.

INGREDIENTS

75g/3oz/6 tbsp butter
50g/2oz/generous ½ cup icing sugar
finely grated rind of 1 small lemon
1 egg yolk
175g/6oz/1½ cups plain flour
pinch of salt

To Decorate
2 egg yolks
red and green edible food colourings

Makes about 12

1 In a large bowl, beat the butter, sugar and lemon rind together until pale and fluffy. Beat in the egg yolk and then sift in the flour and the salt. Knead together to form a smooth dough. Wrap in clear film and chill for 30 minutes.

2 Preheat the oven to 190°C/375°F/Gas 5. On a lightly floured surface, roll out the dough to 3mm/⅛in thick. Using a 6cm/2½in fluted cutter, stamp out as many biscuits as you can, with the cutter dipped in flour to prevent it from sticking to the dough.

3 Transfer the biscuits on to lightly greased baking trays. Mark the tops lightly with a 2.5cm/1in holly leaf cutter and use a 5mm/¼in plain piping nozzle for the berries. Chill for 10 minutes, until firm.

4 Meanwhile, put each egg yolk into a small cup. Mix red food colouring into one and green food colouring into the other. Using a small, clean paintbrush, carefully paint the colours on to the biscuits. Bake the biscuits for 10–12 minutes, or until they begin to colour around the edges. Let them cool slightly on the baking trays, and then transfer them to a wire rack to cool completely.

> 🌿 COOK'S TIP 🌿
>
> *When cooking with young children, things will flow more smoothly if you have all the ingredients prepared before they start to cook. It is a good idea to provide large aprons for all involved!*

GINGER FLORENTINES

These colourful, chewy biscuits are delicious served with ice cream and are certain to disappear

as soon as they are served. Store them in an airtight container.

INGREDIENTS

50g/2oz/4 tbsp butter
115g/4oz/8 tbsp caster sugar
50g/2oz/¼ cup chopped mixed glacé cherries
25g/1oz/2 tbsp chopped orange peel
50g/2oz/½ cup flaked almonds
50g/2oz/½ cup chopped walnuts
25g/1oz/1 tbsp chopped glacé ginger
30ml/2 tbsp plain flour
2.5ml/½ tsp ground ginger

To Finish
50g/2oz plain chocolate
50g/2oz white chocolate

Makes 30

1 Preheat the oven to 180°C/350°F/ Gas 4. Whisk together the butter and sugar in a mixing bowl until they are light and fluffy. Thoroughly mix in all the remaining ingredients, except for the chocolate.

2 Cut a piece of non-stick baking paper large enough to fit your baking trays. Put 4 small spoonfuls of the mixture on to each tray, spacing them well apart to allow for spreading. Gently flatten the biscuits with the palm of your hand and bake them for 5 minutes.

3 Remove the biscuits from the oven and flatten them with a wet fork, shaping them into neat rounds. Return to the oven for 3–4 minutes, until they are golden brown.

4 Allow the biscuits to cool on the baking trays for 2 minutes, to firm up, and then, using a palette knife, carefully transfer them to a wire rack. When the biscuits are cold and firm, melt the plain and the white chocolate. Spread dark chocolate on the undersides of half the biscuits and spread white chocolate on the undersides of the rest.

CHOCOLATE KISSES

These rich little biscuits look attractive mixed together on a plate and dusted with icing sugar.

Serve them with ice cream or simply as a sweet accompaniment to coffee.

INGREDIENTS

75g/3oz plain chocolate, broken into
squares
75g/3oz white chocolate, broken into
squares
115g/4oz/½ cup butter
115g/4oz/8 tbsp caster sugar
2 eggs
225g/8oz/2 cups plain flour
icing sugar, to decorate

Makes 24

1 Put each pile of chocolate squares into a small bowl and, stirring occasionally, melt it over a pan of hot, but not boiling, water Set aside to cool.

2 Whisk together the butter and caster sugar until they are pale and fluffy. Gradually beat in the eggs, one at a time. Then sift in the flour and mix together well.

3 Halve the mixture and divide it between the two bowls of melted chocolate. Mix the chocolate into the dough mixture thoroughly. Knead the doughs until smooth and pliable, wrap them in clear film and set aside to chill them for about 1 hour. Preheat the oven to 190°C/375°F/Gas 5.

4 Shape slightly rounded teaspoonfuls of both doughs roughly into balls. Roll the balls in the palms of your hands to make neater ball shapes. Arrange the balls on greased baking trays and bake them for 10–12 minutes. Dust with sifted icing sugar and then transfer them to a wire rack to cool.

DATE-FILLED PASTRIES

The secret of good pastries is to get as much date filling into the pastry as possible,

but you must make sure to seal the opening well.

INGREDIENTS

*75g/3oz/6 tbsp margarine or butter,
softened
175g/6oz/1½ cups plain flour
5ml/1 tsp rose water
5ml/1 tsp orange flower water
45ml/3 tbsp water*

For the Filling
*115g/4oz/⅔ cup stoned dried dates
2.5ml/½ tsp orange flower water
20ml/4 tsp sifted icing sugar for
sprinkling*

Makes about 25

1 To make the filling, chop the dates finely. Add 50ml/2fl oz/¼ cup boiling water and the orange flower water, beat the mixture and leave to cool.

2 To make the pastries, rub the fat into the flour. Add the flower waters and the water and mix.

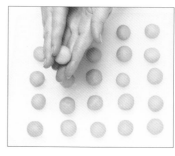

3 Once the dough feels firm, shape it into about 25 small balls.

4 Preheat the oven to 180°C/350°F/ Gas 4. Press your finger into each ball to make a small container, pressing the sides round and round to make the walls thinner. Put about 1.5ml/¼ tsp of the date mixture into each one and seal by pressing the pastry together.

5 Arrange the date pastries, seam side down, on a lightly greased baking sheet and prick each one with a fork. Bake in the preheated oven for 15–20 minutes, then transfer to a wire rack and allow to cool completely.

6 Put the cooled pastries on a plate and lightly sprinkle over the sifted icing sugar. Shake gently to make sure they are well covered. Date-filled pastries will freeze very well until needed.

Cinnamon Rolls

These pretty little pastry whirls, scented with cinnamon, are sure to be coffee-time favourites.

INGREDIENTS

For the Dough
400g/14oz/1⅔ cups strong white flour
2.5ml/½ tsp salt
30ml/2 tbsp sugar
5ml/1 tsp easy-blend dried yeast
45ml/3 tbsp oil
1 egg
120ml/4fl oz/½ cup warm milk
120ml/4fl oz/½ cup warm water

For the Filling
25g/1oz butter, softened
25g/1oz soft dark brown sugar
2.5–5ml/½–1 tsp ground cinnamon
15ml/1 tbsp raisins or sultanas

Makes 24 small rolls

1 Sift the flour into a large mixing bowl, the add the salt and sugar and sprinkle over the yeast. Mix together the oil, egg, milk and water and add the liquid to the flour. Mix to a dough, then knead until smooth. Leave the dough to rise until it has doubled in size and then knock it back again.

2 Roll out the dough into a large rectangle and cut in half vertically. Spread over the soft butter, reserving 15ml/1 tbsp for brushing. Mix the sugar and cinnamon and sprinkle over the top. Dot with the raisins. Roll each piece of dough into a long Swiss roll shape, to enclose the filling.

3 Cut each piece into 2.5cm/1in slices and arrange on a baking sheet. Brush with butter. Leave to rise for 30 minutes.

4 Preheat the oven to 200°C/400°F/Gas 6. Bake the rolls for 20 minutes. Leave to cool on a wire rack.

Amaretti

If bitter almonds are not available, make up the weight with sweet almonds.

INGREDIENTS
150g/5oz/1¼ cups sweet almonds
50g/2oz/½ cup bitter almonds
225g/8oz/1 cup caster sugar
2 egg whites
2.5ml/½ tsp almond extract
5ml/1 tsp vanilla extract
icing sugar, for dusting

Makes about 36

1 Preheat the oven to 160°C/325°F/ Gas 3. Peel the almonds by dropping them into a pan of boiling water for 1–2 minutes. Drain. Rub off the skins.

2 Place the almonds on a baking tray and let them dry out in the oven for 10–15 minutes without browning.

3 Grind the almonds with half of the sugar in a food processor. Beat the egg whites until they hold soft peaks. Sprinkle over half the remaining sugar and continue beating until stiff peaks form. Fold in the remaining sugar, almond extract, vanilla and almonds.

4 Spoon the almond mixture into a pastry bag with a smooth nozzle. Line a flat baking sheet with non-stick baking paper. Dust this with flour.

5 Pipe out the mixture in rounds the size of walnuts. Sprinkle lightly with the icing sugar, and allow to stand for 2 hours. Near the end of this time, turn the oven on again and preheat to 180°C/350°F/Gas 4.

6 Bake the amaretti in the preheated oven for 15 minutes, or until they turn pale gold. Remove from the oven and allow them to cool on a rack. When completely cool, the biscuits may be stored in an airtight container.

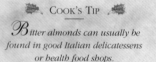
COOK'S TIP
Bitter almonds can usually be found in good Italian delicatessens or health food shops.

Mocha Viennese Swirls

Some temptations just can't be resisted.

Put out a plate of these "melt-in-the-mouth" marvels and watch them vanish.

INGREDIENTS

15g/4oz plain chocolate, broken into
squares
200g/7oz/scant 1 cup unsalted butter,
softened
50g/2oz/6 tbsp icing sugar
30ml/2tbsp strong black coffee
200g/7oz/1¾ cups plain flour
50g/2oz/½ cup cornflour

To Decorate
about 20 blanched almonds
150g/5oz plain chocolate

Makes about 20

> ### 🌿 COOK'S TIP 🌿
>
> *If the mixture is too stiff to pipe,*
> *soften it by adding a little more*
> *black coffee, a little at a time.*

1 Preheat the oven to 190°C/375°F/ Gas 5. Lightly grease two large baking sheets. Melt the chocolate squares in a mixing bowl over hot water. Cream the butter with the icing sugar in a bowl until smooth and pale. Beat in the melted chocolate, then the strong black coffee.

2 Sift the flour and cornflour over the mixture in the bowl. Fold in lightly and evenly to make a soft mixture.

3 Spoon into a piping bag fitted with a large star nozzle and pipe about 20 swirls on the baking sheets.

4 Press an almond into the centre of each of the swirls. Bake for about 15 minutes or until the biscuits are firm and just beginning to brown.

5 Leave the biscuits to cool for about 10 minutes on the baking sheets, then lift them carefully on to a wire rack and allow them to cool completely.

6 When the biscuits have cooled, melt the chocolate and dip the base of each swirl to coat. Place the coated biscuits on a sheet of non-stick baking paper and leave to set.

DOUBLE-CRUST MINCE PIES

Mince pies are an essential part of the culinary tradition and the Christmas season would not be complete without them. This recipe has an extra-special pastry case for maximum delight.

INGREDIENTS

*shortcrust pastry made with 350g/
12oz/3 cups flour
butter, for greasing
flour for dusting
450g/1lb/2 cups mincemeat
milk, for brushing
icing sugar or caster sugar, for dusting*

Makes 24 pies

1 Preheat the oven to 200°C/400°F/ Gas 6. Use a rolling pin to roll out the shortcrust pastry as thinly as possible on a lightly floured board. Using a 7.5cm/3in plain round cutter, cut out 24 circles. With a 5cm/2in plain round cutter, cut out another 24 circles. Carefully lay the circles aside.

2 Grease 24 muffin tins, dust them with flour and line them with the larger circles. Fill each one with mincemeat, then brush the edges with milk. Press the smaller rounds on top and seal the edges. Brush the tops with milk.

3 Bake for 25–30 minutes until the pastry is light golden brown. Cool in the tins, then transfer the pies to a wire rack to become cold. Store them in an air-tight tin. Just before serving, dust the tops with sugar. Serve the pies warm.

COOK'S TIP

Today's mincemeat no longer contains meat or poultry as it once did, except in the form of suet. If you do not wish to eat animal fats, make sure you choose a mincemeat made with vegetarian suet.

Almond Mincemeat Tartlets

Serve these little tartlets warm with brandy- or rum-flavoured custard.

INGREDIENTS

275g/10oz/2½ cups plain flour
75g/3oz/generous ¾ cup icing sugar
5ml/1 tsp ground cinnamon
175g/6oz/¾ cup butter
50g/2oz/⅔ cup ground almonds
1 egg yolk
45ml/3 tbsp milk
450g/1lb jar mincemeat
15ml/1 tbsp brandy or rum

For the Lemon Sponge Filling
115g/4oz/½ cup butter or margarine
115g/4oz/8 tbsp caster sugar
175g/6oz/1½ cups self-raising flour
2 large eggs
finely grated rind of 1 large lemon

For the Lemon Icing
115g/4oz/1 generous cup icing sugar
15ml/1 tbsp lemon juice

Makes 36

3 For the lemon sponge filling, whisk the butter or margarine, sugar, flour, eggs and lemon rind together until smooth. Spoon on top of the mincemeat, dividing it evenly, and level the tops. Bake for 20–30 minutes, or until golden brown and springy to the touch. Remove and leave to cool on a wire rack.

4 For the lemon icing, sift the icing sugar into a bowl and mix with the lemon juice to form a smooth, thick, coating consistency. Spoon into a piping bag and drizzle a zigzag pattern over each of the tartlets. Alternatively, if you're very short of time, simply dust the tartlets with sifted icing sugar before serving.

1 For the pastry, sift the flour, icing sugar and cinnamon into a bowl and rub in the butter until it resembles fine breadcrumbs. Add the ground almonds and bind with the egg yolk and milk to a soft dough. Knead the dough until smooth, wrap and chill for 30 minutes.

2 Preheat the oven to 190°C/375°F/Gas 5. On a lightly floured surface, roll out the pastry and cut out 36 fluted rounds with a pastry cutter, to line the tins. Mix the mincemeat with the brandy or rum and put a teaspoonful in each pastry case. Chill in the fridge.

De Luxe Mincemeat Tart

The mincemeat can be made up and kept in the fridge for up to two weeks.

It can also be used to make individual mince pies.

INGREDIENTS

225g/8oz/2 cups plain flour
10ml/2 tsp ground cinnamon
50g/2oz/⅔ cup finely ground walnuts
115g/4oz/½ cup butter
50g/2oz/4 tbsp caster sugar, plus extra for dusting
1 egg
2 drops vanilla essence
15ml/1 tbsp cold water

For the Mincemeat
2 dessert apples, peeled, cored and coarsely grated
225g/8oz/1⅓ cups raisins
115g/4oz ready-to-eat dried apricots, chopped
115g/4oz ready-to-eat dried figs or prunes, chopped
225g/8oz green grapes, halved and seeded
50g/2oz/½ cup chopped almonds
finely grated rind of 1 lemon
30ml/2 tbsp lemon juice
30ml/2 tbsp brandy or port
1.5ml/¼ tsp mixed spice
115g/4oz/generous ½ cup soft light brown sugar
25g/1oz/2 tbsp butter, melted

Serves 8

1 To make the pastry, put the flour, cinnamon and walnuts in a food processor. Add the butter and process until the mixture resembles fine breadcrumbs. Turn into a bowl and stir in the sugar. Using a fork, beat the egg with the vanilla essence and water. Gradually stir the egg mixture into the dry Ingredients. Gather together with your fingertips to form a soft, pliable dough. Knead briefly on a lightly floured surface until smooth. Then wrap the dough in clear film and chill in the fridge for 30 minutes.

2 Mix all of the mincemeat ingredients together in a large bowl.

3 Cut one-third off the pastry and reserve it for the lattice. Roll out the remainder and use it to line a 23cm/9in, loose-based flan tin. Make a 5mm/¼in rim around the top edge.

4 With a rolling pin, roll off the excess pastry. Fill the case with mincemeat.

5 Roll out the remaining pastry and cut it into 1cm/½in strips. Arrange the strips in a lattice over the top of the pastry, wet the joins and press them together well. Chill for 30 minutes.

6 Preheat the oven to 190°C/375°F/Gas 5. Place a baking sheet in the oven to preheat. Brush the pastry with water and dust it with caster sugar. Bake it on the baking sheet for 30–40 minutes. Transfer to a wire rack and leave to cool for 15 minutes. Then carefully remove the flan tin. Serve warm or cold, with sweetened whipped cream.

> ### COOK'S TIP
> *Mincemeat will taste even better if it is made at least 4 weeks before Christmas and left in a cool, dry, dark place to mature.*

Christmas Treats & Edible Gifts

There's nothing nicer to receive at Christmas-time than a selection of homemade sweets and treats in beautiful festive wrappings. If you're used to shop-bought fudge or Turkish delight, you'll be astounded by the taste of these homemade versions. The same goes for the marshmallow recipe included here, which produces little pillows of mouthwatering delight. Though Marzipan Fruits and Fruit Fondant Chocolates take a little time and effort, the results will be well worth the trouble. Collections of biscuits and individual cakes are a favourite Christmas treat, as are the Mini Black Buns, hiding their luscious filling inside. Try Flavoured Vinegars and Fruits in Liqueurs for special gifts that taste as good as they look.

CREAMY FUDGE

A good selection of fudge always makes a welcome change from chocolates.

Mix and match the flavours to make a gift-wrapped assortment.

INGREDIENTS

50g/2oz/4 tbsp unsalted butter, plus extra for greasing
450g/1lb/2 cups granulated sugar
300ml/1/2 pint/1¼ cups double cream
150ml/¼ pint/⅔ cup milk
45ml/3 tbsp water (this can be replaced with orange, apricot or cherry brandy, or strong coffee)

Flavourings
225g/8oz/1 cup plain or milk chocolate dots
115g/4oz/1 cup chopped almonds, hazelnuts, walnuts or brazil nuts
115g/4oz/½ cup chopped glacé cherries, dates or dried apricots

Makes 900g/2lb

1 Grease a 20cm/8in shallow square tin. Place the butter, sugar, cream, milk and water or other flavourings into a large heavy-based saucepan. Heat very gently, until all the sugar has dissolved.

2 Bring the mixture to a rolling boil, until the fudge reaches the soft ball stage.

3 If you are making chocolate-flavoured fudge, add the chocolate dots to the mixture at this stage. Remove the saucepan from the heat and beat thoroughly until the mixture starts to thicken and become opaque.

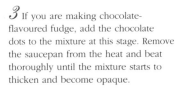

4 Just before this consistency has been reached, add chopped nuts for a nutty fudge, or glacé cherries or dried fruit for a fruit-flavoured fudge. Beat well until evenly blended.

5 Pour the fudge into the prepared tin, taking care as the mixture is very hot. Leave the mixture until cool and almost set. Using a sharp knife, mark the fudge into small squares and leave in the tin until quite firm.

6 Turn the fudge out on to a board and invert. Using a long-bladed knife, cut into neat squares. You can dust some with icing sugar and drizzle others with melted chocolate, if desired.

Orange, Mint and Coffee Meringues

These tiny, crisp meringues are flavoured with orange, coffee and mint chocolate sticks and liqueurs.

Pile them into dry, airtight glass jars or decorative tins.

INGREDIENTS

25g/1oz/8 chocolate mint sticks
25g/1oz/8 chocolate orange sticks
25g/1oz/8 chocolate coffee sticks
2.5ml/½ tsp crème de menthe
2.5ml/½ tsp orange curaçao or Cointreau
2.5ml/½ tsp Tia Maria
3 egg whites
175g/6oz/¾ cup caster sugar
5g/1 tsp cocoa

Makes 90

🍂 COOK'S TIP 🍂

These little meringues are ideal served with coffee after dinner. Alternatively, they make an original topping for ice-cream sundaes.

1 Preheat the oven to 110°C/225°F/ Gas ¼. Line 2–3 baking sheets with non-stick baking paper. Chop each flavour of chocolate stick separately and place each into separate bowls, retaining a teaspoonful of each flavour of stick. Stir in the liquid flavourings to match the flavour of the chocolate sticks in the bowls.

2 Place the egg whites in a clean bowl and whisk until stiff. Gradually add the sugar, whisking well after each addition until thick. Add ⅓ of the meringue to each bowl and fold in gently, using a clean spatula, until evenly blended.

3 Place about 30 teaspoons of each mixture on to the baking sheets, spaced apart. Sprinkle the top of each meringue with the reserved chopped chocolate sticks. Bake for 1 hour or until crisp. Allow to cool, then dust with cocoa.

TURKISH DELIGHT

Turkish Delight is always a favourite at Christmas, and this versatile recipe can be made in minutes. Try

different flavours such as lemon, crème de menthe and orange and vary the colours accordingly.

INGREDIENTS

450g/1lb/2 cups granulated sugar
300ml/½ pint/1¼ cups water
25g/1oz/2 tbsp powdered gelatine
2.5ml/½ tsp tartaric acid
30ml/2 tbsp rose water
pink food colouring
25g/1oz/3 tbsp icing sugar, sifted
15ml/1 tbsp cornflour

Makes 450g/1lb

1 Wet the insides of 2 x 18cm/7in shallow square tins with water. Place the sugar and all but 60ml/4 tbsp of water into a heavy-based saucepan. Heat gently, stirring occasionally, until the sugar has dissolved.

2 Blend the gelatine and remaining water in a small bowl and place over a saucepan of hot water. Stir occasionally until dissolved. Bring the sugar syrup to the boil and boil steadily for about 8 minutes, or until the syrup registers 127°C/260°F on a sugar thermometer. Stir the tartaric acid into the gelatine, then pour into the boiling syrup and stir until well blended. Remove from the heat.

3 Add the rose water and a few drops of pink food colouring and stir, adding a few more drops, as necessary, to tint the mixture pale pink. Pour the mixture into the prepared tins and allow to set for several hours or overnight. Dust a sheet of greaseproof paper with some of the icing sugar and cornflour. Dip the base of the tins in hot water and invert on to the paper. Cut the Turkish Delight into 2.5cm/1in squares, using an oiled knife. Toss the squares in icing sugar to coat evenly.

Glacé Fruits

These luxury sweetmeats are very popular at Christmas and they cost a fraction of the shop price if

made at home. The preparation is done over about 4 weeks, but the result is well worth the effort.

Choose one type of fruit, or select a variety of fruits such as cherries, plums, peaches, apricots,

starfruit, pineapple, apples, oranges, lemons, limes and clementines.

INGREDIENTS

450g/1lb fruit
1kg/2¼lb/4½ cups granulated sugar
115g/4oz/1 cup powdered glucose

Makes 24 pieces

1 Stone cherries, plums, peaches and apricots. Peel and core pineapple and cut into cubes or rings. Peel, core and quarter apples and thinly slice citrus fruits. Prick cherry skins with a cocktail stick to extract the maximum flavour.

2 Place enough prepared fruit in a saucepan to cover the base, keeping individual fruit types together. Add water to cover the fruit and simmer gently, to avoid breaking it, until almost tender. Use a slotted spoon to transfer the fruit to a shallow dish, removing any skins if necessary. Repeat as above until all the fruit has been cooked.

3 Measure 300ml/½ pint/1¼ cups of the liquid, or make up this quantity with water if necessary. Pour into the saucepan and add 50g/2oz/4 tbsp sugar and the glucose. Heat gently, stirring occasionally, until dissolved. Bring to the boil and pour over the fruit in the dish, completely immersing it, and leave overnight.

4 DAY 2. Drain the syrup into the pan and add 50g/2oz/4 tbsp sugar. Dissolve the sugar and bring to the boil. Pour over the fruit and leave overnight. Repeat this process each day, draining off the syrup, dissolving 50g/2oz/4 tbsp sugar, boiling the syrup and immersing the fruit. Leave overnight on Days 3, 4, 5, 6 and 7.

5 DAY 8. Drain the fruit, dissolve 75g/3oz/½ cup sugar in the syrup and bring to the boil. Add the fruit and cook gently for 3 minutes. Return to the dish and leave for 2 days. DAY 10. Repeat as for Day 8. The syrup should now look like honey. Leave in the dish for at least 10 days, or up to 3 weeks.

6 Place a wire rack over a tray and remove each piece of fruit with a slotted spoon. Arrange on the rack. Dry the fruit in a warm, dry place or in the oven at the lowest setting until the surface no longer feels sticky. To coat in sugar, spear each piece of fruit and plunge into boiling water, then roll in granulated sugar. To dip into syrup, place the remaining sugar and 175ml/6fl oz/¾ cup of water in a saucepan. Heat gently until the sugar has dissolved, then boil for 1 minute. Dip each piece of fruit into boiling water, then quickly into the syrup. Place on the wire rack and leave in a warm place until dry. Place the fruits in paper sweet cases and pack into boxes.

FRUIT FONDANT CHOCOLATES

These chocolates are simple to make using pre-formed plastic moulds, yet they look very professional.

Fruit fondant is available from specialist foods shops and comes in a variety of flavours, including coffee

and nut. Try a mixture of flavours, using a small quantity of each, or use just a single flavour.

INGREDIENTS

*225g/8oz/8 squares plain,
milk or white chocolate*
115g/4oz/1 cup real fruit liquid fondant
15–20ml/3–4 tsp cooled boiled water

Decoration
*15ml/1 tbsp melted plain, milk or white
chocolate*

Makes 24

1 Melt the chocolate. Use a piece of cotton wool to polish the insides of the chocolate moulds, ensuring that they are spotlessly clean. Fill up the shapes in one plastic tray to the top, leave for a few seconds, then invert the tray over the bowl of melted chocolate, allowing the excess chocolate to fall back into the bowl. Sit the tray on the work surface and draw a palette knife across the top to remove the excess chocolate and to neaten the edges. Chill until set. Repeat to fill the remaining trays.

2 Sift the fruit fondant mixture into a bowl. Gradually stir in enough water to give it the consistency of thick cream. Place the fondant in a greaseproof paper piping bag, fold down the top and snip off the end. Fill each chocolate case almost to the top by piping in the fondant. Leave for 30 minutes or until a skin has formed on the surface of the fondant.

3 Spoon the remaining melted chocolate over the fondant to fill each mould level to the top. Chill until the chocolate has set hard. Invert the tray and press out the chocolates one by one. Place the melted chocolate of a contrasting colour into a greaseproof paper piping bag, fold down the top, snip off the point and pipe lines across the top of each chocolate. Allow to set, then pack the chocolates in pretty boxes and tie with ribbon.

CHOCOLATE TRUFFLES

These truffles are a Christmas speciality in France.

They can be rolled in cocoa or nuts, or dipped in chocolate.

INGREDIENTS

175ml/6fl oz/¾ cup double cream
275g/10oz plain chocolate, chopped
25g/1oz/2 tbsp unsalted butter,
cut into pieces
30–45ml/2–3 tbsp brandy (optional)

For the Coating
cocoa powder
finely chopped pistachio nuts or hazelnuts
400g/14oz plain, milk or white chocolate

Makes 20–30

1 Bring the cream to the boil. Remove from the heat and add the chocolate, then stir until melted. Stir in the butter and the brandy, if using, then strain into a bowl and cool. Cover and chill overnight.

2 Line a large baking sheet with greaseproof paper. Using two teaspoons, form the chocolate mixture into 20–30 balls and place on the paper. Chill if the mixture becomes soft.

3 To coat the truffles with cocoa, sift the cocoa into a bowl, drop in the truffles, one at a time, and roll to coat well, keeping the round shape. To coat with nuts, roll truffles in finely chopped nuts. Chill, wrapped, for up to 10 days.

4 To coat the truffles with chocolate, freeze the truffles for at least 1 hour. In a small bowl, melt the plain, milk or white chocolate over a saucepan of barely simmering water, stirring until the chocolate has melted and is smooth, then allow to cool slightly.

5 Using a fork, dip the frozen truffles into the cooled chocolate, one at a time, tapping the fork on the edge of the bowl to shake off the excess. Place on a baking sheet lined with non-stick baking paper and chill at once. If the melted chocolate thickens, reheat until smooth. Wrap in clear film and store in a cool place for up to 10 days.

MARSHMALLOWS

These light and fragrant mouthfuls of pale pink mousse are flavoured with rose water.

INGREDIENTS

oil, for greasing
45ml/3 tbsp icing sugar
45ml/3 tbsp cornflour
50ml/2fl oz/¼ cup cold water
45ml/3 tbsp rose water
25g/1oz/1 tbsp powdered gelatine
pink food colouring
450g/1lb/2 cups granulated sugar
30ml/2 level tbsp liquid glucose
250ml/8fl oz/1 cup boiling water
2 egg whites

Makes 500g/1¼lb

1 Lightly oil a 28 x 18cm/11 x 7in Swiss roll tin. Sift together the icing sugar and cornflour and use some to coat the inside of the tin.

2 Mix the cold water, rose water, gelatine and a drop of food colouring in a bowl. Place over a pan of hot water. Stir until the gelatine has dissolved.

3 Place the sugar, liquid glucose and boiling water in a heavy-based saucepan. Stir to dissolve the sugar.

4 Bring the syrup to the boil and boil steadily without stirring until the temperature reaches 127°C/260°F on a sugar thermometer. Remove from the heat and stir in the gelatine mixture.

5 While the syrup is boiling, whisk the egg whites stiffly in a large bowl using an electric hand whisk. Pour a steady stream of syrup on to the egg whites while whisking continuously for about 3 minutes, until the mixture is thick and foamy. At this stage add more food colouring, if the mixture looks too pale.

6 Pour the mixture into the prepared tin and allow to set for about 4 hours or overnight. Sift some of the remaining icing sugar mixture over the surface of the marshmallow and the rest over a board or baking sheet. Ease the mixture away from the tin using an oiled palette knife and invert on to the board. Cut into 2.5cm/1in squares, coating the cut sides with the icing sugar mixture. Pack the marshmallows into glass containers or tins and seal well.

MARZIPAN FRUITS

These eye-catching and realistic fruits will make a perfect gift for lovers of marzipan.

INGREDIENTS

450g/1lb white marzipan
yellow, green, red, orange and burgundy
food colouring dusts
30g/1½oz/2 tbsp whole cloves

Makes 450g/1lb

1 Cover a baking sheet with non-stick baking paper. Cut the marzipan into quarters. Take 1 piece and cut it into 10 even-size pieces. Place a little of each of the food colouring dusts into a food paint palette, or place small amounts spaced apart on a plate. Cut ⅔ of the cloves into 2 pieces, making a stem and core end.

2 Shape the 10 pieces into a neat ball. Dip 1 ball into the yellow food colouring and roll to colour. Re-dip into the green colouring and re-roll to tint a greeny-yellow colour. Roll one end to make a pear shape. Press a clove stem into the top and a core end into the base. Repeat with the remaining balls. Place on the prepared baking sheet.

3 Cut another piece of the marzipan into 10 pieces and shape into neat balls. Dip each piece of marzipan into the green food colouring dust and roll in the palms to colour evenly. Add a spot of red colouring dust and roll gently to blend the colour. Using a ball tool or the end of a fine paint-brush, indent the top and base to make an apple shape. Make a stem and core, using cloves.

4 Repeat as above, using another piece of the marzipan to make 10 orange coloured balls. Roll each over the surface of a fine grater to give the texture of an orange skin. Press a clove core into the base of each.

5 Take the remaining piece of marzipan, reserve a small piece, and mould the rest into lots of tiny marzipan beads. Colour them burgundy with the food colouring. Place a whole clove on the baking sheet. Arrange a cluster of burgundy beads in the shape of a bunch of grapes. Repeat with the remaining burgundy beads of marzipan to make another 3 bunches of grapes.

6 Roll out the remaining piece of marzipan thinly and brush with green food colouring. Using a vine leaf cutter, cut out 8 leaves, mark the veins with a knife and place 2 on each bunch of grapes. Leave the fruits to dry, then pack into gift boxes.

PEPPERMINT CHOCOLATE STICKS

These delicious bite-size chocolate sticks will prove irresistible.

INGREDIENTS

115g/4oz/½ cup granulated sugar
150ml/¼ pint/⅔ cup water
2.5ml/½ tsp peppermint essence
*200g/7oz plain dark chocolate, broken
into squares*
60ml/4 tbsp toasted desiccated coconut

Makes about 80

1 Lightly oil a large baking sheet. Place the sugar and water in a small heavy-based saucepan over a medium-low heat. Allow the water to heat gently, until the sugar has dissolved completely. Stir occasionally.

2 Bring to the boil and boil rapidly until the syrup registers 138°C/280°F on a sugar thermometer. Remove from the heat. Add the peppermint essence and pour on to the greased baking sheet. Leave to set.

3 Break up the peppermint mixture into a small bowl and use the end of a rolling pin to crush it into small pieces.

4 Melt the chocolate in a heatproof bowl over hot water. Remove from the heat and stir in the mint pieces and desiccated coconut.

5 Spread the chocolate mixture over a 30 x 25cm/12 x 10in sheet of non-stick baking paper, to make a rectangle measuring about 25 x 20cm/10 x 8in. Leave to set. When firm, use a sharp knife to cut into thin sticks, each about 6cm/2½in long.

TRUFFLE CHRISTMAS PUDDINGS

Truffles disguised as Christmas puddings are great fun both to make and receive.

Make any flavour truffles, and decorate them as you like.

INGREDIENTS

20 plain chocolate truffles
15ml/1 tbsp cocoa
15ml/1 tbsp icing sugar
225g/8oz/1 cup white chocolate dots, melted
50g/2oz/¼ cup white marzipan
green and red food colourings
yellow food colouring dust

Makes 20

COOK'S TIP

These little truffle puddings are fun to make at home and children will love to help. They may be able to coat the truffles, do some stamping, or pack the finished puddings in a box as a special present.

1 Make the truffles following the recipe on page 247. Sift the cocoa and icing sugar together and coat the truffles.

2 Spread ⅔ of the white chocolate over a piece of non-stick baking paper. Using a small daisy cutter, stamp out 20 rounds. Place a truffle on the centre of each daisy shape, secured with a little of the reserved melted chocolate.

3 Colour ⅔ of the marzipan green and ⅓ red using the food colourings. Roll out the green marzipan thinly and stamp out 40 leaves, using a tiny holly leaf cutter. Mark the veins with a sharp knife. Mould lots of tiny red marzipan beads. Colour the remaining white chocolate with yellow food colouring dust and place in a greaseproof paper piping bag. Fold down the top of the bag, cut off the point and pipe the marzipan over the top of each truffle to resemble custard. Arrange the holly leaves and berries on the top of the puddings. When the truffle puddings have set, arrange them in gift boxes, label and tie with ribbon.

Striped Biscuits

Eat these biscuits with scoops of vanilla ice cream or any light desserts.

INGREDIENTS

25g/1oz/1 square white chocolate, melted
red and green food colouring dusts
2 egg whites
90g/3½oz/¼ cup caster sugar
50g/2oz/½ cup plain flour
50g/2oz/4 tbsp unsalted butter, melted

Makes 25

1 Preheat the oven to 190°C/375°F/ Gas 5. Line 2 baking sheets with non-stick baking paper. Divide the melted chocolate in two and use the food colouring dust to colour the chocolate red and green. Fill 2 greaseproof paper piping bags with each chocolate and fold down the tops. Snip off the points.

2 Place the egg whites in a mixing bowl and whisk until they form stiff peaks. Gradually add the sugar to the bowl, whisking well after each addition, to make a thick meringue. Sift in the flour and melted butter and whisk some more until the mixture is smooth.

3 Drop 4 separate teaspoonfuls of mixture on to the baking sheets and spread into thin rounds. Pipe lines or zigzags of green and red chocolate over each round. Bake in the oven for 3–4 minutes or until pale golden in colour. Loosen the rounds with a palette knife and return to the oven for a few seconds to soften. Have ready 2 or 3 lightly oiled wooden spoon handles at hand.

4 Taking one biscuit out of the oven at a time, roll it around a spoon handle and leave it for a few seconds to set. Repeat to shape the remaining biscuits.

5 When the biscuits are set, leave on a wire rack to cool. Repeat with the remaining mixture and the red and green chocolate until all the mixture has been used.

6 When the biscuits are cold, tie them together with a length of brightly coloured ribbon and pack into airtight boxes, tins or glass jars.

MACAROONS

These little macaroons can be served as petit-fours with coffee.

Dust with icing sugar or cocoa before serving.

INGREDIENTS

50g/2oz/²⁄₃ cup ground almonds
50g/2oz/¼ cup caster sugar
15ml/1 tbsp cornflour
1.5–2.5ml/¼–½ tsp almond essence
1 egg white, whisked
15 flaked almonds
4 glacé cherries, quartered
icing sugar or cocoa, to dust

Makes 30

> #### COOK'S TIP
>
> *To make chocolate-flavoured macaroons, replace the cornflour with the same amount of cocoa powder.*

2 Stir in just enough egg white to form a soft piping consistency. Place the mixture into a nylon piping bag fitted with a 1cm/½ in plain piping nozzle.

3 Pipe about 15 rounds of mixture on to each baking sheet, spaced well apart. Press a flaked almond on to half the macaroons and glacé cherries on to the remainder. Bake for 10–15 minutes.

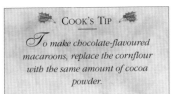

1 Preheat the oven to 160°C/325°F/ Gas 3. Line 2 baking sheets with non-stick baking paper. Place the ground almonds, sugar, cornflour and almond essence into a bowl and mix together well, using a wooden spoon.

Mini Iced Christmas Cakes

A personal Christmas cake makes an extra-special gift.

Experiment with your own designs, decorations and colour schemes.

INGREDIENTS

350g/12oz/1½ cups mixed dried fruit
50g/2oz/¼ cup glacé cherries, sliced
50g/2oz/½ cup flaked almonds
grated rind of ½ lemon
15ml/1 tbsp brandy
115g/4oz/1 cup plain flour
½ tsp ground mixed spice
25g/1oz/¼ cup ground almonds
90g/3½oz/½ cup unsalted butter, softened
90g/3½oz/½ cup dark soft brown sugar
7.5ml/½ tbsp black treacle
2 eggs

For the Icing and Decoration
4 x 10cm/4in square cake boards
60ml/4 tbsp Apricot Glaze (see Christmas Baking)
675g/1½lb white marzipan
900g/2lb ready-to-roll icing
red and green food colourings

Makes 4 cakes

1 Prepare a 15cm/6in square cake tin. Place the mixed dried fruit, cherries, flaked almonds, lemon rind and brandy into a large mixing bowl. Stir until thoroughly blended, cover with clear film and leave for 1 hour or overnight.

2 Preheat the oven to 150°C/300°F/ Gas 2. Sift the flour and mixed spice into another bowl, add the ground almonds, butter, sugar, treacle and eggs. Mix together with a wooden spoon and beat for 2–3 minutes until smooth and glossy. Alternatively use a food mixer or processor for 1 minute. Fold the fruit into the cake mixture until evenly blended. Place the mixture in the prepared tin, level the top and make a slight depression in the centre.

3 Bake the cake in the centre of the oven for 2¼–2½ hours or until a skewer inserted into the centre comes out clean. Leave the cake to cool in the tin. Spoon over a little extra brandy if desired. Remove the cake from the tin and wrap in foil until required.

4 Remove the lining paper and cut the cake into four square pieces. Place each cake on a small cake board and brush evenly with Apricot Glaze. Cut the marzipan into four pieces and roll out a piece large enough to cover one cake. Place over the cake, smooth over the top and sides then trim off the excess marzipan at the base. Repeat to cover the remaining three cakes.

5 Cut the ready-to-roll icing into five pieces. Roll four pieces out thinly to cover each cake, smoothing the top and sides and trimming off the excess icing at the base. Knead the trimmings together with the remaining piece of icing and cut into two pieces. Colour one piece red and the other green, using the food colourings. Roll out half of the red icing into a 25 x 15cm/10 x 6in oblong.

6 Cut the icing into 5mm/¼in strips and place diagonally across the cake, working from corner to corner. Trim the strips at the base of the cake. Brush the ends of the strips with a little water and press on to the cake. Make a few loops of icing and place on top of the cake. Repeat to decorate the remaining cakes with green, and finally red and green strips of icing. Pack into gift boxes when dry.

MINI CHOCOLATE CHRISTMAS CAKES

A striped marzipan Christmas decoration adorns each of these smart cakes.

INGREDIENTS

275g/10oz/2½ cups self-raising flour
15g/1 tbsp baking powder
50g/2oz/½ cup cocoa
250g/9oz/1⅛ cups caster sugar
150ml/¼ pint/⅔ cup sunflower oil
350ml/12fl oz/1½ cups water

For the Icing and Decoration
*4 x 15cm/6in square
silver cake boards*
*90ml/6 tbsp Apricot Glaze (see
Christmas Baking)*
1kg/2¼lb marzipan
900g/2lb chocolate sugarpaste
red, yellow and green food colourings
2m/2yd red ribbon
2m/2yd green ribbon

Makes 4 cakes

3 Cool the cake in the tin for 15 minutes, then turn out, remove the paper and invert on to a wire rack. When completely cold, cut into four equal pieces. Place each piece on a separate cake board and brush with Apricot Glaze.

5 Divide the chocolate sugarpaste into four pieces and repeat the process, rolling out each piece thinly to cover each cake. Colour the remaining marzipan ⅓ red, ⅓ yellow and ⅓ green with the food colourings. Thinly roll out each piece and cut into 1cm/½in strips.

1 Preheat the oven to 160°C/325°F/ Gas 3. Grease a 20cm/8in square cake tin and line with greaseproof paper. Sift the flour, baking powder, cocoa and caster sugar into a mixing bowl.

2 Add the oil and water and mix together with a wooden spoon, beating until smooth and glossy. Pour into the prepared tin and bake in the oven for about 1 hour, or until the cake springs back when pressed in the centre.

4 Divide the marzipan into four equal pieces and roll out a piece large enough to cover one cake. Place over the cake, press neatly into shape and trim off the excess marzipan at the base of the board. Knead the trimmings together and repeat to cover the remaining three cakes.

6 Lay alternate strips together and cut out four Christmas shapes using pastry cutters. Arrange the shapes on top of each cake. Measure and fit the red and green ribbons around each cake and tie in a bow. Pack the cakes into pretty boxes, tie with ribbon and label.

NOVELTY CHRISTMAS CAKES

These individual cakes can be packed in their own little boxes to make unusual gifts for children.

INGREDIENTS

115g/4oz/1 cup self-raising flour
5ml/1 tsp baking powder
15ml/1 tbsp cocoa
115g/4oz/½ cup caster sugar
115g/4oz/½ cup soft margarine
2 eggs

For the Icing and Decoration
45ml/3 tbsp Apricot Glaze (see
Christmas Baking)
2 x 15cm/6in thin round
cake boards
350g/12oz ready-to-
roll icing
350g/12oz white marzipan
red, black, green, yellow and brown
food colourings
white and red edible glitter flakes

Makes 2

3 Brush both the cakes with Apricot Glaze and place on the cake boards. To make the clown cake, roll out one-third of the icing to a round large enough to cover one cake. Place over the cake, smooth the surface and trim off the excess at the base. Mould two ears from the trimmings and press into position.

5 To make the Father Christmas cake, colour the remaining marzipan skin tone using a tiny amount of brown colouring and roll out thinly to cover two-thirds of the second cake. Trim to fit. Roll out three-quarters of the remaining red marzipan thinly and cover the rest of the cake to make the hat. Gather the excess together at one side for the hat. Mould a nose and mouth from the remaining red marzipan.

1 Preheat the oven to 160°C/325°F/ Gas 3. Grease and line the bases of two 15cm/6in round sandwich tins. Place all the cake ingredients into a large mixing bowl. Beat with a wooden spoon for 2–3 minutes until smooth and glossy.

2 Divide the mixture between the two tins, smooth the tops and bake in the oven for 20–25 minutes or until the cakes spring back when pressed in the centre. Loosen the edges of the cakes and invert on to a wire rack. Remove the paper and leave to cool.

4 Colour one-third of the marzipan red and shape a mouth and nose; reserve the remainder. Colour a small piece of marzipan black and roll out thin lengths to outline the mouth and make the eyebrows and two crosses for the eyes. Colour another small piece green for the ruffle. Colour another small piece yellow and grate coarsely to make the hair. Stick in position with Apricot Glaze and sprinkle with white glitter flakes.

6 Coarsely grate the remaining white icing and use to trim the hat and to shape the beard, moustache and eyebrows. Gently press a small ball of grated white icing together to make a bobble for the hat. Shape two black eyes and press in position. Sprinkle red glitter flakes on to the hat to give it a sparkle. Pack each cake into a small box with a lid and write a name tag.

ROUND CHRISTMAS PUDDING

This rich Christmas pudding makes a wonderful novelty gift. Special moulds are available

from kitchen shops in large and small sizes.

INGREDIENTS

350g/12oz/1½ cups mixed dried fruit
200g/7oz/1 cup dried mixed fruit salad,
chopped
50g/2oz/½ cup flaked almonds
1 small carrot, coarsely grated
1 small cooking apple, coarsely grated
grated rind and juice of 1 lemon
15ml/1 tbsp black treacle
90ml/3½fl oz/6 tbsp stout
50g/2oz/1 cup fresh white breadcrumbs
50g/2oz/½ cup plain flour, sifted
5ml/1 tsp ground allspice
50g/2oz/¼ cup dark soft brown sugar
50g/2oz/4 tbsp butter, melted, plus extra
for brushing
1 egg

Makes 1 large or 2 small puddings

1 Place all the dried fruits, nuts, carrot and apple into a large mixing bowl. Mix everything together with a wooden spoon. Stir in the lemon rind and juice, treacle and stout until well blended. Cover with clear film and leave in a cool place for a few hours or overnight.

2 Add the breadcrumbs, flour, allspice, sugar, butter and egg. Mix all the ingredients together with a wooden spoon until thoroughly blended.

3 Lightly butter one 14cm/5½in round Christmas pudding mould or two 7.5cm/3in moulds, and place a disc of non-stick baking paper in the base of each half. Have a saucepan ready into which the mould(s) will fit comfortably.

4 Spoon the mixture into both halves of the mould(s) so they are evenly filled. At this stage insert silver coins or miniature keepsakes wrapped several times in greaseproof paper, if you wish.

5 Place the two halves of the mould(s) together, stand on the base and clip firmly together to secure during cooking. Carefully place the mould(s) into the saucepan. Half-fill the saucepan with boiling water, taking care that the water does not reach any higher than the join of the mould(s). Bring to the boil, cover and simmer very gently for 5–6 hours, being sure to replenish the saucepan with boiling water during the cooking time.

6 Carefully remove half the mould(s) and leave until the pudding is cold. Turn out. To gift-wrap each pudding, wrap in cellophane paper and tie with a festive ribbon. Tuck a sprig of holly into the ribbon bow.

Individual Dundee Cakes

Dundee cakes are traditionally topped with almonds but also look tempting covered with glacé fruits.

INGREDIENTS

225g/8oz/1 cup raisins
225g/8oz/1 cup currants
225g/8oz/1 cup sultanas
50g/2oz/¼ cup sliced glacé cherries
115g/4oz/¾ cup mixed peel
grated rind of 1 orange
300g/11oz/2¾ cups plain flour
2.5ml/½ tsp baking powder
5ml/1 tsp mixed spice
225g/8oz/1 cup unsalted butter, softened
225g/8oz/1 cup caster sugar
5 eggs

Topping

50g/2oz/½ cup whole blanched almonds
50g/2oz/¼ cup halved glacé cherries
50g/2oz/½ cup sliced glacé fruits
45ml/3 tbsp apricot glaze

Makes 3

1 Preheat the oven to 150°C/300°F/ Gas 2. Prepare 3 x 15cm/6in round cake tins. Place all the fruit and the orange rind into a large mixing bowl. Mix together until blended. In another bowl, sift the flour, baking powder and mixed spice. Add the butter, sugar and eggs. Mix together and beat for 2–3 minutes until smooth and glossy. Alternatively use a food mixer or processor for 1 minute.

2 Add the mixed fruit to the cake mixture and fold in, using a spatula, until blended. Divide the cake mixture between the 3 tins and level the tops. Arrange the almonds in circles over the top of one cake, the glacé cherries over the second cake and the mixed glacé fruits over the last one. Bake in the oven for approximately 2–2½ hours or until a skewer inserted into the centre of the cakes comes out clean.

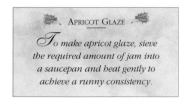

3 Leave the cakes in their tins until completely cold. Turn out, remove the paper and brush the tops with apricot glaze. Leave to set, then wrap in cellophane paper or clear film and place in pretty boxes.

APRICOT GLAZE

To make apricot glaze, sieve the required amount of jam into a saucepan and heat gently to achieve a runny consistency.

MINI BLACK BUNS

This is a traditional Scottish recipe with a rich fruit cake mixture cooked inside a bun dough.

INGREDIENTS

*50g/2oz/4 tbsp butter, melted, plus extra
for brushing
225g/8oz/1 cup mixed dried fruit
50g/2oz/¼ cup glacé cherries, chopped
50g/2oz/½ cup chopped almonds
10ml/2 tsp grated lemon rind
25g/1oz/2 tbsp caster sugar
15ml/1 tbsp whisky
50g/2oz/½ cup plain flour
5ml/1 tsp mixed spice
1 egg, beaten*

Decoration
*30ml/2 tbsp apricot glaze
450g/1lb white marzipan
purple and green food colourings*

Makes 4

1 Preheat the oven to 150°C/300°F/ Gas 2. Cut out 4 x 15cm/6in squares of greaseproof paper and 4 squares of foil. Place the greaseproof paper squares on top of the foil squares and brush with a little melted butter.

2 Place the dried fruit, chopped glacé cherries, chopped almonds, lemon rind, caster sugar, whisky, sifted flour and mixed spice into a large mixing bowl. Using a wooden spoon, stir until all of the ingredients are well mixed. Add the melted butter and egg and beat together until the mixture is well blended.

3 Divide the mixture between the 4 paper and foil squares, draw up the edges to the centre of the foil and twist the squares to mould the mixture into rounds. Place on a baking sheet and bake in the preheated oven for 45 minutes, or until the mixture feels firm when touched. Remove the foil and bake for a further 15 minutes. Open the paper and allow the cakes to cool on a wire rack.

4 Remove the paper and brush each cake with apricot glaze. Cut off ¼ of the marzipan for decoration and put to one side. Cut the remainder into 4 pieces.

5 Roll out each piece of marzipan thinly and cover the cakes. Roll each cake in the palm of your hands to make them into round shapes. Prepare a hot grill and place the cakes on to a baking sheet lined with foil.

6 Grill the cakes until the marzipan is evenly browned. Leave until cold. Colour ½ of the remaining marzipan purple and ½ green with food colourings. Cut out 4 purple thistle shapes, green leaves and stems and arrange them on top of each cake, moistening with a little water to stick. Wrap in cellophane and place into small cake boxes.

FLAVOURED VINEGARS

Flavoured vinegars look extra special if you pour them into beautifully shaped bottles.

INGREDIENTS

*good quality white and red wine vinegar
or cider vinegar*

Herb Vinegar
*15ml/1 tbsp mixed peppercorns
2 lemon slices
4 garlic cloves
rosemary, thyme, tarragon and curry
plant sprigs*
Spice Vinegar
*15ml/1 tbsp allspice berries
2 mace blades
10ml/2 tsp star anise
2 cinnamon sticks
1 orange*

Fruit Vinegar
*450g/1lb/3 cups raspberries
450g/1lb/3 cups gooseberries
450g/1lb/3 cups blackberries or
elderberries*

Makes 600ml/1 pint/2½ cups
of each flavour

1 Sterilize 2 bottles with corks or caps. To the first bottle add the peppercorns, lemon slices and garlic cloves. Place the herb sprigs together and trim the stems so they very in length. Insert them into the bottle, placing the short ones in first.

2 Into the second bottle add the allspice berries, mace, star anise and cinnamon sticks. Cut 2 slices from the orange and insert into the bottle. Pare the rind from the remaining orange and insert into the bottle.

3 Using white wine vinegar, fill the bottle containing the herbs up to the neck. Repeat to fill the bottle containing the spices with red wine vinegar. Cork or cap the bottles and store them in a cool place.

4 Wash the raspberries, gooseberries and blackberries or elderberries separately under cold running water and place them into separate bowls. Crush the fruit with a wooden spoon.

5 Pour each fruit into a separate clean wide-necked jar and add 600ml/1 pint/ 2½ cups of white wine vinegar. Cover the jars and leave for 3–4 days in a cool place. Shake the jars occasionally to mix well.

6 Strain each fruit separately through a jelly bag or a muslin-lined sieve into a stainless steel saucepan and boil for 10 minutes. Pour into sterilized bottles or jars and seal with lids or tops with plastic-coated linings. All the vinegars should be used within 6 months.

PEPPERS IN OLIVE OIL

The wonderful flavour and colour of these peppers will add a Mediterranean

theme to festive meals. Bottle the peppers separately or mix the colours together.

INGREDIENTS

3 red peppers
3 yellow peppers
3 green peppers
300ml/½ pint/1¼ cups olive oil
2.5ml/½ tsp salt
2.5ml/½ tsp freshly ground black pepper
3 thyme sprigs

Makes enough to fill 3 x 450g/1lb jars

COOK'S TIP

This pungent oil should be stored in a cool, dark place and used within a week. The filled bottles also make great decorations for the home, if you choose not to use the oil for cooking.

---

2 Allow the peppers to cool for at least 5 minutes, then peel off the skins. Remove the cores, seeds and stalks. Slice each of the peppers thinly, keeping each colour separate, and place each into a separate dish.

3 Pour ⅓ of the olive oil over each of the peppers. Season and add a sprig of thyme. Stir well. Sterilize 3 jars and lids and fill each with a mixture of peppers. Top up each jar with the oil. Screw the jar lids on firmly and label.

1 Prepare a hot grill or preheat the oven to 200°C/400°F/Gas 6. Put the whole peppers on a grill rack or on to a baking sheet. Place under the grill or in the oven and cook for about 10 minutes, until the skins are charred and blistered all over. Turn the peppers frequently during the cooking time.

Fresh Fruit Preserve

The wonderfully fresh flavour of this fruit spread makes it a welcome gift. To vary the recipe,

use a mixture of soft fruits or other individual fruits such as strawberries or blackberries.

INGREDIENTS

675g/1½lb/3½ cups raspberries
900g/2lb/4 cups caster sugar
30ml/2 tbsp lemon juice
120ml/4fl oz/½ cup liquid pectin

Makes 900g/2lb

COOK'S TIP

The process of leaving the fruit in the sugar for an hour is known as macerating. This process allows the fruit to become very pulpy and sweet, with a more intense flavour.

1 Place the raspberries in a large bowl and lightly crush with a wooden spoon. Stir in the caster sugar. Leave for 1 hour at room temperature, giving the mixture an occasional stir to dissolve the sugar.

2 Sterilize several small jars or containers and their lids, if being used. Add the lemon juice and liquid pectin to the raspberries and stir until thoroughly blended.

3 Spoon the raspberry mixture into the jars, leaving a 1cm/½ in space at the top if the preserve is to be frozen. Cover the surface of each preserve with a greaseproof paper disc, and cover with the jar lid or with cellophane paper and an elastic band. Do not use a screw-topped lid if the preserve is to be frozen. Allow to cool, then label. The preserve can be stored in the freezer for up to 6 months, or refrigerated for up to 4 weeks.

FRUITS IN LIQUEURS

These eye-catching fruits in liqueurs are best made when the fruits are plentiful, cheap and in season.

Choose from apricots, clementines, kumquats, physalis, cherries, raspberries, peaches, plums or seedless

grapes, and team them with rum, brandy, Kirsch or Cointreau, to name just a few.

INGREDIENTS

450g/1lb/3 cups fresh fruit
225g/8oz/1 cup granulated sugar
150ml/¼ pint/⅔ cup liqueur or spirits

Makes 450g/1lb

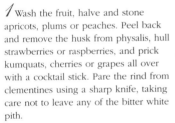

5 Boil the syrup rapidly until it reaches 107°C/225°F, or the thread stage. Test by pressing a small amount of syrup between 2 teaspoons; when they are pulled apart, a thread should form. Allow to cool.

6 Measure the cooled syrup, then add an equal quantity of liqueur or spirit. Mix until blended. Pour over the fruit in the jars until covered. Seal each jar with a screw or clip top, label and keep for up to 4 months.

1 Wash the fruit, halve and stone apricots, plums or peaches. Peel back and remove the husk from physalis, hull strawberries or raspberries, and prick kumquats, cherries or grapes all over with a cocktail stick. Pare the rind from clementines using a sharp knife, taking care not to leave any of the bitter white pith.

2 Place 115g/4oz/½ cup of the sugar and 300ml/½ pint/1¼ cups of water into a large saucepan. Heat gently, stirring occasionally, until the sugar has dissolved. Bring to the boil.

3 Add the fruit to the syrup and simmer gently for 1–2 minutes until the fruit is just tender, but the skins are still intact and the fruits are whole.

4 Carefully remove the fruit using a slotted spoon and arrange neatly in the warmed sterilized jars. Add the remaining sugar to the syrup in the saucepan and stir continuously until it has dissolved.

Festive Drinks & Cocktails

*T*he cheerful custom of the Christmas "wassail" –
a steaming bowl of ale mixed with roasted apples, sugar
and spices – has existed for centuries as a celebration of
good cheer. The modern equivalent to this traditional toast
is the ever-popular Mulled Claret, and there are plenty of
other tempting alcoholic and non-alcoholic alternatives
included in this chapter. Brandied Eggnog is one of the
more warming recipes to lift the spirits and, along with
Irish Chocolate Velvet, it makes the ultimate nightcap.
Cocktail drinks such as Buck's Fizz and Cranberry Kiss
are perfect to get the party started, while for the post-party
breakfast, choose the delightful, sparkling Cranberry Frost.

CRANBERRY FROST

A non-alcoholic cocktail with the colour of holly berries will delight younger and older guests alike.

It is the perfect "one-for-the-road" drink to serve at the end of a gathering.

INGREDIENTS

115g/4oz/½ cup caster sugar
juice of 2 oranges
still water, enough to dissolve the sugar
1 litre/1¾ pints/4 cups sparkling mineral water
100ml/4fl oz/½ cup cranberry juice
fresh cranberries, to decorate
sprigs of mint, to decorate

Serves 10

1 Put the sugar, orange juice and still water into a small pan and stir over a low heat to dissolve the sugar. Bring to the boil and boil for 3 minutes. Set aside to cool. The syrup can be made in advance and stored in a covered container in the refrigerator. Pour the syrup into a chilled bowl, pour on the cranberry juice and mix well. To serve, pour on the mineral water and decorate with cranberries and mint leaves.

COOK'S TIP

To make this fabulous non-alcoholic drink the very essence of festive colour, chill with ice cubes made by freezing fresh red cranberries and tiny mint leaves in the water.

Mulled Claret

This mull is a blend of claret, cider and orange juice. It can be varied to suit the occasion

by increasing or decreasing the proportion of fruit juice or, to give the mull more pep,

by adding up to 150ml/¼ pint/⅔ cup brandy.

Ingredients

1 orange
75ml/5 tbsp clear honey
30ml/2 tbsp seedless raisins
2 clementines
a few cloves
whole nutmeg
60ml/4 tbsp demerara sugar
2 cinnamon sticks
1½ litres/2½ pints/6¼ cups inexpensive claret
600ml/1 pint/2½ cups medium cider
300ml/½ pint/1¼ cups orange juice

Makes 16 x 150ml/¼ pints/⅔ cup glasses

3 Grate a little nutmeg into the sugar and then add it to the pan with the cinnamon sticks. Pour on the wine and heat over a low heat, stirring until the sugar has completely dissolved and the honey melted.

4 Pour the cider and the orange juice into the saucepan and continue to heat the mull over a gentle heat. Do not allow it to boil or all the alcohol will evaporate.

5 Warm a punch bowl or other large serving bowl. Remove the clementines and cinnamon sticks from the saucepan and strain the mull into the bowl to remove the raisins. Add the clementines studded with cloves, and serve the mull hot, in warmed glasses or in glasses containing a silver spoon (to prevent the glass breaking). Using a nutmeg grater, add a little nutmeg over each serving, if you wish.

1 With a sharp knife or a rotary peeler, pare off a long strip of orange peel.

2 Place the orange peel, honey and raisins in a large pan. Stud the clementines all over with the cloves and add them to the saucepan.

BRANDIED EGGNOG

This frothy blend of eggs, milk and spirits definitely comes into the nightcap category of drinks.

INGREDIENTS

4 eggs, separated
30ml/2 tbsp caster sugar
60ml/4 tbsp dark rum
60ml/4 tbsp brandy
300ml/½ pint/1¼ cups milk (or according to the volume of the glasses), hot
whole nutmeg

Serves 4

1 Beat the egg yolks with the sugar. Beat the whites to soft peaks. Mix and pour into 4 heatproof glasses.

2 Pour on the rum and brandy, 15ml/1 tbsp of each in each glass.

3 Top up the glass with hot milk. Grate the nutmeg over the top and serve at once.

COOK'S TIP

You can also make a cold version of this drink using chilled single cream instead of the hot milk.

Irish Chocolate Velvet

This smooth, sophisticated drink will always be appreciated on cold Christmas evenings.

INGREDIENTS

120ml/4fl oz/½ cup double cream
400ml/14fl oz/1⅔ cups milk
30ml/2 tbsp cocoa powder
115g/4oz milk chocolate, broken into squares
60ml/4 tbsp Irish whisky
whipped cream, for topping
chocolate curls, to decorate

Serves 4

COOK'S TIP

If Irish whisky is not available, use brandy or any liqueur which uses whisky or brandy as its base.

1 Whip the cream in a bowl until it is thick enough to hold its shape.

2 Put the milk into a saucepan and whisk in the cocoa powder. Add the chocolate squares and heat gently, stirring, until the chocolate has melted. Bring the chocolate milk to the boil.

3 Remove the saucepan from the heat and add the whipped double cream and Irish whisky. Stir gently for about 1 minute to blend well.

4 Pour quickly into four heatproof mugs or glasses and top each serving with a generous spoonful of whipped cream. Decorate with chocolate curls and serve at once.

Buck's Fizz (Mimosa)

This delightfully refreshing drink, invented by the barman at the Buck's Club in

London in 1921, has achieved star status. In France it is known as "Champagne-orange"

and in Italy and the United States as "Mimosa".

INGREDIENTS

120ml/4fl oz/½ cup fresh orange juice
5ml/1 tsp grenadine syrup
175ml/6fl oz/¾ cup Champagne or other
sparkling white wine, chilled

Makes 1 glass

1 Put the orange juice into a chilled long-stemmed glass. Add the grenadine syrup and stir with a long-handled spoon to blend. Then add the Champagne or white wine and stir again. Serve the cocktail at once, decorated with a slice of fresh orange.

COOK'S TIP

Buck's Fizz, with its refreshing combination of fruit juice and white wine, makes the perfect cocktail drink for Christmas morning.

Brandy Alexander

A warming digestif, made from a blend of crème de cacao, brandy and double cream,

that can be served at the end of the meal with coffee.

Ingredients

crushed ice
20ml/1 measure/1½ tbsp brandy
20ml/1 measure/1½ tbsp
crème de cacao
20ml/1 measure/1½ tbsp double cream
whole nutmeg, grated, to decorate

Serves 1

❧ Variation ❧

Warm the brandy and double cream and whizz in a blender with crème de cacao, until frothy. Serve in a tall glass with a cinnamon stick.

3 Strain the chilled cocktail into a small wine glass.

4 Finely grate a little nutmeg over the top of the cocktail and serve at once.

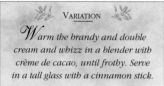

1 Half fill the cocktail shaker with ice and pour in the brandy, crème de cacao and, finally, the cream.

2 Ensure the lid is screwed firmly in place and shake for about 20 seconds, to mix the ingredients together well.

CRANBERRY KISS

A delicious full-flavoured cocktail, with the tang of cranberry and pink

grapefruit juices and the sweetness of Marsala.

INGREDIENTS

redcurrant string, to decorate
1 egg white, lightly beaten, to decorate
15ml/½oz caster sugar, to decorate
crushed ice
45ml/2 measures/3 tbsp cranberry juice
20ml/1 measure/1½ tbsp brandy
45ml/2 measures/3 tbsp pink grapefruit
juice
45ml/2 measures/3 tbsp Marsala

Serves 1

1 Lightly brush the redcurrants with the egg white.

2 Shake caster sugar over the redcurrants, to cover them in a light frosting. Set them aside to dry.

3 Place the cranberry juice with the brandy and grapefruit juice in a cocktail shaker full of crushed ice and shake for 20 seconds to mix thoroughly.

4 Strain the cocktail mixture into a well-chilled glass.

5 Tilt the glass slightly before slowly pouring the Marsala down the side of the glass into the drink.

6 Serve the cocktail decorated with the frosted redcurrant string.

VARIATION

Shake together cranberry and pineapple juice with coconut milk. Add vodka or gin to taste.

FRUIT AND GINGER ALE

An old English mulled drink, served chilled over ice. It can be made with

ready-squeezed apple and orange juices, but roasting the fruit with cloves gives a far superior flavour.

INGREDIENTS

1 cooking apple
1 orange, scrubbed
1 lemon, scrubbed
20 whole cloves
7.5cm/3in fresh root ginger, peeled
25ml/1½ tbsp soft brown sugar
350ml/12fl oz bitter lemon or non-alcoholic wine
wedges of orange rind and whole cloves, to decorate

Serves 4–6

3 Add 300ml/½ pint/1¼ cups boiling water. Using a spoon, squeeze the fruit to release more flavour. Cover the mixing bowl and leave to cool for several hours or overnight.

4 Strain into a jug of cracked ice and use a spoon to press out all the juices from the fruit. Add the bitter lemon or non-alcoholic wine to taste. Decorate with orange rind and cloves.

1 Preheat the oven to 200°C/400°F/ Gas 6. Score the apple around the middle and stud the orange and lemon with the cloves. Bake them in the oven for 25 minutes until soft and cooked.

2 Quarter the orange and lemon and pulp the apple, discarding the skin and the core. Finely grate the ginger. Place the fruit and ginger together in a bowl with the soft brown sugar.

CHRISTMAS SPIRIT

This colourful drink has a sharp but sweet taste. It is excellent served as a winter warmer

or after a meal, but it also makes a good summer drink served with crushed ice.

INGREDIENTS

450g/1lb/2 cups cranberries
2 clementines
450g/1lb/2 cups granulated sugar
1 cinnamon stick
475ml/16fl oz/2 cups vodka

Makes 750ml/1¼ pints/3 cups

1 Crush the cranberries in a food processor and spoon into a large jar. Pare the rind from the clementines and add.

2 Squeeze the juice from the clementines and add to the cranberries and pared rind in the jar. Add the sugar, cinnamon stick and vodka to the jar and seal with the lid or a double thickness of plastic, and tie down securely. Shake the jar well to combine all the ingredients.

3 Store the jar in a cool place for 1 month, shaking the jar daily for 2 weeks, then occasionally. When the drink has matured, sterilize some small pretty bottles and, using a funnel with a filter paper inside, strain the liquid into the bottles and cork immediately. Label the bottles clearly and tie a gift tag around the neck.

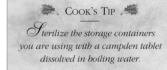

> **COOK'S TIP**
>
> *Sterilize the storage containers you are using with a campden tablet dissolved in boiling water.*

Festive Liqueurs

These are easier to make than wines and may be made with a variety of flavours and spirits.

All these liqueurs should be allowed to mature for 3 months before drinking.

INGREDIENTS

Plum Brandy
450g/1lb plums
225g/8oz/1 cup demerara sugar
600ml/1 pint/2½ cups brandy

Fruit Gin
450g/1lb/3 cups raspberries,
blackcurrants or sloes
350g/12oz/1½ cups granulated sugar
750ml/1¼ pints/3 cups gin

Citrus Whisky
1 large orange
1 small lemon
1 lime
225g/8oz/1 cup granulated sugar
600ml/1 pint/2½ cups whisky

Makes 900ml/1½ pints/3¾ cups
of each liqueur

1 Sterilize 3 jars and lids. Wash and halve the plums, remove the stones and slice. Place the plums in the sterilized jar with the sugar and brandy. Crack 3 of the plum stones, remove the kernels and chop. Add them to the jar and stir until blended.

2 Place the raspberries, blackcurrants or sloes into the prepared jar. If using sloes, prick the surface of the berries using a stainless steel pin to extract the flavour. Add the sugar and gin to the jar and stir until the mixture is well blended.

3 To make the Citrus Whisky, first scrub the fruit. Using a sharp knife or potato peeler, pare the rind from the fruit, taking care not to include the white pith. Squeeze out all of the juice and place in the jar with the fruit rinds. Add the sugar and whisky, and stir until well blended.

4 Cover the jars with lids or double thickness plastic tied down well. Store the jars in a cool, dark place for 3 months.

5 Shake the Fruit Gin every day for 1 month, and then occasionally. Shake the Plum Brandy and Citrus Whisky every day for 2 weeks, then occasionally, Sterilize the chosen bottles and corks or stoppers for each liqueur.

6 When each liqueur is ready to be bottled, strain the liquid through a sieve, then pour it into sterilized bottles through a funnel fitted with a filter paper. Fit the corks or stoppers and label the bottles with a festive label.

Decorations & Gifts for Christmas

Instead of shop-bought decorations, it is very satisfying to make your own decorations for the Christmas tree and table, and to keep them year after year as family heirlooms. Friends and relatives will be enchanted by handmade cards and presents, especially from children, and gifts will mean so much more if you use your own gift-wrap and add a personal touch to the parcel. There are ideas here for projects large and small, and the wide variety of techniques used includes modern crafts such as tin embossing, machine embroidery, wirework, papier-mâché and gilding.

INTRODUCTION

There's no time like Christmas. Sooner or later we all get swept up in its huge, warm embrace. It may be commercialized, expensive and a lot of hard work, but it can also be a magical time of happy gatherings and memorable meals, reaffirming friendships and family ties.

Christmas is an unrivalled opportunity to give free rein to your creativity as you decorate your home and plan your festive table. Brighten the dark days of winter with the glint of gold, the enchanting glow of candlelight and the scent of freshly gathered evergreens. These lovely craft ideas will spark your creative energy and help you make the best of the season.

You'll find suggestions for traditional tree ornaments, or you may prefer an elegant, modern arrangement of gold or silver. If you'd rather get

ABOVE: *Use painted clothes pegs to hang your cards up the stairs.*

LEFT: *Turn plain glass Christmas tree ornaments into opulent gilded decorations by covering them in swirling patterns of gold glass (relief) outliner.*

LEFT: *A glass bowl of oranges, lemons and limes makes a glowing, fragrant centrepiece.*

BELOW: *Transform parcel paper into highly original gift-wraps.*

right away from Christmas glitz, find inspiration in a rustic look, using materials such as homespun fabrics, raffia, and twigs and greenery you could collect on a winter walk.

Don't stop at decorations: make your own gift-wrap and tags – and gifts too. Find out how to make your own crackers and you'll be able to fill them with personalized treats for your guests.

All the projects are simple to make following the detailed step-by-step

RIGHT: *Natural materials make lovely decorations: collect your own evergreens, nuts and cones.*

instructions. Perhaps they'll introduce you to some new skills, such as needlepoint or stencilling, that you'll want to develop after the flurry of Christmas is over. Once you've discovered the satisfaction that comes

from creating your own Christmas you'll no longer be content with ready-made decorations. Collect rich fabrics, gold paper, ribbons, glitter and paint and use them to turn your home into a welcoming haven every Christmas.

PAPERS AND PAINTS

Build up a store of interesting materials for your decorating projects:

save pretty boxes, foil wrapping and packaging material.

crepe paper

copper foil

aluminium foil

willow twigs

CRAYONS AND PENS
Stencil crayons come in a range of plain and metallic colours. They are oil-based and dry out to form a skin which must be scraped away each time they are used. Allow the work to dry thoroughly for a permanent finish. Gold (magic) marker pens are an alternative to paint when you need a fine line.

DECORATIVE PAPERS
The choice is endless here. Look for double-sided and metallic crepe paper, especially in unusual colours such as bronze. Gold papers and foils come in various textures, matt and shiny, and add a touch of luxury to your work. Don't forget the basics: add your own decorations to brown parcel wrap (packaging paper), white paper and card (cardboard).

GLITTER AND GLITTER PAINTS
There is an amazing selection of different types of glitter to choose from now. As well as the old-fashioned tubes of coloured glitter to sprinkle on, you can buy coloured glitter suspended in clear paint and tubes of glittery fabric paints.

LINO-CUTTING TOOL
This can be used to cut decorative grooves in citrus fruit. Another traditional implement, used by chefs, is a canelle knife.

METAL FOILS
Copper and aluminium foils are available from crafts suppliers in a heavier gauge than ordinary kitchen foil.

OIL-BASED PAINTS
These are used for decorating surfaces that will need washing, such as glass and ceramics. Read the manufacturer's instructions before you use them. Clean your brushes with (distilled) turpentine or white spirit (paint thinner). Glass (relief) outliner paint comes in a tube and is squeezed directly on to the surface. It needs a long drying time but sets hard.

OTHER PAINTS
Gold spray paint is useful for covering large areas, but look out for different shades of gold in water-based and oil-based paints. Watercolour inks have a wonderful translucent vibrancy that is quite different to the matt effect of gouache paint.

PAPERS
There is a tremendous range of decorative papers available from stationers and craft suppliers. It is always worth stocking up at Christmas time.

POLYSTYRENE SHAPES (PLASTIC FOAM FORMS)
These are available from craft suppliers and come in a large range of different shapes.

WHITE EMULSION (LATEX) PAINT
This is a cheaper alternative to white gouache paint for covering the surface of papier-mâché. For added strength, mix in some PVA (white) glue.

WILLOW TWIGS
Perfect for rustic decorations, willow twigs grow straight and are very pliable.

metallic
crepe paper

gold spray paint

card
(cardboard)

stencil crayons

gold relief
outliner

white
paper

white emulsion
(latex) paint

oil-based
glass paint

foam
board

gouache

lino-cutting tool

decorative
papers

watercolour inks

gold water-
based paint

glitter paint

glitter

polystyrene shapes
(plastic foam forms)

gold (magic)
marker pen

foil wrappers

FABRICS AND THREADS

One of the joys of making your own decorations lies in using high-quality, sumptuous materials. You can create an impression of luxury with very small amounts of beautiful fabrics, ribbons and braids.

BUTTONS

Many people collect buttons for pleasure. For Christmas, keep a supply of gold buttons and always save real mother-of-pearl buttons from shirts that are no longer used.

CHECKED COTTON, TICKING, WOOL, CALICO, HESSIAN (BURLAP) AND LINEN

As an antidote to all the richness of traditional Christmas fabrics, simple, country-style, homespun materials are perfect for naïve decorations. Age fabrics by washing well, then dipping in strong tea.

CORDS AND BRAIDS

Gold is the most festive colour for cords and braids. Use fine gold cord to make loops for hanging decorations on the tree.

POLYESTER WADDING (BATTING)

This is invaluable for stuffing since it is lightweight and very soft. It can also be purchased in lengths for quilting, which can be cut to shape when a light padding is needed.

RIBBONS

Wide satin ribbon is the kind most often used for the projects in this book. Wire-edged ribbon is very good for making bows.

SEQUINS AND BEADS

Sequins, seed pearls (beads) and glass beads add instant opulence to any decorative piece. They are available from crafts suppliers in a multitude of shapes.

SILKS, TAFFETA, ORGANZA (ORGANDY) AND LAMÉ

Use these luxurious fabrics for decorations and gifts. You'll find plenty of gold shades to choose from in the run-up to Christmas.

STRING AND RAFFIA

Thin garden twine is used for several of the projects in this book: its soft brown colour and rustic appearance suit naïve decorations. Sisal (parcel string) and natural (garden) raffia are also used.

TAPESTRY CANVAS

You will need white canvas with 24 holes to 5cm (12 holes to 1in) for the needlepoint projects in this book.

THREADS

A well-stocked sewing box filled with every shade of sewing thread is every dressmaker's dream. Start with essential black and white and build up your collection as you sew. Stranded embroidery thread (floss) has six strands: for all but the boldest stitches you'll probably want to use two or three. Tapestry wool (yarn) is for canvaswork and is very hardwearing. Don't be tempted to substitute knitting wool (yarn) or you will get constant breaks as you stitch.

VELVET

Available in rich, dark colours, velvet is especially Christmassy. It is available in light weights for dressmaking and heavier weights for furnishing (upholstering).

homespun cotton check

calico

linen

polyester wadding (batting)

tapestry canvas

hessian (burlap)

pleated organza

lamé

cotton ticking

gold netting

velvet

fine gold
cord

decorative
braid

sequin
ribbon

gold braid

silk

mother-of-
pearl buttons

glass
beads

plastic
gemstones

satin
ribbons

sewing
thread

garden
twine

stranded
embroidery
thread (floss)

quilting
wadding
(batting)

sisal
(parcel
string)

natural
(garden)
raffia

tapestry
wool (yarn)

EQUIPMENT

It's sensible to make sure you have everything you need for your Christmas craft project

before you begin. The following list includes artist's materials, office supplies and some

basic equipment you probably already have around the home.

ADHESIVE TAPE
Double-sided adhesive (cellophane) tape allows you to join paper invisibly. It is also a substitute for glue when you don't wish to dampen a surface such as crepe paper.

CRAFT KNIFE
Craft knives have extremely sharp blades. Use them for cutting out stencils and for accurate cutting of paper against a metal ruler. Change the blade frequently and keep out of the reach of children. Always use with a cutting mat.

CUTTING MAT
Use when cutting out with a craft knife to protect your work surface. A self-healing mat is best.

FOAM ROLLERS
These come in assorted sizes and are easily washable. Use them with stencil paint and for sponging water-based paints on to paper or fabrics.

GLUE
PVA (white) glue is a thick liquid that dries to a transparent sheen. It can be diluted with water when making papier-mâché or as a protective coating. After use, wash brushes in water straight away. Glue sticks are excellent for sticking paper and are safe for children to use.

HOLE PUNCH
Useful for making neat holes for the handles of gift bags and for punching holes in gift tags.

HOT GLUE GUN
The nozzle delivers a small dot of hot, melted glue. The glue dries almost instantly.

METAL RULER
This provides a safe edge to work against when cutting paper with a craft knife.

PAINTBRUSHES
Old brushes are useful for applying glue and emulsion (latex) paint mixed with PVA (white) glue. Stencil brushes are wide and stiff. You will need a fine-tipped brush for delicate work and a medium bristle brush for applying metallic craft paint, which should be cleaned with white spirit (paint thinner).

PENCILS, PENS AND MARKERS
A soft pencil that can easily be erased is useful for tracing motifs. Keep an old ballpoint pen that has run out of ink for making embossed foil decorations. For marking light fabrics, use a vanishing fabric marker.

PINS AND NEEDLES
Use dressmaker's pins to hold fabrics in place. Use an ordinary sewing needle for seams and an embroidery needle for embroidery thread (floss). A tapestry needle is fairly broad, with a large eye and a blunt point.

PLASTIC ADHESIVE
This malleable substance is used for attaching objects and paper to surfaces from which it can later be removed cleanly.

SCISSORS
You will need one pair for cutting paper and another for fabrics: never use the latter on paper as it will blunt them very quickly. A small pair of needlework scissors with pointed ends is useful for embroidery.

SECATEURS (PRUNING SHEARS)
Used to cut heavy-duty foliage and for twig decorations.

STAPLER AND STAPLE GUN
A staple gun is indispensable for attaching fabrics to wood or board. An ordinary office stapler will secure paper, fabric and thin card (cardboard).

STENCIL CARD (CARDBOARD)
Specially made for stencilling, this is coated in a water-resistant oil so that you can wipe it clean between stencils, and when changing colours. Transfer your image to the card using a soft pencil and cut it out with a craft knife.

TAPE MEASURE
A tape measure is more flexible than a ruler, and is therefore suitable for measuring lengths of fabric.

TRACING PAPER
Trace a motif and cut it out to use as a pattern. Alternatively, transfer it by rubbing the back of the tracing paper with a soft pencil, positioning the template, and then tracing over the outline again from the front of the paper.

cutting mat

double-sided adhesive
(cellophane tape)

staple gun

foam roller

PVA (white)
glue

craft knife

metal ruler

12pt Rabone Chesterman 10 20 N°4778 30

50 Grimson Quality 60

hole punch

needles

tracing
paper

pins

tape
measure

1 DEAN 2 IN 3 4 FIBREGLASS TAPE

scissors

paintbrush

stapler

stencil
brush

fabric
marker

hot glue
gun

oil card
(board)

ballpoint
pen

permanent
marker

secateurs
(pruning
shears)

fine-tipped
paintbrush

plastic adhesive

pencil

Decorating with Natural Materials

*B*ringing evergreens indoors to decorate the house is very traditional. There are many ideas here for making a welcoming wreath for the front door, a garland for indoors and a gorgeous swag for the mantelpiece. Candle pots make lovely table centrepieces, and you can even create a miniature Topiary Tree. Many natural materials such as blue pine (spruce), cinnamon sticks and dried rosemary have the spicy smell that is the true essence of Christmas. Experiment with new versions of favourite designs such as the Mistletoe Kissing Ring, or for real impact make a stunning Tulip and Holly Wreath.

TRADITIONAL CHRISTMAS WREATH

Blue pine (spruce) releases a glorious fresh scent as you work with it. Here it is used with

dried red roses and amaranthus for a traditional look.

MATERIALS

large copper or steel garland ring
sphagnum moss
silver reel (rose) wire
secateurs (pruning shears)
blue pine (spruce)
dried amaranthus, dyed red
medium stub wires
dried red roses
dried lavender
natural (garden) raffia
twigs
sweet chestnuts
fir cones
dried fungi
strong florist's wire

1 Cover the ring very roughly on both sides with moss – this need not be thick but should be fairly even. Secure the moss in place by winding with silver reel (rose) wire, leaving a space of about 5cm/2in between each loop.

2 Trim the blue pine (spruce) to lengths of about 15–20cm/6–8in. Divide into four piles and begin to tie each stem to the ring with wire, using one pile for each quarter of the ring. Work outward from the inner edge in a zigzag fashion.

3 Trim the amaranthus stems to 20cm/8in and wire into four small bunches, leaving the stub wires untrimmed. Treat the roses in the same way, but cut the stems to 10cm/4in. In each quarter of the ring, push a bunch or roses and a bunch of amaranthus, tying the wires into the back of the ring.

4 Trim the lavender to 20cm/8in and wire into four bunches. Keep a long length of wire hanging from each bunch and wind a bow of raffia around the stems. Push each wire through the blue pine (spruce) and tie to the back.

5 Wire bunches of twigs, chestnuts, fir cones and fungi. Tie bows of raffia around the bunches of twigs. Add these materials in small mixed groups, linking each group around the ring. Add a loop of strong wire to the back of the garland for hanging and tie a raffia bow at the top.

ℰXOTIC 𝒲REATH

This luxurious Christmas wreath combines the rich colours, shapes and textures of dried pomegranates,

artichokes and chillies with traditional evergreen.

MATERIALS

ball of string
large copper or steel garland ring
sphagnum moss
scissors
silver reel (rose) wire
secateurs (pruning shears)
blue pine (spruce)
birch twigs
medium stub wires
freeze-dried artichokes
dried red chillies
dried pomegranates
fir cones
hot glue gun and glue sticks
dried lichen
rope or ribbon

1 Attach the end of the string to the larger of the two circles of the ring. Attach the moss to both sides evenly, winding the string tightly around the ring. Continue until the whole ring is covered, then tie the string firmly and trim the ends.

2 Tie the end of the silver reel (rose) wire to the ring. Snip off several sprigs of blue pine (spruce) and build up a thick layer by staggering them evenly around the ring. Secure each sprig in place by winding the wire tightly around the stem.

3 Continue to build up the blue pine base until the whole ring is covered. Cut off the wire and twist it around itself several times on the underside of the wreath.

4 Make large loops out of birch twigs and place diagonally at intervals around the wreath. Secure with lengths of stub wire bent into U-shaped pins pushed firmly through the middle of the wreath.

5 Wire the larger dried materials individually. Beginning with a group of artichokes, push the wired stems firmly through the body of the wreath.

6 Wire the chillies in threes. Group them together between the artichokes in large clusters.

7 Insert the dried pomegranates in large clusters of at least five to balance the artichoke and chilli groups. Fill in any gaps with smaller clusters of fir cones.

8 Glue the delicate lichen to the wreath. Intertwine the rope or ribbon between the dried materials, then anchor it with wires folded in half.

COUNTRY-STYLE WREATH

This unusual design blends horse chestnut and sweet chestnut cases, dried red chillies

and bunches of cinnamon sticks in a small wreath.

MATERIALS

short cinnamon sticks
natural (garden) raffia
scissors
small dried red chillies
fine silver wire
wirecutters
medium stub wires
25cm/10in diameter vine wreath base
hot glue gun
horse chestnuts
sweet chestnut cases
shiny ribbon (optional)

1 Tie the cinnamon sticks into bundles with raffia. Thread the chillies in clusters on to fine silver wire.

2 Cut the stub wires in half, bend into U-shapes to make staples and push through the raffia ties. Fix the cinnamon bunches to the wreath base by pushing the wires between the vine twigs. Glue the horse chestnuts and sweet chestnut cases at random around the ring, adding the red chillies last, as colour accents.

3 Tie the ribbon in a bow, if using, and attach to the wreath with a wire.

WINTER GARLAND

Nuts and fir cones make a richly textured display.

MATERIALS

*hot glue gun
ready-made vine garland
fir cones
brazil nuts
walnuts
hazelnuts (filberts)
red paper ribbon
stub wire
gold spray paint (optional)*

2 Add the nuts, either in groups of one variety or mixed together. Make sure that you fill the spaces between the fir cones to hide as much of the garland as possible. Arrange the nuts so that they graduate from a thin layer at the top to a thicker one at the bottom.

3 Tie the paper ribbon in a large bow. Pass a stub wire through the back of the knot and thread the wire through the garland. For a smarter effect, spray the bow lightly with gold paint.

> ### CRAFT TIP
>
> *When the garland of nuts and cones is beginning to look a little tired, you can freshen it up with a coat of spray paint. Silver, gold and white provide the most successful frosting effect because some of the natural colour of the materials in the garland will show through from underneath the paint. For the merest hint of colour, spray-paint the nuts only.*

1 Using a glue gun, stick the fir cones to the vine garland. Glue them to the ring in groups of four to five, leaving a good space between each group. Stick larger cones to the bottom of the garland and use smaller ones on the sides and the top.

KUMQUAT WREATH

Vibrant orange kumquats and green chillies give a traditional wreath a new lease of life.

MATERIALS

secateurs (pruning shears)
sprigs of bay leaves
blue pine (spruce)
medium stub wires
kumquats
green chillies
small fir cones
small willow or
vine wreath base
scissors
wide wire-edged ribbon
dressmaker's pin

2 Twist a piece of wire around each stem, leaving a length to insert into the willow wreath base.

5 Reserving a short length of ribbon for the centre of the bow, join the ends together with a pin.

1 Trim the bay leaves and blue pine (spruce) into sprigs suitable for the size of the wreath, wiring pieces together here and there to fill them out.

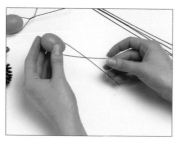

3 Wire the kumquats and chillies by sticking a piece of wire through the base, then bending the ends down and twisting them together. Wind a piece of wire around the base of each fir cone.

6 Fold the ribbon over on itself to make four loops.

7 Pinch the centre of the loops together and secure with a wire. Cover this with the remaining piece of ribbon and wire the bow to the top of the wreath.

CRAFT TIP

Ready-made rings made from natural materials such as willow and vines are available from florists in many different sizes. You could also make your own ring using vines or twigs cut when they are green.

4 Attach the greenery, kumquats, chillies and fir cones to the wreath, twisting the ends of the wires to secure them.

CLEMENTINE WREATH

This colourful wreath is very modern in its regular geometry and its

bold use of tightly grouped materials and vivid colours.

MATERIALS

medium stub wires
clementines
30cm/12in diameter florist's foam ring
secateurs (pruning shears)
pyracanthus branches, with
berries and leaves
ivy leaves

3 Cut the pyracanthus into stems about 6cm/2½in long. Push the stems into the outer side of the plastic ring and between the two rings of clementines, making sure it is evenly distributed.

1 Push a stub wire across and through the base of each clementine from one side to the other, and bend the two projecting ends down. Bend another wire to form a hairpin shape and push the ends right through the middle of each clementine so that the bend in the wire is sitting flush with the top of the fruit. Cut the projecting wires to about 4cm/1½in.

4 Cut the ivy leaves into individual stems about 7cm/3in long. Push the stems into the plastic, positioning a leaf between each clementine.

2 Soak the plastic foam ring in water. Arrange two rows of wired clementines in tight circles on the ring by pushing their projecting wire legs into the foam.

Tulip and Holly Wreath

This gorgeous wreath can be used on a door or, with candles, as a table centrepiece.

MATERIALS

25cm/10in diameter florist's foam ring
100 white tulips
scissors
holly with berries

1 Soak the plastic foam ring in water. Cut the tulips to a stem length of approximately 3cm/1¼in. Starting at the centre, work outwards in concentric circles to cover the whole surface of the plastic foam with tulip heads.

2 Cover any exposed foam and the outside of the ring with holly leaves by pushing the stems into the foam and overlapping them flat against the edge of the ring. Make sure you don't leave any gaps in the foam.

3 Cut 12 stems of holly with berries approximately 4cm/1½in long. Push them into the foam in two concentric circles around the ring, one towards the inside and the other towards the outside. Make sure no foam is still visible.

CRAFT TIP

The tulip stems are pushed fully into the foam in tight masses, so that only their heads are visible.

Mistletoe Kissing Ring

A traditional kissing ring can be hung up as a Christmas decoration to serve

as a focal point for a seasonal kiss.

MATERIALS

scissors
7 stems of winterberry, with berries
large bunch of mistletoe
twine
twisted cane ring
tartan (plaid) ribbon

1 Cut the stems of the winterberry into 18cm/7in lengths. Divide the mistletoe into 14 substantial stems and make the smaller sprigs into bunches by tying with twine. Attach some winterberry on to the outside of the cane ring with the twine. Add a stem, or bunch, of mistletoe so that it overlaps about one-third of the length of winterberry, and bind in place. Bind on another stem of winterberry, overlapping the mistletoe.

2 Repeat the sequence until the outside of the ring is covered in a "herringbone" pattern of materials. Cut four lengths of ribbon of approximately 60cm/24in each. Tie one end of each piece of ribbon to the decorated ring at four equidistant points around its circumference. Bring the ends of the ribbon up above the ring and tie in a bow for hanging.

Topiary Tree

Make a small ornamental tree for indoors, or a large tree to place outside the front door.

MATERIALS

terracotta flowerpot
setting clay
small tree trunk or thick branch
florist's foam sphere
strong glue
silver reel (rose) wire
secateurs (pruning shears)
blue pine (spruce)
sphagnum moss
medium stub wires
small dried red roses
fir cones
hand drill and vice or hot glue gun
assorted nuts
cinnamon sticks
dried rosemary stalks
natural (garden) raffia

2 Using stub wires, wire the roses into small bunches, leaving a long length of wire to insert into the foam sphere. Add the roses to the tree at random, pressing the stub wires well into each area of the round foam shape.

5 Tie stub wires around the cinnamon sticks and rosemary stalks to make small bundles, again leaving long lengths of wire. Cover the wire with raffia tied in a bow. Add the bundles to the tree.

1 Cover the inside of the flowerpot with setting clay, then push the trunk into the centre. Add more clay to half-fill the pot. Leave to set hard. Push the foam sphere on to the top of the trunk, then glue in place. Tie the end of the silver reel (rose) wire to the trunk and wind it round the sphere to secure. Cut the blue pine (spruce) into 15cm/6in lengths and trim the foliage from the stems. Push the bare stems into the sphere. Fill small gaps with moss.

3 Thread a stub wire through the bottom "leaves" of each fir cone, leaving a long length of wire. Add them to the tree, standing back to check the shape.

4 Carefully drill a hole through the base of each nut, holding it in a vice. Push a stub wire through the hole so it extends equally either side, then cross the ends and twist together. Insert into the tree. (Alternatively, you can attach the nuts to the tree with a glue gun.)

6 Cover the base of the trunk and the pot with handfuls of moss. To decorate the large tree, use a bunch of garden canes cut to length and tied with a ribbon bow.

ROSEHIP TREE

Scarlet rosehips are the perfect decoration for this little evergreen "tree", which is very simple to make.

MATERIALS

damp sphagnum moss
2.5cm/1in wire mesh netting
wirecutters
18cm/7in diameter flowerpot
florist's adhesive tape
secateurs (pruning shears)
clippings of glossy evergreens,
e.g. box (boxwood)
rosehips
false berries (optional)

1 Place the moss on the wire mesh netting, turn the corners into the centre to enclose the moss and crush the wire into a ball shape. Tuck in or cut off any stray ends with wirecutters. Place the wire ball on the flowerpot and secure it with two or three short lengths of adhesive tape. Cut the evergreens to more or less equal lengths and push the stems into the wire ball.

2 Continue filling in the ball with evergreens, then push in the rosehips and, if you are using them, the stems of false berries.

> CRAFT TIP
>
> *Put this pretty rosehip tree in a porch, fireplace or a room corner where there is enough light to enhance the colour of the leaves. It makes a nice alternative to an evergreen Christmas tree.*

CANDY CENTREPIECE

Silvery lavender makes an unusual tree, decorated with ribbon and shiny wrapped candies.

MATERIALS

plastic florist's spike
23cm/9in high florist's foam cone
florist's adhesive clay
pedestal cake stand
scissors
lavender
wirecutters
medium stub wires
shiny wrapped candies
1.5cm/½in wide ribbon

3 Cut the stub wires in half, push them through the candy paper wrappings (not through the candy itself) and twist the ends. Insert the candies at intervals all around the cone.

4 Twist a wire around the centre of two lengths of ribbon and press the ends into the top of the cone.

1 Insert the spike into the base of the foam cone. Press a piece of florist's clay on to the base of the spike and press it on to the cake stand. The surface should be absolutely dry.

2 Cut the lavender stems to graduated lengths, the longest extending beyond the rim of the stand and the others successively shorter, to achieve a conical shape. Position the stems around the foam cone.

CRAFT TIP

To further enhance the glamorous effect of this irresistible centrepiece, you could first spray-paint the branches gold or silver. The finished decoration will look its best under a spotlight or in the middle of a table.

Mini Christmas Tree

Mixed evergreens, traditionally decorated with baubles and ribbon,

make the most of clippings from a garden.

MATERIALS

damp sphagnum moss
2.5cm/1in wire mesh netting
wirecutters
florist's adhesive clay
pinholder
18cm/7in diameter round basket
stout twig
medium stub wires
secateurs (pruning shears)
evergreens, such as cypress, sage and
box (boxwood)
dried hydrangeas
gold baubles
7.5cm/3in wide gold ribbon

1 Place the moss on the wire mesh netting and shape it into a cone. Trim off the excess netting at the top and tuck in any stray ends of wire. Press a large piece of adhesive clay on to the base of the pinholder, then press the pinholder on to the base of the basket. Push the twig on to the pinholder. Secure it using two stub wires attached to the sides of the basket, wrapping the wires around the twig. Place the cone on the twig and secure it by taking wires from side to side and around the twig.

2 Arrange the evergreens to form a conical shape. Decorate the tree with dried hydrangeas and gold baubles. Glue a gold bow at the front of the basket to finish.

CRAFT TIP

Save all the evergreen cuttings from your garden and choose only the best ones to make this decorated tree. The grey-green colours of the tree contrast beautifully with the gold baubles.

CHRISTMAS SWAG

Honesty, poppies and Chinese lanterns (winter cherry) make a lovely

indoor decoration, studded with metallic birds.

MATERIALS

secateurs (pruning shears)
dried honesty, poppy and Chinese lantern
(winter cherry) seedheads
dried sage
silver reel (rose) wire
ready-made raffia plait (braid), available
from florist's suppliers
hot glue gun or medium stub wires
bird tree decorations, on wires

1 Cut all the dried materials into stems of equal length. Using silver reel (rose) wire, bind them into mixed bunches. Attach the bunches to the raffia plait (braid), using a glue gun or stub wires bent into U-shaped staples, so that some face to either side.

2 Insert the wires of each bird through the plait (braid). With the birds in place, the swag is ready to hang on an interior door. The dried materials are too fragile to brave harsh winter climates.

ROSEMARY HEART

Fragrant rosemary, symbolizing remembrance, is ideal for a "token of affection".

Add a seasonal posy of holly, ivy and rosebuds.

MATERIALS

strong, flexible wire
silver reel (rose) wire
rosemary
dried red and cream rosebuds
honesty, holly and ivy
hollow wheat straw
ribbon

1 Bend the strong, flexible wire into a circle and bind the ends securely with silver reel (rose) wire. Bend the shape into a heart.

2 Cover the frame with short sprigs of rosemary, so that the tips of each cover the stem ends of the one before.

3 Bind the rosebuds, honesty, holly and ivy on to the wheat straw to give the appearance of a posy. Use the silver reel (rose) wire to bind the posy to the wire heart. Decorate the finished heart with ribbon.

❧ CRAFT TIP ❧

In a year when holly is richly endowed with berries, it is a good idea to strip some stalks of the leaves. This will go some way towards reducing the amount of berries, and yet stay within the bounds of tradition.

Door Posy

Gilded wheat and evergreens create a gorgeous, informal posy, tied with a floppy gold bow.

MATERIALS

*newspaper or
scrap paper
wheat stalks
silver reel (rose) wire
ivy
gold spray paint
evergreens, such as blue
pine (spruce), cypress and yew
dried grasses
wide gold ribbon*

1 Cover the work surface with newspaper or scrap paper. Gather 10–12 wheat stalks to form a bunch and bind with silver reel (rose) wire. Spray the wheat and ivy with gold paint and leave to dry.

2 Place the largest component in the posy on the work surface and arrange the other materials over it. Bind the stems lightly with wire. Tie the ribbon over the wire and make a large, loose bow. Cut the ribbon ends neatly in a "swallowtail" V shape.

311

TABLE CENTREPIECE

Arrange fresh flowers, fruits and evergreens in a rich display that would steal the limelight

on a sideboard or buffet table.

MATERIALS

scissors
florist's adhesive clay
2 plastic florist's spikes
large, flat plate
2 blocks of florist's foam, soaked in water
florist's scissors
evergreens, such as mahonia, yew,
cypress, ivy and eucalyptus
pineapple
carnations
roses
spray chrysanthemums
iris berries
clear quick-setting glue or hot glue gun
lychees
assorted nuts
satsumas
gold spray paint

2 Lean the pineapple against the central foam block. Secure with a stub wire wrapped around the stem and with the ends pushed into the foam. Position the carnations and roses behind the pineapple, creating a fan shape.

4 Using clear, quick-setting glue or a hot glue gun, glue several lychees into a cluster. Push a stub wire through a gap between the lychee cases, twist the ends and push them into the foam. Form a nut cluster in a similar way and position it on the other side of the design. Thread a stub wire through the back of a satsuma, twist the ends and push into the foam above the lychees.

5 Complete the design with sprays of ivy spattered with gold spray paint. Turn the arrangement around and complete the back of the centrepiece with sprays of ivy and cypress.

1 Cut two strips of adhesive clay and press one on to the underside of each plastic spike. Making sure that the plate is absolutely dry, press the spikes on to it, one just behind the centre and one in front to the right. Push the blocks of foam on to the spikes. Outline the arrangement with evergreens, the tallest ones at the centre back and low on the right.

3 Position short stems of ivy and spray chrysanthemums as "fillers" between the main flowers. Arrange the iris berries on stems of graduating height to distribute their contrasting texture throughout the design.

> **· CRAFT TIP ·**
>
> *Make your selection of fruits, flowers and nuts with an eye to colour, scale and texture. Your arrangement will look most effective when contrasting shapes are positioned next to each other.*

Citrus Centrepiece

The warm, spicy smell of oranges readily evokes the festive season.

Materials

oranges, lemons and limes
V-shaped lino-cutting tool or
canelle knife
sharp knife
scissors
wire-edged ribbon
medium stub wire
glass dish or bowl
secateurs (pruning shears)
sprigs of fresh bay leaves

3 Cut thin spirals of orange peel as long as possible to drape over the arrangement.

1 Use a lino-cutting tool or canelle knife to cut grooves in the peel of some of the fruits and reveal the white pith beneath. When doing this, you can either follow the contours of the fruit in a spiral or make straight cuts.

4 Cut short lengths of wire-edged ribbon, fold into loops and secure the ends with a stub wire.

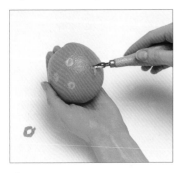

2 On other fruits, try making an overall pattern of small circles. Practise the patterns on spare fruits first.

5 Arrange the fruits in a glass dish or bowl. Tuck in the ribbon loops and add a few sprigs of bay leaves.

COUNTRY CANDLE-HOLDERS

Small pumpkins and weathered flowerpots make enchanting containers for candles.

MATERIALS

For the Pumpkin Candle-holders
sharp knife
small pumpkins
yellow and orange candles
florist's adhesive clay (optional)

For the Flowerpot Candle-holders
2 weathered terracotta flowerpots
gravel chippings
damp hay
dark green candles, in varying heights

1 For the Pumpkin Candle-holders:
Using a knife, slice off the bottom of
each pumpkin if necessary so that it
will sit steadily without toppling over.
Break off the stalk and gouge out a
shallow hole wide enough to hold a
candle. If the flesh is very hard, fix the
candle firmly in place with florist's
adhesive clay.

2 For the Flowerpot Candle-holders:
Fill the flowerpots with gravel chippings
to just below the rim. Cover lightly with
damp hay to conceal the gravel. Push
the candles firmly into the gravel.

CHRISTMAS CANDLE POT

A candle pot makes a wonderful, rich centrepiece for the table.

MATERIALS

knife
1 block florist's foam
terracotta pot
candle
medium stub wires
florist's tape (stem-wrap tape)
hay
blue pine (spruce)
secateurs (pruning shears)
reindeer moss
mossing (floral) pins
small dried red roses
fir cones
dried mushrooms and dried kutchi fruit (alternatively, use cinnamon sticks and slices of dried orange)

2 Add slightly shorter pieces of pine to make a layer above the first. Continue to build up a pyramid shape, keeping the pine well away from the candle. Use stub wires to strengthen or lengthen the shorter pieces.

3 Fill any large spaces in the display with moss, attaching it with mossing (floral) pins. Put plenty of moss around the base of the candle to hide the tape.

1 Cut the foam to fit the pot, then secure the candle on top, using stub wires and florist's tape (stem-wrap tape). Fix the foam into the pot, packing any spaces with hay. Group the blue pine (spruce) into pieces of various sizes. Trim the needles from the ends of the stems. Push the largest pieces into the base of the foam, so they lean down slightly.

4 Wire the roses into bunches, using stub wires, then wire the fir cones and other material. Add to spaces in the display to create a balanced arrangement.

Advent Candle Centrepiece

Traditionally, the four Advent candles are burned for an hour on each Sunday

leading up to Christmas. On the first Sunday, one candle is burned for an hour;

on the second Sunday it is burned alongside the second candle, and so on.

MATERIALS

florist's foam brick
plate
church or beeswax candles
bunch of tree ivy
secateurs (pruning shears)
picture framer's gilt wax
fine wire
wirecutters
10 Chinese lanterns (winter cherries)

1 Soak the florist's foam brick in water and set it on a plate. Carefully push the candles into the foam.

2 Cut the tree ivy stems to size and push them into the florist's foam. Gild the berries with picture framer's gilt wax.

3 Pass a wire through the base of each Chinese lantern (winter cherry), then twist the ends together. Push the twisted wire ends into the florist's foam base.

EVERGREEN WINTER CANDLES

Candlelight in a window gives pleasure to those inside the room and to others who pass by outside.

MATERIALS

knife
florist's adhesive clay
florist's foam holders
florist's foam,
soaked in water
tall green and white candles
wirecutters
medium stub wires
lichen
miniature evergreen tree, in
pot (optional)
selection of mixed evergreens
fir cones
fallen leaves,
sprayed gold

2 Cut the stub wires in half and bend each one in half to make U-shaped staples. Fix clumps of lichen to the foam, to conceal the fixings. Add the miniature evergreen tree in its pot, if using.

3 Arrange the evergreens in a dense mass of varying greens until all the foam is covered. Twist stub wires around the fir cones and push them into the foam at intervals throughout the design. Add the gilded leaves.

1 Cut strips of adhesive clay and press them to the undersides of the florist's foam holders. Press the soaked foam into the holders. Press the candles into the foam.

*M*ANTELPIECE *S*WAG

This grand swag is very simply created using string and sprigs of fresh,

supple blue pine (spruce) as a base.

MATERIALS

string
silver reel (rose) wire
scissors
secateurs (pruning shears)
blue pine (spruce)
wirecutters
medium stub wires
freeze-dried artichokes
dried pomegranates
fir cones
dried red chillies
thick rope or wide ribbon

1 Make a loop of string and attach the silver reel (rose) wire to its base, twisting it around several times to secure. Measure the string to the desired length of the swag and cut. Cut sprigs of blue pine (spruce) of roughly equal length.

2 Place a sprig of blue pine over the loop, then secure with wire as tightly as possible. Continue to add a few sprigs at a time along the string.

3 Alternate sides and rotate the swag to achieve a fully rounded effect. The string should be wound into the centre of the swag to act as a core and to ensure flexibility. When you reach the end, make another loop, tie with the wire and cut.

4 Wire the artichokes and pomegranates individually. Insert them into the body of the swag in clusters of three, starting with the artichokes. Space each group evenly along the whole length of the swag.

5 Push the wires firmly through the body of the swag at a diagonal, then wind the ends tightly around one another to secure. Place groups of pomegranates at regular intervals between the artichoke clusters.

6 Wire the fir cones between the natural "teeth" of the cone, as close to the base as possible. Add the fir cones in groups of three at regular intervals.

7 To prepare the chillies, take three at a time and wire the stalks together. Add to the swag in large clusters between the other main groups of materials.

8 Feed rope or ribbon between the various groups. Secure it to the swag at strategic points with U-shaped pins made of short lengths of bent stub wire. Do not pull the rope or ribbon too tightly.

MANTELPIECE DECORATION

Place this elegant arrangement in front of a mirror

to make it doubly effective.

MATERIALS

polystyrene (plastic foam) balls
double-sided adhesive (cellophane) tape
scissors
reindeer moss
ivory candles of various sizes and heights
foil dishes
plastic adhesive
silver reel (rose) wire
ivy

3 Arrange the candles on foil dishes, then secure them in place with pieces of plastic adhesive.

1 Completely cover the polystyrene balls with double-sided adhesive (cellophane) tape.

4 Wire together small bunches of ivy, then attach them to longer main stems to make lush garlands. Arrange the candles on the mantelpiece and drape the ivy garlands in front. Place the moss balls around the candles.

2 Press the reindeer moss gently on to the balls to cover the polystyrene. Leave to dry.

CRAFT TIP

Never leave burning candles unattended and do not allow them to burn down to within 5cm/2in of foliage or other decorative material.

Christmas Crafts to Make & Sew

*I*nstead of buying expensive commercial Christmas decorations, it is far more satisfying to make your own. None of these designs involves difficult techniques and many of them use basic materials or offcuts of fabric and yarn, which you can collect throughout the year. Among the simple but effective ideas are a rich Silk-wrapped Candle Pot, which you can quickly assemble at the last minute, a Silver Crown Candle-holder made of aluminium foil embossed with a ballpoint pen, and stockings for gifts. You can tailor the colours and design to create a personal handmade present that is sure to please.

CHRISTMAS LANTERN

Put a welcoming light in your window at Christmas with this simple etched lantern.

MATERIALS

ruler or tape measure
tin lantern
paper
re-usable adhesive
black contour paste
self-adhesive vinyl
etching paste
small decorator's paintbrush
craft knife

3 Apply self-adhesive vinyl to all the parts of the lantern that you are not working on.

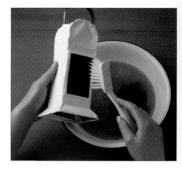

5 Remove all of the etching paste with cold water. If the design is not sufficiently etched, repeat step 4.

1 Measure the size of the glass in your lantern. Draw a simple star shape on paper to fit. Stick the design to the back of one of the glass panels with re-usable adhesive and trace the design on to the glass with black contour paste.

4 Working in a well ventilated area, apply the etching paste with a paintbrush and leave for the length of time specified in the manufacturer's instructions.

6 Peel off the self-adhesive vinyl. Lift up a corner of the contour paste with a craft knife and peel it off to reveal the completed design. Scrub in warm soapy water to remove any residual traces of contour paste.

2 Fill in all of the areas between the design with contour paste. Leave to dry. If any areas of contour paste look patchy, apply a second layer.

CRAFT TIP

If you wish to etch on to large areas of glass, PVA wood glue could be used instead of the contour paste. To remove PVA, wrap the item in a warm towel, which should help the glue to peel off easily.

STAR CANDLE-HOLDER

This star-shaped chocolate box makes a perfect Christmas candle-holder.

MATERIALS

small, rigid chocolate box, with a lid
metal screw-cap from a bottle
pen
craft knife
newspaper
PVA (white) glue
artist's paintbrush
white emulsion (latex) paint
gold (magic) marker pen
watercolour inks

SAFETY TIP

Never leave lit candles unattended. Extinguish the candle before it reaches the candle-holder.

1 Place the bottle cap exactly in the centre of the box lid and draw around it.

2 Divide the circle into narrow "pie" sections and cut them with a craft knife. Fold them down into the box. Push the bottle cap into the hole so that its rim is just below the surface of the box (this will hold the candle).

3 Tear the newspaper into strips about 1 x 5cm/½ x 2in. Dilute the PVA (white) glue slightly with water. Paint a strip liberally with glue on both sides and stick it on to the box, flattening it with the paintbrush loaded with more glue. Apply a layer of newspaper all over the box in this way, beginning around the bottle cap to cover the join. Press the paper neatly over awkward corners. When the first layer is dry, apply a second layer and leave to dry thoroughly.

4 Mix a little white emulsion (latex) paint with the glue and paint the whole box white.

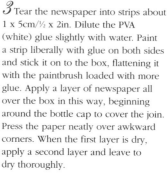

5 Outline the edges with a gold (magic) marker pen, then decorate the box with watercolour inks. The white paint will resist the inks a little, so apply two coats for a colour-washed effect.

Silk-wrapped Candle Pot

This is a simple way to incorporate a beautiful piece of silk into your decorative scheme.

Materials

*selection of coloured candles in
various sizes
terracotta flowerpot
scissors
corrugated card (cardboard)
gold paper
marker pen
double-sided adhesive (cellophane) tape
square of silk fabric, to fit comfortably
around the pot
newspaper or tissue paper
plastic adhesive*

1 Place the candles in the flowerpot to find a suitable height. Cut out a circle of cardboard to fit in the pot at this level as a base for the candles.

2 Cut a larger circle of gold paper and use it to cover the cardboard. Fold the edges under neatly and secure with double-sided adhesive (cellophane) tape.

3 Neaten the edges of the silk fabric and stand the flowerpot in the centre. Take two opposite corners and bring them up over the sides of the pot, tucking them inside. Tie the other two corners together at the front.

4 Pad the pot with newspaper or tissue paper, place the gold disc inside and arrange the candles, securing them with small pieces of plastic adhesive.

332

PAINTED CANDLES

Decorate plain candles with gold paint and gift-wrap to match.

MATERIALS

*artist's paintbrush
coloured candles
gold paint
ribbon
tube of fabric glitter paint
gold gift-wrap
pencil
scissors
cartridge (heavy) paper
watercolour inks*

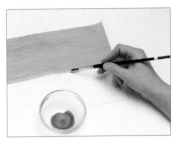

3 Fold a strip of gold gift-wrap over several times. Mark a semi-circle at the top and bottom in pencil and cut it out. Unfold the paper to reveal a scalloped edge.

4 Paint a sheet of cartridge (heavy) paper in watercolour ink to co-ordinate with the candles. Allow to dry, then tear into strips. Wrap a set of candles in the scalloped gold paper, then a strip of painted paper, finishing with a bow of dotted glitter ribbon.

1 Paint the candles with spots or stripes, building up the colour in several layers if the candles resist the paint. Allow to dry between coats.

2 Apply gold dots on the ribbon with fabric glitter paint. The glitter effect will begin to show only as the paint dries.

APPLIQUÉ CHRISTMAS TREE

This charmingly simple little picture can be framed or mounted as a seasonal greeting for a special person.

MATERIALS

scraps of homespun fabrics in greens, red and orange
scissors
matching sewing threads
needle
coarse off-white cotton
dressmaker's pins
stranded embroidery thread (floss)
gold embroidery thread (floss)
embroidery needle

1 Cut out the pieces for a simple tree shape from three different shades and textures of green fabric. Cut out a red rectangle for the background and an orange tree trunk. Join the three sections of the tree with running stitches, using matching sewing thread.

2 Pin all the pieces to a piece of off-white cotton large enough to fill the picture frame or mount.

3 Using matching threads, sew the pieces together invisibly in slip-stitch, tucking the edges under with your needle as you sew. Aim for a slightly uneven, naïve appearance. Add gold stars and coloured stitch details using three strands of embroidery thread (floss). Press the appliqué picture gently before framing or mounting.

CRAFT TIP

For the best effect, use homespun fabrics in contrasting textures and colours, with simple, childlike stitches.

HEAVENLY GOLD STAR

Collect as many different kinds of gold paper as you can find to give subtle variations of texture.

MATERIALS

assorted gold papers – candy wrappers,
metallic crepe paper, gift-wrap, etc
PVA (white) glue
artist's paintbrush
polystyrene (plastic foam) star
fine wire
scissors
masking tape
gold glitter paint

3 Make a loop of wire and stick the ends into the back of the star for hanging. Secure with masking tape. Cover the back with gold paper in the same way as the front.

4 Leave the glue until it is completely dry, then cover the whole star with a coat of gold glitter paint.

1 Tear the various gold papers into odd shapes of slightly different sizes.

2 Dilute PVA (white) glue with a little water. Paint it on to the back of a piece of gold paper and stick on to the polystyrene (plastic foam) star. Paint more glue over the piece to secure it. Work all over the front of the star, using different papers to vary the texture and colour.

Advent Calendar

Decorate this exotic calendar with plenty of ornate motifs and patterns to make a stunning decoration.

MATERIALS

*pencil
tracing paper
large piece of thin white
card (cardboard)
craft knife
metal ruler
cutting mat
artist's paintbrush
gouache paints
white cartridge (heavy) paper
watercolour inks
gold (magic) marker pen
scissors
glue stick
white polystyrene (plastic foam-
filled) mounting board
cup sequins*

3 Using the front tracing again, mark the window frames on cartridge (heavy) paper and draw on the inside motifs. Paint with watercolour inks, then draw in details with a gold (magic) marker pen. Cut out and attach with a glue stick.

5 Mount the three sections on the boards, gluing the edges, then glue the sections together. Paint the front of the calendar, carefully avoiding getting any paint inside the windows. Add details and number the windows with gold pen. Paint the edges of the mounting boards.

1 Using a photocopier, enlarge the template at the back of the book to twice the size. Trace this and transfer on to the white card (cardboard). Using a craft knife, metal ruler and cutting mat, cut out three sides of each window.

2 Turn over the card and paint the backs of the windows and a little of the area around them with gouache paint, so that they will look neat when the windows are opened.

4 Cut the work into three sections; the first the main doorway and lower windows, the second the three middle windows and two towers, and the third the top central panel. Cut three pieces of mounting board, the largest the size of the whole calendar with two more graded steps to go in front.

6 Finish the calendar with shiny cup sequins. Using a glue stick, attach them all around the edges of the calendar.

SAFETY TIP

Change the blade of your craft knife frequently, and keep it out of the reach of children. Be very careful when cutting – a craft knife is very sharp. When cutting out your calendar, use a cutting mat to protect your work surface. A self-healing mat is best.

NEEDLEPOINT PINCUSHION

This seasonal pincushion would make a lovely gift for a needlework enthusiast.

MATERIALS

23cm/9in square of white needlepoint canvas with 24 holes per 5cm (12 holes per in)
ruler
waterproof (magic) marker pen
masking tape
small lengths of tapestry wool (yarn) in 12 shades
scissors
tapestry needle
co-ordinating furnishing fabric, for the backing
dressmaker's pins
matching sewing thread
sewing needle
polyester wadding (batting)
70cm/28in decorative cord

1 To prepare the canvas, draw a vertical line down the centre and a horizontal line across the centre with a waterproof (magic) marker pen.

2 Bind the edges of the canvas with masking tape to prevent the yarn from catching as you work. Select three colours for each corner star.

3 Work the design from the chart at the back of the book in tent stitch, beginning in the centre and counting each square as one intersection of canvas threads. Complete all four squares. Remove the masking tape. Press with a steam iron, pulling the canvas gently back into a square. Dry it quickly so that the canvas does not distort.

4 Cut a square of backing fabric and pin it to the canvas, right sides together. Machine or hand stitch around the edges, leaving a gap on one side. Trim the seams and corners and turn to the right side. Stuff with polyester wadding (batting) to make a nice plump shape.

5 Beginning near the opening, hand stitch the cord around the edges of the cushion. Make a knot in the cord as you reach each corner. Push both ends of the cord into the opening and sew it up neatly, securing the cord as you stitch.

CRAFT TIP

This pincushion is ideal for using up small quantities of tapestry wool (yarn) left over from other projects, but if you do use scraps make sure you will have enough to complete the design.

Sparkling Flowerpot

This attractive container is covered with the foil wrapped around chocolates and candies.

Fill it with baubles (balls) for a table decoration.

Materials

coloured foil candy wrappers
terracotta flowerpot
decorator's paintbrush
PVA (white) glue and brush

1 Smooth out the coloured foils and select as many rectangular shapes as possible. If any have tears, you may be able to overlap them.

2 Paint the flowerpot all over with PVA (white) glue to seal the surface.

3 Coat the back of a piece of foil with glue and apply it to the pot, smoothing it with the brush and brushing on more glue to secure it. Continue adding the oil in an attractive geometric pattern. When the pot is completely covered, seal it with another coat of glue.

Craft Tip

Although you can arrange the foils in a haphazard manner for a crazy patchwork effect, this project looks best if you keep to a more regular design by placing the foil pieces horizontally and vertically.

Silver Crown Candle-Holder

Dress nightlights (tealights) up for Christmas with these easy foil crowns.

Materials

scissors
heavy-gauge aluminium foil
ruler
nightlight (tealight)
masking tape
dried-out ballpoint pen
glue stick

3 Remove the tape and lay the foil flat on a protected surface. Emboss a design on the foil with a dried-out ballpoint pen, making sure that it will meet neatly when the crown is joined up.

4 Roll the finished design tightly around the nightlight to get a good candle shape, then stick it together with a glue stick. Press the foil ends together to ensure a smooth join.

1 Cut a rectangle of foil to fit around the nightlight (tealight) and overlap by about 4cm/1½in. The foil should stand at least 3cm/1¼in higher than the light.

2 Wrap the foil in a circle around the candle and secure with a piece of masking tape. Cut the points of the crown freehand with scissors.

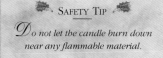

· Safety Tip ·

*D*o not let the candle burn down near any flammable material.

Velvet Fruit

These sumptuous apples and pears express the richness

of the festive season.

MATERIALS

pencil
tracing paper
scissors
dressmaker's pins
small pieces of dressweight velvet in red,
plum and green
sewing machine
matching sewing threads
sewing needle
polyester wadding (batting)

3 Cut two pieces of green velvet for each leaf. Machine stitch the pieces together, leaving the end open, and turn to the right side. Gather the end, using a needle and thread, to give a realistic leaf shape.

1 Trace the pear, apple and leaf shapes at the back of the book and enlarge as required. Transfer to paper and cut out. Pin to the velvet and cut out, adding a 5mm/¼in seam allowance all around. You will need four sections for the pear and three for the apple.

4 Stuff each fruit with polyester wadding (batting). Sew up the opening at the top with a needle and thread, catching in the leaf as you sew.

2 Wrong sides together, pin together the side seams and machine stitch, leaving the top of the fruit open. Turn to the right side.

ABSTRACT CHRISTMAS TREE

This stylish white-and-gold tree makes a lovely modern alternative to traditional decorations.

It looks best as part of a cool, monochrome arrangement in white or gold.

MATERIALS

hot glue gun
coarse sisal (parcel) string
large polystyrene (plastic foam) cone
scissors
small polystyrene (plastic foam) star
white emulsion (latex) paint
artist's paintbrush
gold paint

CRAFT TIP

When winding the coarse sisal (parcel) string on to the cone, make sure the ends of the string are evenly spaced around the base so that the tree stands upright.

1 Using a hot glue gun, attach the end of the string to the base of the cone. Wind the string up the cone towards the point, then down to the base again, gluing it as you work and securing it when it crosses. Each time you reach the base, cut the string and start again from another point so that the cone is evenly covered.

2 Wind a short length of string in a coil and glue it to the top of the cone. This coil will act as a base for the star to sit on.

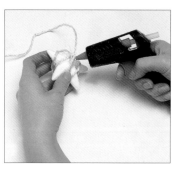

3 Wind and glue string around the star in the same way. Hide the raw ends under the string. Glue the star to the top of the cone.

4 Paint the cone and star with several coats of white emulsion (latex) paint, covering the string and filling in any dents in the polystyrene (plastic foam).

5 Finish by brushing roughly over the string with gold paint.

Santa's Toy Sack

Leave this gorgeous sack by the fireplace on Christmas Eve. Alternatively, it would be

a wonderful way to deliver gifts when you visit friends.

MATERIALS

tape measure
scissors
1.6 x 1.1m/63 x 43in hessian (burlap),
washed
dressmaker's pins
sewing machine
selection of contrasting satin ribbons,
3.5–4.5cm/1¼–1¾in wide
bodkin or safety pin
matching sewing threads
needle

1 Trim the hessian (burlap) so that it measures 1 x 1.5m/39 x 59in. Fold it in half, right sides together, bringing the shorter sides together. Pin across the bottom and up the side, making a seam allowance of approximately 4cm/1½in.

2 Machine stitch the bottom and one side of the sack.

3 Still working on the wrong side, turn down the top edge by approximately 7cm/3in. Pin, then cover the raw edge with a length of satin ribbon. Fold under the raw ends of the ribbon to leave an opening. Machine stitch close to the top and bottom edges of the ribbon.

4 Using a bodkin or safety pin, thread a length of contrasting ribbon through the channel you have created. It should be long enough to make a generous bow when the top of the sack is gathered up. Turn the sack right side out.

5 Using a double thread, stitch along one edge of a length of ribbon in running stitch. Draw the ribbon up into gathers. Cut to length, allowing for joining the ends, flatten out and measure how much you need to make a rosette. Cut all the ribbons to this length. Gather each ribbon and secure tightly, then join the raw edges invisibly from the wrong side.

6 Make enough rosettes in assorted colours to make a pleasing arrangement on the front of the sack. Stitch on the rosettes by hand, using matching thread.

Velvet Stocking

This grown-up stocking is just asking to be filled with exquisite treats and presents.

MATERIALS

pencil
paper for templates
gold satin fabric
dressmaker's pins
tailor's chalk
scissors
dressweight velvet in three
toning colours
sewing machine
matching sewing thread
decorative braid
sequin ribbon
sewing needle
gold buttons

1 Copy the template for the cuff from the back of the book and enlarge to the size required. Place the template against a folded edge of gold satin. Pin, then draw around the pattern piece with tailor's chalk. Cut out two cuffs, adding a narrow seam allowance.

2 Make a template for the stocking in the same way and divide into three sections. Place the template for each section on a double thickness of each colour of velvet. Pin and draw around each piece with tailor's chalk. Cut out, leaving a narrow seam and pin together.

3 When the three sections of velvet and the gold cuff for each side have been pinned together, machine stitch each seam and tidy any loose ends of thread.

4 On the right side of each piece, pin a strip of decorative braid and a strip of sequin ribbon. Sew these on invisibly by hand.

5 Right sides together, machine stitch the two sides of the stocking and the cuff together. Turn through, then fold down the gold satin inside to form a deep cuff. Turn in the raw edge of the cuff and stitch down to neaten, catching it to the seams of the velvet stocking.

6 Trim the satin cuff with a few gold buttons. To finish, attach a loop of gold braid for hanging.

ANGEL STOCKING

Different shades of denim work well together to make an unusual Christmas stocking.

MATERIALS

*pencil
tracing paper
paper for templates
scissors
iron-on fusible
bonding web
scraps of denim,
in different shades
dressmaker's pencil or
fading fabric marker
embroidery needle
embroidery threads (floss)
buttons
dressmaker's pins
ribbon
sewing machine
matching sewing threads
pinking shears
gingham fabric*

1 Trace the angel shapes at the back of the book and transfer on to paper to make templates. Iron fusible bonding web on to the back of scraps of denim. Draw around the templates on to the bonding web with a dressmaker's pencil or fabric marker. Cut out the shapes.

2 Draw a large stocking shape on paper and cut out to make a template. Draw around the template on to two pieces of denim and cut out. Remove the backing paper from the bonding web. Position the appliqué shapes on the right side of one stocking piece and iron in place.

3 Decorate the angel with different embroidery stitches. Stitch features on to the face and the hair.

4 Sew buttons around the angel and scatter over the rest of the stocking.

5 Right sides facing, pin the two stocking pieces together, leaving the top edge open. Cut a 12cm/4½in length of ribbon, fold in half and trap between the two stocking pieces on one side, approximately 6cm/2½in below the top. Machine stitch the pieces, leaving a 1cm/½in seam. Neaten the raw edges with pinking shears.

6 For the lining, use pinking shears to cut two stocking shapes from gingham fabric. Right sides facing, pin them together, leaving the top edge open. Stitch, leaving a 1cm/½in seam and a 15cm/6in gap along one side.

7 Place the denim stocking inside the lining stocking, matching the top raw edges. Pin the denim and lining together around the top opening. Stitch, leaving a 1cm/½in seam.

8 Push the denim stocking through the gap in the lining, then push the lining inside the denim stocking. Slip-stitch the gap. Stitch a line of running stitch around the top edge of the stocking.

CHRISTMAS CRACKERS

Making your own Christmas crackers is very rewarding, and you can collect small gifts to put in them.

MATERIALS

double-sided crepe paper
craft knife
metal ruler
cutting mat
thin card (cardboard) in
white and black
double-sided adhesive
(cellophane) tape
gold crepe paper
gold paper-backed foil
corrugated card (cardboard)
fine gold cord
cracker snaps
paper hats, jokes and
small gifts
narrow black ribbon

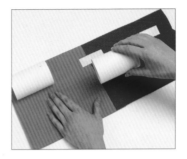

2 Cut three pieces of thin white card (cardboard) 22 x 10cm/9 x 4in. Roll each into a cylinder, overlapping the short ends by 3.5cm/1¼in. Lay strips of double-sided adhesive (cellophane) tape across the crepe paper with which to attach the card cylinders: one in the centre and the other two about 4cm/1½ in from each end of the crepe rectangle. Roll up and secure the edge with double-sided tape.

4 Insert a cracker snap and place a paper hat, joke and gift in the central section of the cracker.

5 Tie up the ends of the cracker with narrow black ribbon, easing the crepe paper gently so that you can tie the knots very tightly. Tie each ribbon into a large, neat bow.

1 For each cracker, cut two rectangles of crepe paper 25 x 20cm/10 x 8in, using a craft knife and cutting mat. Join, overlapping the ends, to make a rectangle 45 x 20cm/18 x 8in.

3 Decorate the cracker with strips of gold paper. To make the gold corrugated paper, lay a strip of paper-backed foil over a piece of corrugated card (cardboard) and ease the foil into the ridges with your thumb. Cut a simple star shape out of thin black card (cardboard), wrap some fine gold cord around it and stick it on top of the gold decoration.

6 Complete the cracker by folding the edges of the crepe paper neatly over the ends of the cardboard cylinders.

WILLOW TWIG NAPKIN RINGS

A row of twigs makes a lovely natural decoration on these simple napkin rings.

MATERIALS

willow or other straight twigs
secateurs (pruning shears)
11 x 22cm/4¼ x 8½in cotton fabric for
each napkin ring
fabric glue and brush
stranded embroidery thread (floss)
embroidery needle
dressmaker's pins
matching sewing thread

1 For each napkin ring, cut four pieces of willow or other straight twigs, each 9cm/3½in long, using secateurs (pruning shears).

2 Make a 1cm/½in hem along one short end of the fabric and glue it down. Fold the long sides of the fabric rectangle to the centre and glue.

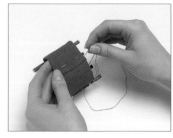

3 Position the twigs evenly across the centre of the right side of the fabric. Using three strands of embroidery thread (floss) and an embroidery needle, oversew the twigs on to the napkin ring.

4 Pin the ends of the napkin ring together, tucking the raw edge into the folded edge. Slip-stitch together, using matching sewing thread.

HOLLY LEAF NAPKIN

A simply embroidered outline motif is a lovely decoration for the Christmas table.

MATERIALS

pencil
paper for template
scissors
dressmaker's pins
50cm/20in square of washable
cotton fabric
tailor's chalk
embroidery needle
stranded embroidery thread
(floss) in acid green,
acid yellow and
bright orange

3 Fold the edge of the fabric under and pin a 5mm/¼in double hem all around the cotton square.

4 Using three strands of bright orange embroidery thread (floss), work a neat running stitch evenly around the hem.

1 Trace the holly leaf motif from the back of the book and make a paper template. Pin it on to one corner of the cotton fabric, allowing room for a hem, and draw around it with tailor's chalk.

2 Using three strands of embroidery thread (floss) and working in stem stitch, use the acid green colour to embroider the outline of the holly leaf, and use the acid yellow colour to embroider the veins.

GOLD CROWN TABLECLOTH

Set the festive tone with this lovely white-and-gold tablecloth, decorated with stencilled motifs.

MATERIALS

135cm/54in square of white cotton fabric
dressmaker's pins
pencil
tracing paper
stencil card (cardboard)
craft knife
cutting mat
masking tape
stencil brush
gold stencil paint
fine artist's paintbrush
sewing machine
white sewing thread

1 Iron the fabric to remove creases, then fold in quarters and press the folds. Fold each quarter to find the centre point, press and mark with pins. Trace the crown and shooting star templates from the back of the book, transfer on to stencil card (cardboard) and cut out with a craft knife. Stencil crowns in the corners of the tablecloth, then the edges and centre.

2 Taking care not to overload your brush, stencil shooting stars between the crowns, all pointing in the same direction around the edge of the cloth.

3 Complete the stars by touching up the gaps left by the stencil with a fine paintbrush and gold stencil paint.

4 Press on the wrong side of the fabric to fix the paint. Hem the fabric all around the edge on a sewing machine, using matching thread.

FESTIVE WINE GLASSES

Transform plain wine glasses with stained-glass colours, to give the effect of a medieval feast.

MATERIALS

plain wine glasses
white spirit (paint thinner)
gold glass (relief) outliner
oil-based glass paints
fine artist's paintbrush
old glass or jar

3 Check the colour and get the feel of the glass paint by practising on an old glass or jar first. Use a fine paintbrush to colour in your design, and be careful not to get paint on the gold outliner. Try to finish each colour before changing to the next one. Clean the brush with white spirit between each colour.

1 Wash the glasses with detergent, then wipe over with white spirit (paint thinner) to remove all traces of grease.

2 Pipe your design directly on to the glass with gold glass (relief) outliner. (It's best to avoid the rim of the glass as the outliner will feel bumpy against the drinker's lips.) Leave to dry thoroughly for at least 24 hours.

HAND-PAINTED PLATE

Turn a plain white plate into a brilliant work of art, using ceramic paints.

MATERIALS

pencil
tracing paper
carbon paper
scissors
27cm/10½in diameter glazed white plate
masking tape
fine and medium artist's paintbrushes
oil-based ceramic paints in several colours
including gold
clear polyurethane varnish and brush

1 Trace the crown, star and swirl from the back of the book. Cut pieces of carbon paper to the size of the tracings.

2 Starting with the crown, secure the carbon paper and the tracing to the plate with masking tape. Draw over the motif to transfer it to the plate. Plan the positions of the stars and swirls, spacing them evenly around the rim, and transfer them in the same way.

3 Using a fine paintbrush, paint in the coloured areas of the crown, the centres of the stars and the swirls with ceramic paints, following the manufacturer's instructions. Start at the centre and work outwards so that your hand does not smudge the paint. Fill in the background with a medium brush.

4 Leave the paint to dry for about 24 hours, then paint in the gold details. You may need two coats for a rich gold effect. Leave to dry again for 24 hours.

5 Cover the plate with a coat of clear varnish to protect the surface. Leave to dry thoroughly.

CRAFT TIP

This plate isn't suitable for serving food. Use it instead as a decoration on a dresser or side table.

Christmas Tree Decorations

*D*ecorations for the Christmas tree can be made from an enormous array of different materials, including reflective papers, gingerbread, papier-maché and modelling clay. You can make tassels or delicate insects out of embroidery threads (floss), or gild fruit, eggs or shells with gold or silver spray paint, gilt cream or metal leaf. Salt dough shapes and tin decorations have great folk art appeal, and the lovely Wire Angel and the Button Garland have the same simple charm. For a traditional Victorian tree, choose spangly decorations such as the Sequinned Baubles, or you can experiment with the spectacular Byzantine Decorations.

Shiny Snowflakes

These sparkling decorations are easy to make by cutting geometric patterns out of reflective paper.

MATERIALS

sharp pencil
compass
reflective papers in gold, silver and other colours
scissors
tracing paper
craft knife
cutting mat
gold thread

1 Draw a circle on the back of a piece of reflective paper and cut out. Fold the circle in half three times. Photocopy the patterns from the back of the book, enlarging them if necessary.

2 Trace one of the photocopied snowflake patterns and transfer it on to the folded paper. Use a sharp pencil as the detail is intricate and must be precise.

3 Cut out the traced pattern, using a craft knife to make small, internal cuts. Unfold the circle and flatten. Do the same with the other papers and patterns.

4 For the curved patterns, unfold once and fold in half the other way, then cut out triangular notches along the fold line. Attach lengths of gold thread to hang all the snowflakes.

HARLEQUIN EGGS

These rich, metallic-effect ornaments are in fact blown eggs, carefully decorated

with gold and silver gilt cream.

MATERIALS

hen's eggs
pale blue acrylic paint
flat artist's paintbrush
white pencil
fine paintbrush
gilt cream in gold and silver
soft cloth
wire egg-holders

3 Using a fine paintbrush, paint gold gilt cream in alternate squares, taking care to keep the edges neat. Leave to dry. Paint silver squares in the same way and leave to dry.

4 Carefully polish the egg with a soft cloth to a high shine. Hold the two prongs of the wire egg-holder firmly together and push them into the hole at the top of the egg for hanging.

1 Blow the eggs by making a hole at either end and blowing the contents out. Paint half of each egg with pale blue acrylic paint, using a flat paintbrush. Leave to dry, then paint the other half in the same colour.

2 Using a white pencil, and with a steady hand, draw horizontal and vertical lines over the egg to make a checked pattern or your own design.

ℰXOTIC 𝒮HELLS

The intricate shapes of shells look beautiful gilded with precious metal leaf.

MATERIALS

assorted shells
small decorator's paintbrushes
blue emulsion (latex) paint
water-based gold size
Dutch metal leaf in aluminium or gold,
on transfer paper
pale shellac varnish and brush
strong glue
ribbon

1 Wash the shells thoroughly to remove any sand. Paint each shell with two coats of blue emulsion (latex) paint and leave to dry. Using another brush, apply size over the shell, smoothing out air bubbles with the brush. Leave until the size becomes clear.

2 Press a sheet of metal leaf on to the shell, using a dry brush to remove any excess. Varnish the gilded shells and leave to dry. Dab glue on to the tip of each shell and attach a length of ribbon for hanging.

CRAFT TIP

Be careful not to take rare shells from the beach, or any that are not empty.

A Touch of Gold

A quick and easy way to create gilded Christmas ornaments is with gold (or silver) spray paint.

MATERIALS

nuts
gold or silver spray paint
strong glue
stub wire
colourful ribbons
dried fungi
biscuits (cookies)
edible gold spray paint

2 Be bold in your choice of subjects to spray: dried fungi are an unusual choice. Dry them in an airing cupboard (linen closet) or an oven at the lowest setting with the door slightly open. After spraying, tie them singly, in pairs or in groups with colourful ribbons.

3 Biscuits (cookies) in fun shapes make wonderful subjects for gilding. You can buy edible gold spray from specialist cake decorating outlets.

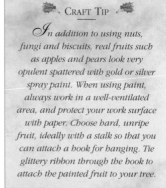

CRAFT TIP

In addition to using nuts, fungi and biscuits, real fruits such as apples and pears look very opulent spattered with gold or silver spray paint. When using paint, always work in a well-ventilated area, and protect your work surface with paper. Choose hard, unripe fruit, ideally with a stalk so that you can attach a hook for hanging. Tie glittery ribbon through the hook to attach the painted fruit to your tree.

1 Paint nuts with gold or silver spray paint, then glue them together in clusters, either keeping the same variety together or mixing interesting-shaped nuts. When the glue has set firm, push a stub wire through a gap between the nuts, twist it to make a loop and tie on a decorative ribbon or bow.

GINGERBREAD PLAQUES

These pretty, edible tree decorations can be made very quickly using a ready-made gingerbread mix.

MATERIALS

2 large baking sheets
golden gingerbread dough
flour
rolling pin
8cm/3¼in gingerbread man pastry
(cookie) cutter
skewer
wire rack
royal icing
piping bag, fitted with writing nozzles
2 bowls
food colouring in green and blue
lemon juice
silver dragees
narrow gingham ribbon

1 Preheat the oven to 180°C/350°F/ Gas 4. Grease the baking sheets. Roll out the gingerbread dough on a floured surface and cut out the gingerbread figures. Space them well apart on the baking sheets.

2 Re-roll the dough trimmings and cut into strips, 1cm/½in wide and 28cm/11in long. Place a strip around each figure and make a hole in the top with a skewer. Bake for 12–15 minutes, then cool on a wire rack.

3 Pipe on the details with icing. Divide the remaining icing into two bowls, then colour one green and the other blue. Thin the icing with lemon juice.

4 Ice the body of each figure and add a row of dragee "buttons". Leave to set for 2 hours. Decorate the edges with white icing, then thread with ribbon.

DRIED FRUITS AND FLOWERS

These pretty, natural decorations complement an evergreen tree perfectly.

MATERIALS

For the Floral Stars and Trees
knife
block of florist's foam
pastry (cookie) cutters in star and
Christmas tree shapes
loose, dried lavender
gold dust powder
plastic bag, with no holes
florist's adhesive
loose, dried tulip and rose petals
(optional)
cranberries (optional)
gold cord
scissors

For the Dried Fruit Decorations
gold cord
dried oranges and limes
florist's adhesive
dried red and yellow rose heads
cinnamon sticks

FLORAL STARS AND TREES

1 Cut the block of foam into slices approximately 2.5cm/1in thick. Using the pastry (cookie) cutters, press out star and tree shapes. Put the lavender with 2 tablespoons of gold dust powder in the plastic bag and shake to mix. Liberally coat all the surfaces of the foam shapes with florist's adhesive.

2 Place the shapes in the plastic bag and shake. As a variation, press dried tulip and rose petals on to the shapes before putting them in the bag; only the exposed glued areas will pick up the lavender. You can glue a cranberry to the centre of each star. Make a small hole in each shape and thread with gold cord for hanging.

DRIED FRUIT DECORATIONS

3 Tie gold cord around each fruit, and knot it on top to form a hanging loop. Using florist's adhesive, stick a rose head to the top next to the knotted cord. Dab adhesive on to short pieces of cinnamon stick and place them next to the rose.

Rococo Star

This magnificent papier-mâché star will take pride of place on the Christmas tree.

MATERIALS

paper for template
corrugated card (cardboard)
pen or pencil
craft knife
cutting mat
newspaper
PVA (white) glue, diluted with water,
and brush
gold spray paint
gold relief paint
gold glitter
gold braid (optional)
all-purpose glue (optional)

1 Using a photocopier, enlarge the star template from the back of the book to the size required. Cut out the paper star, then draw around it on to corrugated card (cardboard), using a craft knife and cutting mat. Tear newspaper into small strips and brush watered-down glue on to both sides. Stick the strips on to the star.

2 Neatly cover the edges and points of the star with the newspaper strips. Allow to dry, then apply a second layer. If the star begins to buckle, place it under a heavy weight. When completely dry, spray both sides with gold paint and leave to dry.

3 Draw a design on one side in gold relief paint and sprinkle with glitter while wet. Allow to dry completely before repeating the design on the other side. If you wish to hang the star, attach gold braid to one point with a dab of glue.

TWIRLING TASSELS

These delicate tassels make stunning ornaments, especially on the Christmas tree.

MATERIALS

scissors
silk or metallic embroidery thread (floss)
thin polyester thread
cord
comb
fine twine

1 Cut and fold equal lengths of embroidery thread and place them on top of the polyester thread. Loop a length of cord, knot the ends and place on the embroidery threads as shown. Tie the polyester thread tightly around the cord.

3 Working from the top to the bottom of the ball of the tassel, neatly bind the twine tightly around the top of the tassel. Pass the end of the twine through the loop.

4 Pull the twine up into the binding and snip off the ends. Make a loop in a strand of the cord and pass the cord through the loop. Trim the cut ends of the tassel neatly.

2 Cut neatly through the folded ends of the embroidery threads, then comb out the tassel. Make a small loop with the fine twine.

JUGGLERS MOBILE

This inventive Christmas tree decoration is made from a wire coathanger and small pieces of polymer clay.

MATERIALS

pliers
wire coathanger
gold spray paint
epoxy resin glue
¼ block modelling polymer clay
earring wires, with loops
sandpaper
modelling tools
star-shaped pastry (cookie) cutters
thick needle
acrylic paints
fine artist's paintbrush
varnish and brush
nylon fishing line
shell-shaped jewellery findings
gold cord

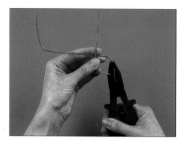

1 Using a pair of pliers, cut the hook and twisted section off the wire coathanger. Twist half the remaining wire into a double-diamond-shaped frame. Spray the frame with gold paint, then glue the wires together where they cross.

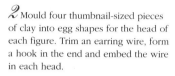

2 Mould four thumbnail-sized pieces of clay into egg shapes for the head of each figure. Trim an earring wire, form a hook in the end and embed the wire in each head.

3 Roll small pieces of clay for the limbs and an oblong for each torso. Assemble the bodies and smooth any seams with sandpaper. Cut five stars with a small pastry (cookie) cutter, two a little larger. Roll five bead shapes and pierce the centres with a needle. Bake all the clay shapes following the manufacturer's instructions.

4 Paint the figures, beads and stars, then varnish. Assemble the figures and stars on the frame using fishing line and jewellery findings. Tie a piece of gold cord to the top for hanging, then glue the large stars on either side, sandwiching the wire.

EMBROIDERED DRAGONFLIES

These charming ornaments make very delicate and original decorations for your tree.

MATERIALS

pencil
tracing paper
water-soluble fabric
embroidery hoop
opalescent cellophane
small pieces of sheer synthetic organdie in brown and green
dressmaker's pins
sewing machine with fine needle
metallic thread in two thicknesses
scissors
spray varnish
glittery pipecleaners
sewing needle
small glass beads
fine wire
all-purpose glue

3 Spray varnish the insects and leave to dry. Cut a pipecleaner longer than each body and sew to the underside as far as the head. Thread glass beads on to fine wire, twist into antennae and attach to each head.

4 Trim and bend the embroidery under the head and body to cover the pipecleaner. Fold the wings into a raised position and stitch them on to the insects by hand. Glue the insects directly to the branches of the tree.

1 Trace the templates at the back of the book and transfer on to water-soluble fabric stretched in a hoop. Place the cellophane between two pieces of organdie and pin under the hoop. Stitch around the wings in straight stitch, using metallic thread.

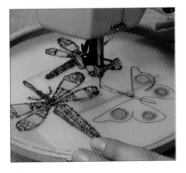

2 Using fine metallic thread in the needle and thick thread in the bobbin, sew the outlines in straight stitch. Fill in the shapes. Remove the hoop and dissolve the fabric in water.

FRUIT AND SPICE ORNAMENTS

Natural materials add a splash of colour and a delightful fresh scent to the Christmas tree.

1 Tie decorative bundles of cinnamon sticks together with ribbon for a spicy decoration, then glue red cranberries to the ribbon. Thread garlands of cranberries on to sewing thread and drape over the tree.

3 Deck the tree with tiny egg-shaped kumquats by threading them on to medium stub wires. Loop the kumquat circlets over the tree branches, or tie them with ribbon. You could also use satsumas, tangerines or clementines.

2 Thick dried orange rings look good enough to eat. Cut 5mm/ ¼in slices from a large orange, place on a rack and dry in an oven at a low temperature for about 1 hour. Push a knife through each slice just below the peel and thread with ribbon.

4 These unusual ornaments are made by gluing a small white cake candle to the base of a white curtain ring. Cut a piece of gold sequin trim to fit the curtain ring and glue it on the back of the ring. Spray a star anise gold and glue to the front.

Spicy Pomanders

Pomanders have been a favourite Christmas decoration since Elizabethan times.

MATERIALS

navel or thin-skinned oranges
cloves
masking tape
large paperclips
narrow ribbon

CRAFT TIP

There are many classic pomander designs based on geometric patterns such as circles, squares and stars. The pomanders shown here were slashed vertically with a knife in a design reminiscent of a Renaissance doublet.

1 Stud the oranges with cloves. For a traditional design, wrap masking tape around the fruit in a criss-cross fashion to divide it into four equal sections, then outline the tape with cloves.

2 Push the loop of a large paperclip deep into the top of each fruit to make a loop. Keep the fruit in a warm cupboard for 1–2 weeks, then thread ribbon through the loops for hanging.

GILDED GLASS

Transform plain Christmas tree balls into unique ornaments – simple designs such as

circles, triangles and stars work best.

MATERIALS

plain glass balls
detergent
white spirit (paint thinner)
gold glass (relief) outliner
kitchen paper
jam jars
wire-edged or other wide ribbon
scissors

1 Clean the balls carefully with detergent and white spirit. Working on one side, squeeze outliner on to the glass in a simple design. Wipe off any mistakes with kitchen paper before they dry.

2 Rest each ball in an empty jam jar and leave for 24 hours to dry thoroughly. Decorate the other side and leave to dry again. Thread ribbon through the hanging loop and tie in a bow.

CRAFT TIP

Simple, bold shapes look best on small balls. Take your inspiration from stained glass windows in churches, mixing geometric shapes with elegant curves or curlicues.

BUTTON GARLAND

Ordinary buttons make an attractive garland for the Christmas tree.

MATERIALS

buttons in various sizes and colours
garden twine
scissors
hot glue gun or strong glue

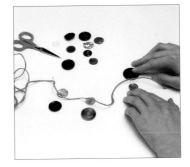

1 Spread all the buttons out on a tabletop and choose a variety of colours and sizes. Alternate small ones with larger ones along a length of garden twine.

2 Put a small dab of glue on the back of the first button. Lay the twine on top and wait until the glue hardens. Glue all the buttons in the same way, spacing them evenly along the twine.

EDIBLE TREE ORNAMENTS

These tasty ornaments will appeal to both children and adults. This recipe makes approximately 12.

MATERIALS

2 baking sheets
non-stick baking paper (parchment)
175g/6oz/1½ cups plain flour
75g/3oz/6 tbsp butter
40g/1½oz/3 tbsp caster (superfine) sugar
egg white
30ml/2 tbsp orange juice
rolling pin
Christmas tree pastry (cookie) cutter
round 1cm/½in pastry (cookie) cutter
225g/8oz coloured fruit sweets (candies)
wire rack
narrow ribbon

1 Preheat the oven to 180°C/350°F/ Gas 4. Line the baking sheets with baking paper (parchment). Sift the flour into a mixing bowl. Cut the butter into pieces and rub into the flour until it resembles breadcrumbs. Stir in the sugar, egg white and enough orange juice to form a soft dough. Knead on a lightly floured surface until smooth.

2 Roll the dough out thinly and stamp out as many shapes as possible, using a Christmas tree cutter. Transfer to the baking sheets, spacing them well apart. Using a round cutter, stamp out six circles from each tree. Cut each sweet into three slices and place a piece in each circle. Make a small hole at the top of each tree for hanging.

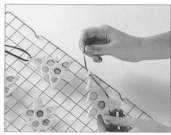

3 Bake in the oven for 15–20 minutes until the trees are golden and the sweets have melted, filling the holes. Leave on the baking sheets for 5 minutes, then transfer to a wire rack to cool. Thread ribbon through the holes at the top. Store in an airtight container until ready to use.

INDIAN-STYLE DECORATIONS

These unusual salt dough ornaments evoke the vivid colours of an Indian festival.

MATERIALS

*2 cups plain flour,
plus extra for dusting
1 cup salt
1 cup tepid water
rolling pin
baking paper (parchment)
scissors
sharp knife
cocktail stick (toothpick) or drinking straw
baking sheet
medium and fine artist's paintbrushes
acrylic gesso
paints in bright colours
strong glue
selection of beads and sequins
matt acrylic varnish and brush
narrow ribbon*

3 Make smaller templates of the relief designs, cut out in dough and stick them to the ornaments. Place on a baking sheet and bake at 120°C/250°F/Gas ½ for 5 hours. Cool.

4 Prime with acrylic gesso. Leave to dry, then paint in bright colours. Glue on beads and sequins. Coat with acrylic varnish when dry. Thread ribbon through the holes for hanging.

1 Mix the flour, salt and half the water, then gradually add more water. Knead for 10 minutes. Roll out the dough on baking paper (parchment). Enlarge the templates from the back of the book on a photocopier. Carefully cut out the templates, place on the dough and cut out the designs with a sharp knife.

2 Dust the dough with flour. Make the patterns and details in the dough using a cocktail stick (toothpick) or drinking straw. Make a hole in the top of each shape for hanging. Moisten the ornaments with a little water.

Sequinned Stars

Shimmering sequins and tiny beads make these lovely decorations really shine.

Materials

*polystyrene (plastic foam) star with
hanging loop
gold spray paint
small piece of modelling clay
brown paper
multicoloured glass seed beads
multicoloured sequins
seed pearl beads
special design sequins
1.5cm/⅝in brass-beaded pins
thin gold braid
scissors*

1 Spray the polystyrene (plastic foam) star with gold paint, anchoring it with a piece of modelling clay to some brown paper to stop it moving. Allow to dry.

2 While the star is drying, sort all the beads, sequins and pins into separate containers to make it easier to choose colours and shapes as you work.

3 Thread a glass bead on to a pin, followed by a multicoloured sequin. Push it gently into the star. Repeat to complete the design, covering the whole star. Pin a seed pearl bead and special design sequin in the centre of each side of the star.

4 For an alternative design, decorate the edges of the star with lines of sequins in contrasting colours. Pick out the ridges of the star in the same way, leaving the inner sections gold. Thread gold braid through the loops of the stars for hanging.

Glittering Fir Cones

The intricate shape of fir cones looks wonderful highlighted with gold and silver paint and glitter.

MATERIALS

fir cones
red oxide spray primer
spray paints in gold and silver
hot glue gun or all-purpose glue and
an old, fine paintbrush
assorted glitters
saucer
ribbon

3 Heat a glue gun and apply a little glue to the tips of each cone, taking care not to apply too much. Alternatively, apply small dabs of glue on to the cone tips with an old, fine paintbrush.

4 Working quickly, sprinkle glitter on to the fir cones so that it sticks to the glued tips. Use a saucer to catch the excess glitter. When dry, glue a length of ribbon to the base of each cone.

1 To provide a good base colour for the spray paint, spray the fir cones with red oxide primer. Leave to dry for 1–2 hours, then check that all the recesses and details are well covered.

2 Spray each cone several times with gold or silver spray. Hold the can 25–30cm/10–12in away from the cone as you spray and take care to cover the whole cone. Set the cones aside until they are completely dry.

Heraldic Decorations

These stylish salt dough decorations look good enough to eat, but are purely ornamental.

MATERIALS

2 cups plain flour
1 cup salt
1 cup tepid water
rolling pin
baking paper (parchment)
pencil
tracing paper
scissors
small, sharp knife
boiled sweets (hard candies)
cocktail stick (toothpick)
artist's paintbrushes
acrylic gesso
gold craft paint
water-based satin varnish
jewels or sequins (optional)
strong glue (optional)
fine gold cord

1 Mix the flour, salt and water to a firm dough. Knead for 10 minutes. Roll the dough out flat on baking paper (parchment) to a thickness of 5mm/¼in. Trace the templates at the back of the book and cut out of the dough. Dust with flour and place a sweet in the centre. Cut around each sweet, adding a 2mm/⅛in margin.

2 Make a hole in the top of each shape with a cocktail stick (toothpick). Transfer the ornaments, without the sweets, on the paper to a baking sheet and bake at 120°C/250°F/Gas ½ for 9 hours. Place a boiled sweet in each hole and return to the oven for 30 minutes. Remove from the oven and set aside to cool.

3 Paint the shapes with gesso and allow to dry. Then paint with gold paint and allow to dry overnight. Apply five coats of varnish, leaving to dry between applications. Jewels or sequins can also be added at this stage by gluing them on to the surface of the decorations. Thread gold cord through the holes for hanging.

CRAFT TIP

Jewels, sequins and colourful painted patterns can be used to enhance classic shapes such as fleurs-de-lys and stars.

PAPIER-MÂCHÉ DECORATIONS

These colourful ornaments are easy to make from scraps of newspaper.

MATERIALS

pencil
tracing paper
thin card (cardboard)
craft knife
cutting mat
strong clear glue and brush
small metal jewellery findings
newspaper
PVA (white) glue, diluted with water
artist's paintbrushes
white emulsion (latex) paint
pencil
poster paints
clear gloss varnish and brush
thin cord

1 Trace the shapes from the back of the book and transfer to card (cardboard). Cut out, using a craft knife and cutting mat. Glue a jewellery finding on to the top of each shape, at the back. When the glue is dry, cover the card shapes with three layers of thin newspaper strips soaked in diluted PVA (white) glue. Dry overnight, then prime with a coat of white emulsion (latex) paint.

2 When dry, draw a design on each shape in pencil, then paint with poster paints. Seal with a coat of varnish. Thread cord through the findings and tie the ends in a knot for hanging.

BYZANTINE DECORATIONS

Exotic shapes dripping with beads make wonderfully ornate hanging decorations.

MATERIALS

pencil
tracing paper
thin card (cardboard)
small scissors
craft knife
metal ruler
cutting mat
bradawl (awl)
beads
flat-headed pins
long-nosed pliers
thin cord

1 Trace the templates at the back of the book. Draw around them on to the card (cardboard), allowing two pieces for each decoration. Cut out.

2 Mark the slotting slits down the centre of each piece and cut out with a craft knife, using a metal ruler and cutting mat. Don't over-cut the slits or the pieces will not fit together tightly.

3 Using a bradawl (awl), make a small hole close to the bottom edge of one piece for the central bead drop, a hole at the top of the corresponding piece for the hanging loop, and holes close to the edges underneath the top curling shapes to hang more beads.

4 Thread the beads on to flat-headed pins to make the droplets, one for the base centre and one for each of the four top curls.

CRAFT TIP

Old boxes are the best source of card (cardboard), and you can flatten them out easily. Choose a strong box, remove any tape that is holding it together, and press the box down flat. Cut the box into pieces, ready for use in any projects that require card.

5 Using long-nosed pliers, bend each pin wire close to the top of the beads, then hook it through a hole in the card. Wrap the wire ends around the pin a few times to secure, then neatly trim off the ends.

6 Slot the two beaded card pieces together so they match at the top and bottom edges, to make a three-dimensional shape. Thread cord through the hole at the top of the decoration and tie the ends to make a hanging loop.

Sequinned Baubles

Sequins make wonderful Christmas decorations, twinkling and sparkling as they catch the light.

MATERIALS

marker pen
2 compressed cotton spheres,
6cm/2¼in diameter
5mm/¼in diameter round concave
sequins in various colours,
including metallic
lill pins
beading needle
beading thread
small bronze-coloured glass beads
fruited metal beads
dressmaker's pins
silver pointed oval sequins
ribbon (optional)

1 Using a marker pen, divide the surface of the first cotton sphere into quarters, as shown. Mark around the middle of the sphere to divide it into eight sections.

CRAFT TIP

Collect as many different colours and shapes of sequins as you can for making these sparkly Christmas baubles. Sequins come in all shapes and sizes, including circles, stars and flower shapes.

2 Outline the sections with round concave sequins, using a variety of different colours. Use lill pins to attach the sequins to the sphere and overlap each one slightly.

3 Fill in the sections, again overlapping the sequins slightly.

4 Using a beading needle and thread, make several small stitches in the top of the sphere. Thread on 8cm/3in of small bronze glass beads, then make several stitches to make a loop for hanging. Thread a metal bead on to a pin and press into the sphere to secure the loop.

5 To make the star bauble, mark several horizontal stripes. Press in a sequin at the top and bottom. Working outwards from these points, press in silver pointed sequins to form a star shape.

6 Fill in the rest of sphere with round sequins, as in steps 2 and 3. As an alternative hanging loop, attach a 10cm/4in piece of ribbon to the top, using a dressmaker's pin and metal bead as in step 4.

WIRE ANGEL

Soft wire bends easily into loops and curls to make a beautiful adornment to hang

from the tree or from a Christmas wreath.

MATERIALS

1mm/0.039in thick silver- or gold-plated
copper wire
round-nosed pliers
parallel (channel-type) pliers
wirecutters
narrow ribbon
star-shaped bead or crystal droplet

1 Use the template at the back of the book as a guide for shaping the wire, either at the same size or enlarged.

2 Leaving 5cm/2in at the end, start bending the wire around the template, using round-nosed pliers and your fingers. Make the hair curls and the forehead up to the eye. Make the lower lid of the eye first and then the upper lid. Halfway along the upper lid, make a loop around the end of the round-nosed pliers to form the pupil. Squeeze the corner of the eye with parallel (channel-type) pliers.

3 Shape the nose and make a larger loop around the end of the round-nosed pliers for the nostril. Shape the mouth, closing the lips with parallel pliers, then shape the chin.

4 Loop the wire around the bottom of the hair to make the cheek. This loop will help to keep the structure flat and more manageable.

5 Follow the template along the arm. Make loops with the round-nosed pliers for the fingers, then shape the bottom line of the arm.

6 Make the shoulder by carefully looping the wire around the point where the arm joins the neck.

7 At the waist, bend the wire across to form the waistband. Make a series of long horizontal loops with slightly curled ends back along the waistband. When you have made seven loops, secure with a tight twist at the bend.

8 Make a large curve for the lower part of the skirt. Shape a wavy hem around the thickest part of the round-nosed pliers. The legs interrupt the wavy hemline. Make the toes in the same way as the fingers, but they should be shorter and rounder. Shape the heels and make a small decorative loop at each ankle.

9 Complete the wavy hemline and the back of the skirt. Secure by twisting the wire tightly around the waistband.

10 Make loops along the bottom of the wing and close slightly to neaten. Form the curved top of the wing.

11 Loop the wire around the back of the shoulder and under the bottom of the wing. Finish off with a coil and cut off the wire.

12 Using the 5cm/2in of wire left at the start, bind the shoulder and wing together. Cut off the end. Thread ribbon through the loops in the waistband and hang a star-shaped bead or crystal droplet from the angel's hand.

FESTIVE FIGURES

Use Christmas-themed pastry (cookie) cutters to make these clay shapes,

then embellish them with bronze powder and rhinestones.

MATERIALS

polymer clay
rolling pin
Christmas-themed pastry
(cookie) cutters
modelling tool
paintbrush
plastic straw
bronze powders in various colours
varnish and brush
rhinestones
glue
toothpick
ribbon

2 Draw on markings with a modelling tool. Make small indentations for the rhinestones with the end of a paintbrush.

5 When cool, use a paintbrush to apply a coat of varnish. This will protect the figure from scratches.

1 Roll out some clay and press out a shape using a pastry (cookie) cutter.

3 Using a plastic straw, make a hole in the centre top for hanging.

6 Glue rhinestones in the indentations, with the aid of a toothpick. Thread ribbon through the hole for hanging.

CRAFT TIP

Polymer clay is actually a plastic, but has all the advantages of clay: it can be moulded, modelled, sculpted, stretched and embossed prior to being baked. It does not require firing at high temperatures: bake it in an ordinary domestic oven at 102–135°C/215–275°F/Gas ½–1 according to the manufacturer's instructions. This trasforms the clay from a malleable substance into a solid one. Once baked, the clay can be sanded, sawn, drilled and glued.

4 Brush on different-coloured bronze powders and blend together. Bake the figures in the oven, following the manufacturer's instructions.

FELT STARS

Red and green, the traditional festive colours, are mixed and matched in these two simple designs.

MATERIALS

*pencil
paper or thin card (cardboard)
scissors
tailor's chalk
red and green felt
embroidery scissors
needle
matching sewing threads
scraps of patterned fabric
ribbon*

4 Stitch the red border to one of the green stars with small, even running stitches and matching thread.

7 For a different decoration, take a green felt star and cut a small circle from the centre. Place on top of a red star, with a small piece of patterned fabric showing through the hole. Sew neatly around the hole in running stitch.

1 Draw a star shape on to paper or thin card (cardboard) and make a template. Using tailor's chalk, draw around the template on to felt.

5 Centre a small red star as cut out in step 3 on a green star. Stitch in place.

8 Stitch the two stars together around the edges with stab stitch.

2 Use a pair of embroidery scissors to cut equal numbers of red and green stars from the felt.

3 Using the point of the embroidery scissors, pierce one of the red stars 5mm/¼in from the edge. Cut out a smaller star, leaving a 5mm/¼in border all around.

6 Place the stars from steps 4 and 5 together, sandwiching a plain red star in the middle. Stitch the three stars together at the inner points, as shown.

9 Use a loop of coloured ribbon for hanging. Alternatively, wrap sewing thread around all four fingers, then stitch a loop on to a point of each star with small stitches.

*R*IBBONS AND *B*OWS

Hang these lovely, delicate decorations on the tree or on a length of gold ribbon

strung across the mantelpiece.

MATERIALS

For the Baubles
pencil
polystyrene (plastic foam) balls,
7.5 or 5cm/3 or 2in
in diameter
gold, brown and cream ribbons,
1m x 3–9mm/40in x ⅛–⅜in
dressmaker's pins
scissors
toning patterned ribbon,
2m x 3–9mm/2¼yd x ⅛–⅜in
tiny gold beads
gold-coin pendants
large, ornate gold beads

For the Fir Cone Parcels
gold, lemon or brown ribbon, 4cm/
1½in wide
gold or brown ribbon, 3mm/⅛in wide
fir cones
all-purpose glue

For the Golden Tassels
scissors
cotton-pulp ball, 2.5cm/1in in diameter
gold grosgrain ribbon, 9.9m x 3mm/
11yd x ⅛in
tape measure
crewel needle
all-purpose glue

BAUBLES

1 Use a pencil to divide a polystyrene (plastic foam) ball into quarters vertically, then into eighths with a horizontal line around the middle. Place a length of ribbon across one section, pin at each end on the drawn lines and cut off the ribbon. Continue filling in the section, using the assorted ribbons like patchwork, overlapping the ribbon edges and laying the ribbon smoothly over the ball.

2 Fill in all the sections, completely covering the ball. Lay the patterned ribbon along the drawn lines, covering the pins and ribbon ends. Pin in position at each point where the pencil lines cross, turning the ribbon ends under to neaten. To make a loop for hanging, slip a 25cm/10in length of ribbon under one intersection. Knot the ends together.

3 Take several pins and slip a tiny gold bead followed by a gold-coin pendant on to each one. Pin them in a row around the bauble. Thread a small bead and then a large, ornate bead on to the last pin and stick it into the base to complete.

FIR CONE PARCELS

4 Make a bow with the wide ribbon. Wrap the narrow ribbon around the fir cone as if wrapping a parcel. Tie the ribbon ends together 10cm/4in above the top of the cone to make a hanging loop. Glue the bow on top of the cone.

GOLDEN TASSELS

5 Use scissors to make a hole through the centre of the cotton-pulp ball. Pull out some of the fibre to enlarge the hole to 1cm/½in diameter.

6 Cut a 25cm/10in length from the ribbon and cut the remainder into 30cm/12in lengths. Put the 25cm/10in length and one 30cm/12in length to one side and insert the remainder through the hole, a few at a time. Use the crewel needle to thread them through if necessary. Allow 12.5cm/5in of each ribbon to hang below the ball. Dab a little glue on to the ball and fold down the ribbons protruding from the top around the outside of the ball. Continue until the ball is completely covered with ribbon.

7 Thread the needle with the 25cm/10in length of ribbon. Glue one end around the ribbons close to the base of the ball. Wrap the ribbon tightly around the tassel.

8 Insert the needle behind the binding ribbon and pull tightly. Unthread the needle, allowing the ribbon end to hang down with the other ribbons. Do not trim at this stage.

9 To suspend the tassel, double the 30cm/12in length of ribbon and thread it on to the needle. Insert the needle down through the hole in the ball. Remove the needle, knot the ends neatly together and trim. Gently pull the loop taut, hiding the knot among the ribbons. Trim the ribbon ends to an even length.

Shiny Tin Decorations

These attractive folk art designs are easy to make using soft aluminium foil.

MATERIALS

soft pencil
tracing paper
thin card (cardboard)
scissors
36-gauge (0.005in)
aluminium foil
sharp pencil
embroidery scissors
marker pen
ruler
dressmaker's wheel
dried-out ballpoint pen
small block of wood
bradawl (awl)
fine wire

1 Trace the templates at the back of the book, enlarging them on a photocopier if you wish. Transfer them on to thin card (cardboard) and cut out. Cut a small piece of aluminium foil. Place the template on the foil and draw around the outside using a sharp pencil.

2 Using embroidery scissors, cut out the foil shape. Cut slowly and carefully to ensure that there are no rough edges around the decoration.

3 Following the picture as a guide, carefully mark the basic lines of the design on the back of the decoration using a marker pen and ruler.

4 Place the decoration face down on a sheet of thin card. Trace over the pen lines with a dressmaker's wheel to emboss a row of raised dots on the front of the decoration. Trace a second line of dots inside the first, in the centre.

5 Using the picture as a guide, draw all of the fine details on to the back of the decoration using a dried-out ballpoint pen.

6 Place the decoration face up on a small block of wood. Using a bradawl (awl), make a hole in the top. Tie fine wire through the hole for hanging.

CRAFT TIP

There are many traditional folk art motifs that could be used to continue the set of decorations, such as hearts, birds and flowers. The finished decorations can be polished with a soft cloth after embossing to brighten the metal.

PRETTY PURSES

Ribbons are available in a great range of fabrics, widths and colours, and you need

only a small amount to make these delicate little decorations.

MATERIALS

scissors
silk, satin and organza (organdy) ribbons
dressmaker's pins
matching sewing thread
needle
sewing machine (optional)
fine gold cord
polyester wadding (batting)

1 For each purse, cut enough ribbon to make a pleasing purse shape when folded in two, short sides together, allowing for the raw edges to be folded down at the top. To make a striped purse, pin and stitch three narrower lengths together, using running stitch.

2 Wrong sides together, sew up the sides of the purse by hand, or using a sewing machine if you prefer.

3 Turn the purse right side out and tuck the raw edges inside. Stitch on a loop of fine gold cord for hanging. Stuff lightly with polyester wadding (batting).

4 Gather the top of the purse together and tie with another piece of ribbon, finishing with a pretty bow.

Victorian Boot

Make this enchanting period decoration in the richest fabrics you can find.

Materials

pencil
tracing paper
thin card (cardboard)
stapler
scissors
fabric glue and brush
scraps of fabric (eg silk, satin, taffeta)
thin gold cord

3 Cut out each boot, leaving an extra allowance of barely 1cm/½in. Snip the excess fabric around all the curves and stick down firmly to the back of the card.

4 Glue a loop of cord to the back of one card for hanging. Glue the two sides of the boot together and leave to dry thoroughly.

1 Trace the template at the back of the book and transfer it on to thin card (cardboard). Fold the card in two and staple the layers together at the edges so that you can cut out two exactly matching templates.

2 Separate the templates. Turn one over and glue each on to different pieces of fabric.

Glitter Keys

Transform everyday objects into fantasy tree decorations.

MATERIALS

old keys in various shapes and sizes
PVA (white) glue
old paintbrush
sheets of scrap paper
coloured glitter
fine gold cord

1 Using an old paintbrush, cover one side of a key with a coat of undiluted PVA (white) glue.

2 Lay the key on a sheet of scrap paper and sprinkle generously with glitter. Repeat with the other keys, using a separate sheet of paper for each one. Allow to dry completely.

3 Remove the keys. Pinch the paper to make a groove for the spare glitter to run into, then pour it back into the container. Glue the remaining uncovered areas of the keys and repeat the process. Add further layers of glitter to build up quite a thick coating. Tie a loop of gold cord to each key for hanging.

CRAFT TIP

PVA (white) glue dries to a transparent glaze, so you can brush it on over glitter you have already applied.

JEWELLED KEYS

Gold paint and fake gems turn a bunch of old keys into something fit to unlock

a fairy-tale castle or treasure chest.

MATERIALS

old keys in assorted shapes and sizes
newspaper
gold spray paint
gold braid
hot glue gun
flat-backed fake gems in
assorted colours

3 Cover the ends of the gold braid by gluing fake gems over them. Arrange two or three more jewels on the key and glue them on. Allow all the finished keys to dry thoroughly before hanging them on the Christmas tree.

1 Make sure the keys are free of rust. Working with one side at a time and over newspaper, spray each key with gold paint and allow to dry.

2 Cut the gold braid to a suitable length for hanging the key. Fold in half and attach the ends to the key with a hot glue gun.

CARNIVAL MASK

This stunning decoration is inspired by the traditional costume of the masked Harlequin.

MATERIALS

soft pencil
tracing paper
thin white card (cardboard)
scissors
ruler
metallic crayons in gold and lilac
glitter paint
PVA (white) glue and brush
glitter
foil candy wrappers
gold sequins
gold doily
matt gold paper
glue stick
fine gold cord
gold button

1 Trace the template from the back of the book and transfer it to thin white card (cardboard). Cut out the mask shape and two holes for the eyes. Use a soft pencil and ruler to draw in the diagonal lines where the diamonds will be be painted.

2 Decorate the diamonds in different colours and textures. Use metallic crayons and glitter paint on some, and add PVA (white) glue and glitter on to others. When dry, coat with more glue to fix the glitter. Glue diamonds from candy wrappers to cover any edges.

3 Trim the eye holes with rows of gold sequins and the edging cut from a doily.

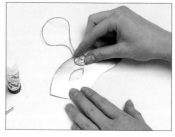

4 Use the template to cut a second mask shape from matt gold paper. Glue to the back of the mask with a glue stick. Attach a loop of gold cord for hanging, covering the ends with a button.

Lacy Silver Gloves

Dainty Victorian ladies' gloves make a pretty motif for a glittering tree ornament.

MATERIALS

tracing paper
heavy-gauge aluminium foil
masking tape
dried-out ballpoint pen
scissors
artist's paintbrush
oil-based glass paints
fine gold cord

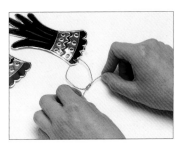

3 Paint the design with glass paints, keeping the colours within the embossed outlines. Allow to dry completely for at least 24 hours.

4 Thread a loop of thin gold cord through the hole for hanging. The completed gloves can be hung from the Christmas tree or mantelpiece.

1 Trace the template from the back of the book. Attach the tracing to a piece of foil with masking tape. Draw over the design to transfer it to the foil. Remove the tracing and complete the embossing with a dried-out ballpoint pen.

2 Cut out the glove, leaving a narrow border all around the edge; don't cut into the embossed outline. Make a hole in one corner of the glove with the point of the scissors.

Sumptuous Rosettes

These flower-like ornaments can be hung on the tree or used to decorate a gift for someone special.

MATERIALS

*pencil
paper for template
scissors
small pieces of silk, gold lamé or
dressweight velvet
dressmaker's pins
scissors
matching sewing thread
needle
fine gold cord
hot glue gun or strong glue
ornate buttons*

1 Draw and cut out a circular template about 12cm/4½in in diameter. Pin it to a single layer of fabric and cut out (there is no need for a seam allowance).

2 Using double thread, sew in running stitch all around the circle 5mm/¼in from the edge. Pull the thread taut to form a rosette and fasten off the ends.

3 Thread a loop of fine gold cord through the top of the rosette for hanging the decoration.

4 Using a hot glue gun, attach a button in the centre of the rosette to cover the raw edges. Alternatively, use strong glue.

ℰXOTIC 𝒪RNAMENTS

These sequinned and beaded balls look like priceless Fabergé treasures, yet they're simple and fun to make.

MATERIALS

scissors
paper
dressmaker's pins
gold netting
silk-covered polystyrene (plastic foam) balls
double-sided adhesive (cellophane) tape
gold braid
sequins in a variety of shapes and colours
small glass and pearl beads
1cm/½in long brass-headed pins
narrow ribbon

3 For an alternative design, cut lengths of gold braid and pin around the ball to make a framework for the rows of sequins.

> **❦ CRAFT TIP ❦**
>
> *When you are working out your designs, use simple repeating patterns and avoid having too many colours on the same ball.*

4 Attach a loop of gold thread to the ball with a brass-headed pin. Thread a bead and sequin on to a brass-headed pin and gently press into the ball. Repeat until your chosen design is complete. Thread ribbon through the loops for hanging on the Christmas tree.

1 Cut a circle of paper to completely cover the ball. Pin it to a piece of gold netting and cut out.

2 Remove the paper and attach the gold netting to the ball using tiny pieces of double-sided adhesive (cellophane) tape. The tape and raw edges will be hidden later by the sequins.

COUNTRY ANGEL

This endearing character is bound to be a friend for many Christmases to come.

MATERIALS

40 x 24cm/16 x 10in natural calico
40 x 26cm/16 x 10¼in small-scale
gingham
30 x 22cm/12 x 9in blue-and-white
ticking
tea
pencil
paper for templates
scissors
fabric marker pen
sewing machine
matching sewing threads
polyester wadding (batting)
twigs
secateurs (pruning shears)
fine permanent (magic) marker
stranded embroidery thread (floss)
in brown
sewing needle
scrap of red woollen fabric
garden twine
fabric stiffener (starch)
copper wire
all-purpose glue

1 Begin by washing all the fabrics. While they are still damp, soak them in tea. Don't worry if the colouring is uneven as this adds to their rustic appearance. Trace the patterns for the head, dress and wings from the back of the book. Cut the head and torso out of doubled calico, leaving a 1cm/½in seam allowance.

2 Right sides together, machine stitch the two body pieces leaving the lower edge open. Clip the curves and turn to the right side. Stuff softly with polyester wadding (batting). Cut two twigs about 20cm/8in long and stick them into the body to make the legs. Sew up the opening, securing the legs as you go.

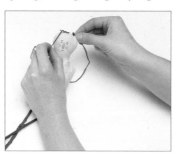

3 With a fine permanent (magic) marker, draw the eyes, nose and mouth on to the face. Make heavy French knots with brown embroidery thread (floss) around the top of the face for the hair.

❦ CRAFT TIP ❦

To make a French knot, make a stitch, and with the needle still in the fabric, pick up the thread and wrap it three times around the needle. Pull the needle out through the threads, then secure the stitch by pulling the needle back through the fabric.

4 Use the paper pattern to cut out the dress from the gingham fabric. Sew up the sides, leaving the sleeves and hem with raw edges. Cut a slit in the top for the neck and turn the dress to the right side. Cut a small heart from the red woollen fabric and attach to the dress with a single cross stitch in brown embroidery thread (floss). Put the dress on the angel, then place short twigs inside the sleeves, securing them tightly at the wrists with garden twine. The twigs should be short enough to let the arms bend forwards.

5 Cut the wings out of the ticking and fray the raw edges slightly. Apply fabric stiffener (starch) liberally to the wings to soak them thoroughly. Lay them completely flat to dry.

6 Make a halo from copper wire, leaving a long end to glue to the wings. Stitch the wings securely to the back of the body through the dress.

NATURAL RAFFIA

For a natural Christmas tree, hang up these little balls covered in creamy undyed raffia.

MATERIALS

scissors
fine copper wire
small polystyrene (plastic foam) balls
double-sided adhesive
(cellophane) tape
natural (garden) raffia

CRAFT TIP

Use coloured raffia such as red or green for a quite different effect.

1 Cut a short piece of wire and bend it into a loop. Push the ends into a polystyrene (plastic foam) ball.

2 Cover the ball in double-sided adhesive (cellophane) tape, making sure there are no gaps.

3 Arrange the hank of raffia so that you can remove lengths without tangling them. Holding the first 10cm/4in of the strand at the top of the ball, wind the raffia around the ball from top to bottom

4 When you have finished covering the ball, tie the end of the raffia to the 10cm/4in length you left free at the beginning. Using a few lengths of raffia together, form a loop for hanging and finish with a loose, floppy bow.

Twiggy Stars

These pretty stars would look equally effective hanging on the tree or in a window.

MATERIALS

willow twigs
secateurs (pruning shears)
stranded embroidery thread (floss)
scissors
check cotton fabric
natural (garden) raffia

3 Using a sharp pair of scissors, cut the check cotton fabric into strips measuring approximately 15 x 2cm/ 6 x ¾in.

4 Tie a fabric strip in a double knot over the thread securing each point of the star. Attach a loop of raffia to one point to hang the decoration.

1 Cut the twigs into lengths of 15cm/ 6in using the secateurs (pruning shears). You will need five for each star.

2 Tie the first pair of twigs together near the ends with a length of embroidery thread (floss), winding it around and between to form a "V" shape. Repeat with the remaining twigs, arranging them under and over each other as shown to form a five-pointed star.

❀ CRAFT TIP ❀

Any straight twigs would be suitable for this project. Collect them on a winter walk.

Tiny Knitted Sock

This would be a charming addition to the tree, and especially appropriate for a baby's first Christmas.

ABBREVIATIONS

K: knit
P: purl
st: stitch
Sl: slip st from one needle to the other
psso: pass the slipped stitch
over the one just worked
K2 tog: pick up two stitches and
knot them together

MATERIALS

4-ply knitting yarn in off-white
set of four double-ended knitting needles
in a size suitable for your yarn
polyester wadding (batting)
large-eyed sewing needle

1 Cast on 36 stitches, 12 stitches on each of three needles.

2 Work rib of K2, P2 for 2.5cm/1in.

3 Work a further 5.5cm/2¼in in stocking stitch. Shape the heel: knot 10 rows in stocking stitch on one set of 12 sts only. Continuing on these 12 stitches only, K3, Sl1, K1, psso, K2, K2 tog, K3, turn and P back. Next row: K2, Sl1, K1, psso, K2, K2 tog, K2, turn and P back. Next row: K1, Sl1, K1, psso, K2, K2 tog, K1. Turn and P back. Next bow: K1, Sl1, K1, psso, K2 tog, K1. This leaves 4 stitches on the needle.

4 Turn the heel. Pick up 10 stitches along each side of the heel and arrange 16 stitches on each needle, with one division at the centre of the heel just worked: this will be the beginning of the round. Now work around the whole sock in continuous rows. 1st round: K13, K2 tog, K1; K1, Sl1, K1, psso, K10, K2 tog, K1; K1, Sl1, K1, psso, K13. 2nd round: K12, K2 tog, K1; K1, Sl1, K1, psso, K8, K2 tog, K1; K1, Sl1, K1, psso, K12. 3rd round: K11, K2 tog, K1; K1, Sl1, K1, psso, K6, K2 tog, K1; K1, Sl1, K1, psso, K11. 4th round: K10, K2 tog, K1; K10; K1, Sl1, K1, psso, K10.

5 Work 22 plain rounds in K for the foot.

6 Shape the toe: 1st round: K1, Sl1, K1, psso, K6, K2 tog, K1 (12 sts); K1, Sl1, K1, psso, K4, K2 tog, K1 (10 sts); K1, Sl1, K1, psso, K6, K2 tog, K1 (12 sts). 2nd round: K1, Sl1, K1, psso, K4, K2 tog, K1 (10 sts); K1, Sl1, K1, psso, K2, K2 tog, K1 (8 sts); K1, Sl1, K1, psso, K4, K2 tog, K1 (10 sts). 3rd round: K1, Sl1, K1, psso, K2, K2 tog, K1 (8 sts); K1, Sl1, K1, psso, K2, K2 tog, K1 (8 sts); K1, Sl1, K1, psso, K2, K2 tog, K1 (8 sts). 4th round: K1, Sl1, K1, psso, K1, K2 tog, K1 (7 sts); K1, Sl1, K1, psso, K2 tog, K1 (7 sts); K1, Sl1, K1, psso, K1, K2 tog, K1 (7 sts).

7 Break off the wool, thread all the remaining stitches on it, draw up and fasten securely. Press gently using steam and pad lightly with polyester wadding (batting). Make a loop at the top of the sock for hanging, using the cast-on end and a large-eyed needle.

CRAFT TIP

Instead of wadding (batting), wrap a tiny present to peep out of the top of the stock.

PEARLY HOUSE AND HEART

Buttons make lovely tree decorations, especially real mother-of-pearl buttons.

MATERIALS

*pencil
paper for templates
scissors
plain corrugated card (cardboard)
masking tape
craft knife
cutting mat
garden twine
hot glue gun
small buttons, in different
shapes and sizes*

1 Draw simple paper templates for the house and heart, cut them out and secure them to the corrugated cardboard with masking tape. Draw around the templates.

2 Cut out the cardboard shapes using a craft knife and cutting mat. Cut a short length of garden twine and glue it in a loop at the top, using a glue gun.

3 Arrange the buttons all over the cardboard shapes, covering them completely. Choose different sizes to fit neatly together. When you are happy with your arrangement, attach the buttons individually with the glue gun.

4 On the back of each decoration, conceal the ends of the twine by gluing a button over them.

WOOLLY HEART

A plump, soft heart edged in blanket stitch is an original addition to a rustic tree.

MATERIALS

pencil
paper for template
scissors
scraps of two co-ordinating
woollen fabrics
polyester wadding (batting)
dressmaker's pins
contrasting stranded
embroidery thread (floss)
needle
garden twine

3 Pin all the layers together, sandwiching the wadding between the fabric hearts. Make a loop of twine for hanging the ornament and insert the ends in the top.

4 Stitch all around the edges in blanket stitch, using three strands of embroidery thread. Make sure the twine loop is secured as you stitch across the top.

1 Draw a heart shape on paper, 7.5cm/3in wide and use it to cut out two hearts, one from each fabric. Cut two small strips for the appliqué cross. Use the template again to cut out a piece of wadding (batting), then trim off about 1cm/½in all around the edge

2 Pin the cross pieces on to the contrasting fabric and attach with large oversewing stitches, using three strands of embroidery thread (floss).

Christmas Cards & Wrapping

*M*aking your own cards and gift-wrap is an absorbing
project for all members of the family on the evenings leading up
to Christmas. Handmade cards are far more personal than any
bought card could ever be, and are often kept and treasured.

Creating wrapping paper is just as fun and often quite
inexpensive. Several identical sheets of gift-wrap can be produced
by repeat methods such as stencilling, stamping or sponging, or
you can create an impressive one-off design for a special present.

Show off your creativity by placing gifts wrapped in Antique
Manuscript Gift-wrap or Bold Stripes under the Christmas tree.

STENCILLED TREE CARDS

This is made from a simple stencil and painted in three seasonal colours – green, red and gold.

MATERIALS

scissors
plain card (cardboard)
pencil
craft knife
cutting mat
sponge
poster paints in green and red
artist's paintbrush
gold paint

1 Cut plain card (cardboard) to make the Christmas card blanks. Fold the cards in half along the long sides. Draw a tree outline on a small piece of card. Cut out the shape with a craft knife, using a cutting mat.

2 Dampen a sponge and dip it into green paint. Place the stencil on the front of the card blank and dab on the green paint. It is more effective if the paint is not applied too evenly. Colour the rest of the cards and leave to dry.

3 Using a paintbrush and red paint, fill in the outline for the tree trunk and pot, and paint shapes to represent bells hanging on the tree branches. Wash the brush and paint gold stars on the tree shape and a crescent moon above it.

CUT-OUT MANGER CARD

This cut-out card is quite simple to make and looks very effective when folded.

Use a silver felt-tipped pen to create a sky full of stars.

MATERIALS

craft knife
cutting mat
stiff card
(cardboard)
ruler
pencil
tracing paper
silver felt-tipped pen

1 Using a craft knife and cutting mat, cut card (cardboard) blanks to measure 19 x 13.5cm/7½ x 5¼in. Measure the centre along the two long edges and draw a thin pencil line from top to bottom. Measure the centre of both the lefthand and righthand sections and draw thin vertical lines. The card will now be marked into four equal sections. Trace the outline of the cut-out section from the template at the back of the book. Place the tracing in the centre section of the card, with the base of the tracing 4.5cm/1¾in from the base of the card. Draw over the traced outline on to the card.

2 Using the craft knife, cut around the imprinted outlines on the card. As the shapes are cut out, the outline of the Holy Family and the manger will appear. Measure and mark a point on the centre line 4cm/1½in above the top of the cut-out. This will form the roof of the manger. Draw a thin pencil line from this point to the top of the cut-out section on each side.

3 To complete the card, fold the two outside edges inwards to the centre. Fold along the centre line in the opposite direction. The card will now fold into a long narrow strip. Fold the two diagonal lines marking the stable roof outwards and the centre line between them inwards. Draw stars and write the word "Peace" in silver felt-tipped pen on the front of the card.

❋ CRAFT TIP ❋

Children can help by tracing the template outline on the card blanks, but the design itself should be cut out by adults or older children. Always use a cutting mat to protect your work surface from the sharp blade of the craft knife.

GOLDEN PLACE CARDS

Touches of gold turn small cards available from stationers into seasonal place cards.

MATERIALS

small, round-cornered cards
ruler
craft knife
cutting mat
gold (magic) marker pen
stick-on "jewels" (optional)
stems of foliage
gold paint
small artist's paintbrush
all-purpose glue
paper ribbon (optional)

1 Score across the midway point of each card using a ruler and craft knife. Fold the card at this point. Write the guest's name on the front in gold, and add a stick-on "jewel" if you like.

2 Choose the best stems of foliage and, using gold paint and a small artist's paintbrush, paint the leaves evenly. Glue the finished gilded leaves on to the side of each card.

3 The simplest cards can enhance a table setting. Here, a white card is decorated with a twirl of paper ribbon, lightly glued in position.

CLOTHES LINE CARD HOLDER

If your mantelpieces and shelves are filled with beautiful decorations, this is

an attractive way to display your Christmas cards.

MATERIALS

wooden clothes pegs (pins)
gouache paints in bright colours
jam jar
artist's paintbrush
thick cotton twine
scissors

1 Separate the halves of each clothes peg (pin) by removing the spring.

2 Paint the clothes pegs with gouache paint in an assortment of bright colours. Allow the pegs to dry, then reassemble them with their springs.

3 Paint the cotton twine in a bright colour. Allow to dry. Attach the pegs to the twine at regular intervals, or according to the sizes of cards you are hanging. Leave a good length at each end of the twine for tying.

EDIBLE LABELS

These cookie labels are good enough to eat!

MATERIALS

*ready-mixed cookie dough
rolling pin
board
pastry (cookie) cutters
skewer
ready-mixed icing
narrow ribbon*

❧ CRAFT TIP ❧

Remember to make a hole in each cookie before you bake it, so that you can thread a ribbon through and attach the label to your gift.

1 Roll out the dough to 1cm/½in thick and cut out the cookies using different-shaped cutters. Make holes for the ribbon, using a skewer. Bake in the oven at 180°C/350°F/Gas 4 for 10–12 minutes. Transfer to a wire rack to cool.

2 Decorate the cookies by piping on ready-mixed icing.

3 Thread a piece of ribbon through the hole in each cookie label.

4 Tie ribbon around the gift and secure the edible label so that it lies flat on top of the parcel.

EMBOSSED CARDS

This subtle technique looks very expensive but in fact is very easy to do.

MATERIALS

ready-made stencil
thick coloured paper
embossing tool
scissors
PVA (white) glue
card (cardboard) in
contrasting colour
small envelopes, to fit the
finished cards
hole punch
narrow ribbon

2 Using an embossing tool, begin rubbing the paper gently over the cut-out area to define the shape. Increase the pressure until the shape shows up as a clear indentation. Turn the paper over to reveal the embossed shape.

3 Trim the paper to shape and stick it on to a contrasting card (cardboard) background using PVA (white) glue. Pair it up with an envelope or punch a hole in it, thread with ribbon and use it as a gift tag.

1 Place the stencil on a flat work surface and cover it with the thick coloured paper.

❄ CRAFT TIP ❄

Experiment with different papers, they all give different results. Remember that if the paper is too thin it will tear easily.

CHRISTMAS TREE GIFT TAGS

Mix different stencil motifs and papers to create these stylish labels.

MATERIALS

craft knife
metal ruler
cutting mat
thin card (cardboard) in
various colours
pencil
paper for template
cellulose kitchen sponge
scissors
corrugated cardboard
glue stick
stencil card (cardboard)
stencil paint in gold and black
white cartridge (heavy) paper
artist's paintbrush
watercolour inks
white oil-crayon
brown parcel wrap
(packaging paper)
hole punch
fine gold cord

2 Draw a triangular Christmas tree on to paper to make a template. Draw around this on a rectangle of kitchen sponge and cut out carefully with scissors, so that you have a positive and negative image to use as stamps. Mount each stamp on a piece of cardboard with a glue stick. Stamp both motifs in gold on to a selection of papers in different textures and colours.

5 Use a white oil-crayon to scribble spots on brown parcel wrap (packaging paper) to represent snowflakes. Tear them out individually, leaving a border of brown paper around each one.

6 Cut or tear out various motifs and arrange them on the gift tags. Attach with the glue stick. Punch a hole in the top and thread each tag with a loop of fine gold cord.

1 Using a craft knife and a metal ruler, cut out gift tags from thin card (cardboard) in various colours.

· CRAFT TIP ·

Experiment with delicate papers such as tracing paper as well as heavier papers.

3 Draw a stylized branch pattern and transfer it to a piece of stencil card (cardboard). Cut out using a craft knife and stencil in black and gold on to a selection of papers and also on to some of the stamped tree motifs.

4 Paint plain white cartridge (heavy) paper with watercolour inks in bright colours, then cut out a simple star motif.

CRAYON GIFT-WRAP

Transform humble parcel wrap (packaging paper) into stylish and original wrapping paper.

MATERIALS

brown parcel wrap (packaging paper)
masking tape
gold paint
old plate
sponge roller
oil pastel crayons in black,
white and other colours
gold oil crayon

⟡ CRAFT TIP ⟡

The oil pastel crayons may
take 24 hours, or even longer,
to dry completely.

1 Secure the brown parcel wrap (packaging paper) with masking tape. Spread gold paint on an old plate. Using a sponge roller, apply the paint in wide gold lines up the sheet. Leave to dry completely.

2 Add coloured or black and white stripes to the gold, using oil pastel crayons. Leave the paper to dry thoroughly before using.

3 For an alternative look, draw vertical stripes down a piece of brown parcel wrap with a chunky gold oil crayon. Experiment with different groupings and spacings for the stripes.

ANTIQUE MANUSCRIPT GIFT-WRAP

Ancient and modern combine to make this unusual wrapping paper.

MATERIALS

piece of old manuscript
plain paper
saucers
*watercolour paints in yellow
ochre and pink*
artist's paintbrush
adhesive (cellophane) tape
scissors
ribbon

1 Photocopy a section of your chosen manuscript on to plain paper. Enlarge the copy by 200%, then make a copy of it on to larger paper.

2 Use diluted watercolour paint to tint the paper with streaks of yellow ochre and pink, giving it an antique effect. Leave to dry.

3 To wrap a round box, place it in the middle of the paper and begin pulling up the edges, sticking each section down with tape as you go. Cut a paper disc slightly smaller than the box top, and glue this on top to cover the edges.

4 Cut three equal lengths of ribbon and tie in simple knots on top of the box. Trim the ends of the ribbon to the same length.

BOLD STRIPES

Often the most stylishly wrapped presents are relatively plain, but create a dramatic effect.

MATERIALS

*brown parcel wrap (packaging paper)
ruler
7.5cm/3in decorator's rollers and tray (or
small sponge brush, for smaller stripes)
emulsion (latex) paint in
dark green and white
scissors
double-sided adhesive (cellophane) tape
broad red moiré satin ribbon
florist's wire*

3 Using the gift as a measuring guide, trim off any excess paper. Wrap the gift, securing the edges invisibly with double-sided tape.

5 Make a bow by looping the ribbon over three times on each side. Secure the loops together by winding florist's wire around the ribbon.

1 Lay some parcel wrap (packaging paper) on scrap paper. Use a roller to paint a white stripe, just in from the edge. Allow a roller's width plus 2cm/¾in, then paint the next stripe. Repeat and leave to dry.

4 Cut a long length of ribbon, taking it around the parcel, crossing it underneath and tying it at the centre point on the top.

6 Attach the bow to the parcel with an extra piece of ribbon tied around the wire to conceal it.

2 Using a fresh roller, paint the dark green stripe about 1.5cm/⅝in away from the first white stripe, so that a small stripe of brown shows through. Repeat three times to complete the striped paper, and leave to dry.

❦ CRAFT TIP ❦

You can use a small decorating roller or cut a sponge roller in half to make a narrower stripe, if your gift is not large enough to show off the broad stripes.

TREE COLLAGE GIFT-WRAP

Simple stencilled, stamped and torn motifs are combined in this richly

textured paper and matching labels.

MATERIALS

artist's paintbrush
foreign-language newspaper
watercolour inks in
bright colours
pencil
paper for template
stencil card (cardboard)
craft knife
cutting mat
white cartridge (heavy) paper
stencil brush
stencil paint in gold and black
scissors
cellulose kitchen sponge
all-purpose glue
corrugated cardboard
gold gift-wrap
glue stick

2 Draw a simple branch shape on paper to make the template. Transfer it to stencil card (cardboard) and cut out, using a craft knife and cutting mat. Paint pieces of white cartridge (heavy) paper, using different colours of watercolour inks. Using a stencil brush and gold or black stencil paint, stencil a branch motif on top of each piece of painted paper.

4 Tear strips, rectangles and simple tree shapes from the rest of the coloured newspaper. Tear around some of the stamped and stencilled motifs, and cut others out with scissors to give different textures.

1 Using an artist's paintbrush, paint sections of the newspaper with watercolour paints.

CRAFT TIP

Look on a newspaper stand for interesting foreign scripts to incorporate in your collage. Use coloured card (cardboard) instead of the white cartridge (heavy) paper if you wish.

3 Cut a triangular Christmas tree shape out of kitchen sponge and glue to a piece of corrugated cardboard, using all-purpose glue. Using gold stencil paint, stamp some of the coloured newspaper with gold trees.

5 Arrange all the tree motifs on the gold gift-wrap to make an interesting design. Secure the motifs in place with a glue stick.

$\mathcal{S}$PONGE-PATTERNED $\mathcal{P}$APER

Sponging is one of the most instantly effective ways of changing plain white paper into gorgeous gift-wrap.

MATERIALS

saucers for the paint
acrylic paints in Indian red,
gold, cobalt blue, viridian green
sponge (synthetic or
natural)
kitchen (paper) towel
plain white paper
scissors
double-sided adhesive (cellophane) tape
broad satin ribbon

1 Fill a saucer with diluted Indian red paint. Dampen the sponge, squeeze it out, then dip it into the paint. Print first on to kitchen (paper) towel then, beginning in one corner, lightly press the sponge on to the paper. Turn the sponge in your hand and make another print. Recharge the sponge with paint as necessary.

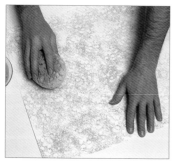

2 Leave the first printing to dry and wash the red out of the sponge. Fill a saucer with gold paint, dilute it, then overprint the Indian red. The effect should be like soft marbling. Try not to overdo the sponging; the gold will shine through the red paint as it dries, and catch the light.

3 As a variation, use cobalt blue paint for the first print. Once again, use a light touch and rotate the sponge each time you print.

4 Leave the paper to dry, wash out the sponge, then print over the blue with viridian green. The colour is denser than the red and gold. Experiment with different colours and try sponging on to coloured papers; each printing will be different.

5 Leave the paper until it is bone dry, then use it to wrap your present. Measure accurately to avoid bulky overlaps and use double-sided adhesive (cellophane) tape to secure the edges together invisibly.

6 Because the pattern on this paper is so subtle, you can afford to use a very bold colour of ribbon. Make a gift tag to match, using a square of ribbon glued diagonally on to a folded piece of sponged paper.

MARBLED PAPER

Florentine marbled paper is the best in the world, so use expensive paper like this

to wrap small boxes or books.

MATERIALS

sheet of marbled paper
scissors
double-sided adhesive (cellophane) tape
narrow black satin ribbon

1 This is very precious paper, so measure accurately to avoid waste. You will need a 2.5cm/1in overlap on the top, and the side flaps should measure two-thirds the height of the box or book.

2 Tuck one edge under the other and use double-sided adhesive (cellophane) tape along the edge nearest you, peeling off the backing and pulling the paper taut before pressing one edge down on to the slight overlap.

3 Fold down the top flap, smooth around the side flaps and sharpen their edges between finger and thumbnail. Place a small piece of double-sided adhesive (cellophane) tape at the apex of the bottom flap, then fold it up and press it into the side.

4 Tie a narrow black ribbon in a simple bow for the perfect, understated way to show off this exquisite paper. Bows and decorations should be kept simple so as not to detract from the impact of the beautiful paper.

Stamped Gold Stars

There is something sumptuous about red tissue paper, stamped here with large gold stars.

MATERIALS

red tissue paper
scrap paper
star rubber stamp
gold ink
saucer
adhesive (cellophane) tape
scissors
gold ribbon

3 Trim the gift with a gold ribbon tied on top in a large bow.

4 Cut the ribbon ends at an angle for a professional finish.

1 Lay a sheet of tissue paper on scrap paper. Beginning in one corner, work diagonally across the sheet, stamping stars about 5cm/2in apart. Leave to dry.

2 Wrap the gift using a lining of one or two sheets of plain red tissue paper under the stamped sheet. Use adhesive (cellophane) tape to secure the ends.

CRAFT TIP

Cutting the ribbon ends at an angle looks smart and also prevents the ribbon from fraying.

Naturally Simple

A subtle blend of understated decorations creates a stylish modern look.

MATERIALS

scissors
brown parcel wrap (packaging paper)
double-sided adhesive (cellophane) tape
pencil
tracing paper
dark blue and orange tissue paper
white chalk
PVA (white) glue
thick coarse string
scissors
selection of dried fir cones and seed pods
hot glue gun

1 Using the item to be wrapped as a measuring guide, cut out the parcel wrap (packaging paper) to size.

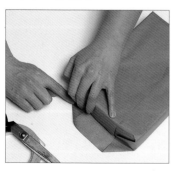

2 Wrap the gift, using double-sided adhesive (cellophane) tape.

3 Draw simple shapes on to tracing paper. Cut them out of blue and orange tissue paper. You will need to use chalk to transfer the shapes on to the darker paper. The number you will need depends upon the size of your gift.

4 Experiment with the positioning of the shapes until you are happy with the arrangement, then apply a thin layer of glue, spread with your finger, directly on to the paper. Quickly smooth the tissue shapes on to the glue.

5 Tie coarse string around the gift, crossing it over underneath and knotting it securely on the top. Untwist the string ends and fluff them out to make a simple tassel, then trim the ends off neatly.

6 Use a glue gun to stick a small arrangement of miniature fir cones and seed pods to the knotting string.

GIANT SNOWFLAKE BOX

This gorgeous gift-wrap is ideal for a large present. Use the stencilled paper on its own for smaller gifts.

MATERIALS

pencil
tracing paper
scissors
stencil card (cardboard)
craft knife
cutting mat
bright blue paper
small sponge
white watercolour paint
adhesive (cellophane) tape
roll of clear, wide cellophane
(plastic wrap)
silver foil ribbon
Christmas decorations

1 Trace the snowflake templates at the back of the book on to tracing paper, then cut them out. Transfer the motifs to stencil card (cardboard) and cut out, using a craft knife and cutting mat.

· CRAFT TIP ·

Stencil paints should always be on the dry side to prevent any from seeping under the stencil.

2 Place scrap paper on your work surface and use a small sponge to apply the white paint. Dip the sponge in a bowl of water, then squeeze it out thoroughly. Apply the snowflakes randomly all over the blue paper and right over the edges. Allow the paint to dry thoroughly.

3 If one sheet of paper is not big enough to cover the box, lay two sheets side by side and run adhesive (cellophane) tape along the join. Repeat with other sheets until you have a single sheet large enough for the box. Wrap up the box, using adhesive tape.

4 Unroll a length of cellophane (plastic wrap) long enough to pass under the box, up the sides and allowing at least 30cm/12in extra on both ends. Do the same in the other direction, to cross over the first sheet under the box.

5 Gather up the cellophane on top of the box, making sure that the sides of the box are completely covered, then tape around the bunch, close to the top of the box.

6 Cover the adhesive tape with silver foil ribbon and attach some decorations for a final Christmas touch.

GOLD ON GOLD

For a really lavish gift, nothing beats all-gold paper, ribbon and decoration.

MATERIALS

box
gold wrapping paper
scissors
double-sided adhesive (cellophane) tape
wide gold ribbon
florist's wire
plastic pear and grapes
antique gold spray paint

1 If your gift is not already boxed, find a box of a suitable size. Using the side of the box as a measuring guide, trim the paper to fit. You need no more than a 7.5cm/3in overlap and the ends of the paper should fold into neat triangles, with no bulky seams.

2 Use double-sided adhesive (cellophane) tape inside the top seam and at the centre points of the ends, to seal the paper invisibly.

3 Cut a long length of gold ribbon and tie it around the box, crossing it over underneath and tying it firmly on the top. Trim off the ends.

4 Make a large bow, securing the loops of ribbon in the centre with a binding of florist's wire. Cover the wire with a double thickness of ribbon, tying it loosely and tucking the ends under the bow. Use the ribbon ends to tie the bow to the box ribbons.

✿ CRAFT TIP ✿

You can spray plastic fruit with antique gold spray paint, or use gilt cream, which is simply rubbed on to the surface and buffed when dry.

5 Spray the plastic pear and grapes with antique gold spray paint. When dry, make an arrangement with the gilded fruit.

6 Attach the fruit to the top of the box by twisting a piece of florist's wire around the ribbon.

PLACE MARKER GIFT BAGS

Arrange your seating plan using these sensational gift bags with embossed copper foil tags.

MATERIALS

*bronze metallic crepe paper
craft knife
metal ruler
cutting mat
double-sided adhesive (cellophane) tape
tracing paper
scissors
heavy-gauge copper foil
dried-out ballpoint pen
hole punch
fine gold cord
small gifts
ribbon*

3 Use double-sided adhesive (cellophane) tape to stick together the sides of the bag and then stick down the bottom edge of the bag.

5 Cut out the numeral with scissors. Use a hole punch to punch a small hole in the top, then thread the hole with fine gold cord.

1 Using a craft knife and metal ruler, cut a rectangle of the metallic crepe paper 45 x 42cm/18 x 16½in.

4 Trace the numerals needed from the back of the book and cut them out. Transfer the design in reverse to the copper foil, embossing it with a dried-out ballpoint pen.

6 Fill the bag with a suitable gift, then close. Tie the ribbon in a bow around the neck of the bag and attach the copper foil tag.

2 Fold over 15cm/6in along one of the long sides, for the top, and 1.5cm/⅝in along the other for the bottom of the bag.

CRAFT TIP

When you're embossing metallic foil, remember that you will be working from the back of the finished design, so always draw the motif on to the foil in reverse.

WRAPPING AND TRIMMING

Not all gifts come in convenient shapes and sizes for wrapping.

WRAPPING A TEDDY BEAR

Successful gift-wrapping should both conceal and enhance your gift, adding mystery and an irresistible temptation to open up and see what is inside. An unusual shape looks great with tissue paper wrapped over cardboard.

1 Decide on a surface that is going to be the base, in this case the teddy is able to sit up. Cut out a regular shape, either square, rectangular or round, from thick cardboard. Cover with a piece of gift-wrap.

2 Place the cardboard in the middle of a large sheet of paper, or cross two lengths over for a larger gift.

3 Pull up the paper from opposite sides and bunch it up on top of the gift. Tissue paper works well for this because it creases in an attractive way. If you are using thicker paper gather and pleat it as you make the bunch.

4 Tie a ribbon or card firmly around the bunch, then arrange the paper into a balanced decorative shape. An ornament hanging down from the ribbon will help to draw attention back down to the gift.

TYING A BASIC BOW

The finishing touches to your wrapped gift are all-important. As well as using paper in a range of colours and textures, enjoy using ribbon, string and decorations to turn something ordinary into something spectacular.

1 Pass the ribbon under the gift so that you have two ends of equal length. Tie the two together on the top.

2 Knot the tied ends so that both your hands are freed for tying the bow.

3 Form two loops and tie together to make a simple bow.

4 Finish off the box by cutting the ribbon ends into swallow tails – fold the ribbon down the middle, then cut from the fold towards the open edges at an angle.

STRING & RIBBON

A combination of coarse, thick string and smooth, silky ribbon can be used to give your gift a highly textured look. For the best effect, use a range of contrasting colours.

TAPED RIBBON

This technique produces a plain look that is very simple and yet highly elegant. Make sure that you use a good-quality ribbon; when finished, this gift needs no extra decoration.

GOLD TASSELS

Tassels like these metallic gold ones are perfect for a rich, opulent look – purple and gold make a classic combination. This style is particularly easy because you don't have to tie a bow.

COLOUR-COORDINATED

Instead of using contrasting colours, try decorating a gift with small decorations of the same colour for a really original touch – any small Christmas decorations of the same colour will look great.

1 Wrap the gift in tissue paper, then wind coarse string around the box at least four times in each direction.

1 Use a broad fancy ribbon on a plain background. Cross the ribbon over on top, then take the ends underneath.

1 Wrap a gift box in several layers of deep purple tissue paper, then surround it with thick gold cord.

1 Wrap the gift in pink tissue paper and tie it with a matching pink spotted ribbon and a bow.

2 Take a short, narrow ribbon and use it to gather all the string together at the centre point. Tie a simple bow in the ribbon, then separate the strands of string out towards opposite edges of the box.

2 Instead of tying the ribbon in a bow or knot, use double-sided adhesive (cellophane) tape to join it and give a taut, flat finish without the need for additional decoration.

2 Tie a double knot and let the tasselled ends fall across the gift as a decoration. Experiment with scarves, curtain tie-backs and even pyjama cords (pajama belts).

2 Thread a Christmas pastry (cookie) cutter on to the ribbon and tie a small bow on the top to secure it. Try other small Christmas tree decorations as well.

Kids' Christmas

*C*hildren love to make their own cards and gifts for
family and friends, and to wrap them in creative ways.
They will also enjoy getting involved in decorating the
Christmas tree and their bedrooms with things they have made
themselves. All of these craft projects are easy to do, using
simple techniques such as potato prints or rope stamps,
although children may need help when using a sharp knife.
Among the most inventive ideas for gifts and cards are the
Snowstorm Shaker, the three-dimensional Spinning Stars Card
and the Glittery Gift Boxes, not forgetting the fabulous Dove
Decoration for the tree. The hardest thing is to keep everything
hidden out of sight until the presents are ready to wrap.

FESTIVE CAT CARD

This charming felt picture would be an ideal gift for a child to make.

MATERIALS

scissors
coloured card (cardboard)
pencil
tracing paper
black felt-tip pen
felt squares in various colours
single hole punch
PVA (white) glue and brush
squeezy paints or felt-tip pens
in various colours
artificial gemstone

1 Cut a rectangle of card (cardboard) and fold in half to make a square greetings card. Trace the templates at the back of the book and cut out. Using a black felt-tip pen, draw around the templates on the reverse side of appropriate colours of felt.

CRAFT TIP

Alternatively, you can frame the cat picture to make a more long-lasting present.

2 Cut out the shapes. Cut the pieces for the background out of felt.

3 To make the snowflakes, pinch small dots from white felt, using a single hole punch.

4 Position all the felt shapes on a background square of felt and glue in place with PVA (white) glue.

5 Using squeeze paints or felt-tip pens, decorate the cat's face to give it eyes, whiskers and a smile. Glue an artificial gemstone on to the cat's collar.

6 Apply a few dabs of glue on the reverse of the fabric picture and glue it firmly in place on to one side of the folded card.

POLKA-DOT PAPER

You will have great fun stamping and printing to make this gift-wrap.

MATERIALS

coloured paper
smaller roller sponge
poster paints in various colours
cork
scissors
scourer pad (sponge)
card (cardboard)
single hole punch
string

CRAFT TIP

This project uses a sponge roller and a cork to print with. Be adventurous and see what else you can use to make a printed shape.

1 Lay the coloured paper on a flat, well-covered surface. Dab the end of the roller sponge in one of the paint colours. Carefully stamp dots on the paper to make a triangle shape for the Christmas tree. You may need to add more paint to the roller between prints.

2 Dab a cork in a different colour of paint and print a line of smaller dots under the tree to make the tree trunk.

3 Cut a scourer pad (sponge) to look like a flowerpot. Dab it in a new colour and print it under the tree trunk.

4 To make a gift tag, dab a scrap piece of scourer pad in paint and print a star shape on card (cardboard). When dry, cut around the shape. Punch a hole in the top of the tag and thread with string.

ROPE-PRINTED PAPER

This spiral design is simple to do but looks very stylish.

MATERIALS

pencil
wooden block
PVA (white) glue and
brush
thin rope
artist's paintbrush
poster paint
scissors
coloured paper
single hole punch
ribbon

3 Make sure you are working on a well-covered surface before you start to paint. Cover the rope generously with paint, then stamp the design on the paper. You will need to re-paint the rope for each print you make.

4 Make a gift tag to go with the paper. Print the design on coloured paper. When the paint is dry, cut around the design and punch a hole in the edge. Pull a length of ribbon through the hole for attaching the tag to a present.

1 Draw a spiral shape on a block of wood, using a pencil so that you can rub out any mistakes. Paint a coat of PVA (white) glue over the spiral shape.

2 Begin laying the rope in place before the glue dries. Starting in the centre of the spiral, carefully wind the rope around, following the spiral design. Hold the rope in place as you work, so that it does not spring off.

CHRISTMAS TREE CARD

Scourer pads (sponges) are usually used in the kitchen, but they can also be cut

into shapes and used to decorate cards.

MATERIALS

*coloured card
(cardboard)
pencil
paper for templates
scissors
scourer pads (sponges) in
various colours
dressmaker's pins
single hole punch
sequins
glitter glue
PVA (white) glue*

CRAFT TIP

*Use the same technique to make a
gift tag with a star motif.*

1 Fold a piece of coloured card (cardboard) in half. Draw a simple Christmas tree shape on paper, then draw a rectangle for the tree trunk and a flowerpot shape for the base. Cut out all three templates. Lay the templates on different coloured scourer pads (sponges) and pin them in place to make them easier to cut out.

2 Carefully cut around the templates, using scissors, then remove the pins.

3 Punch holes out of the flowerpot shape. Punch dots out of a scrap of scourer pad in a contrasting colour to the flowerpot shape. Place the dots in the holes.

4 Decorate the tree with sequins and glitter glue. When the glue has dried, glue the finished tree on to the folded piece of card.

Paper Mosaic Gift Box

This glitzy box is ideal for any presents you find too difficult to wrap in paper.

MATERIALS

scissors
shiny papers in various colours
cardboard box
PVA (white) glue and brush
glitter glue

1 Cut strips of shiny coloured paper, then cut some of the strips into small squares. The bigger your box, the more strips and squares you will need.

2 Glue the paper squares on to the lid of the box, leaving small gaps between them. Continue until you have covered the whole of the box lid.

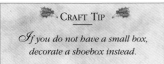

❈ CRAFT TIP ❈

If you do not have a small box, decorate a shoebox instead.

3 Glue the strips of paper all around the sides of the box, leaving a small gap between each strip. Set the lid and the box aside until the glue is completely dry.

4 Carefully apply the glitter glue on the lid of the box where the gaps are. Leave it to dry: it takes quite a long time. If you don't have any glitter glue, use ordinary glitter and glue instead.

POTATO PRINT GIFT-WRAP

A humble potato is an easy way to stamp your own design on to paper.

MATERIALS

pencil
paper for template
card (cardboard)
knife
potato
felt-tip pen
squeeze paints in
various colours
paper towels
sheets of plain wrapping paper
glitter glue

1 Draw a crown shape on paper, cut out and transfer on to card (cardboard). Cut the potato in half. Using a felt-tip pen, draw around the card template on to one cut surface of the potato. Position the template in the centre of the potato.

CRAFT TIP

For this potato print gift-wrap you can use any kind of wrapping paper. This project uses handmade textured paper, but you could also use plain wrapping paper for an equally regal effect.

2 With the help of an adult, cut out the area around the crown shape. It is important that the shape is cut out as neatly as possible, so that the potato gives a nicely shaped print.

3 Squeeze a large dab of paint on to a thick pad of paper towels for dipping the potato into.

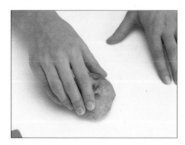

4 Gently dip the potato in the paint. You can add paint directly on to the potato shape if you prefer. Stamp the potato on the wrapping paper to make a print. Slowly remove the potato to reveal the print you have made.

5 Use a paper towel to tidy up the printing area of the potato before you apply more paint on the paper towels or directly on to the potato. Continue printing until you have covered the paper. Let the paint dry completely before decorating the crowns.

6 Add your own decoration to the printed crowns with squeeze paints and leave to dry. For a finishing touch, add a few dabs of glitter glue.

Spinning Stars Card

Make a stunning Christmas card and matching gift tags using this simple three-dimensional design.

MATERIALS

pencil
paper for templates
coloured card (cardboard) in
several colours
scissors
coloured papers in several colours
PVA (white) glue and brush
paper fasteners
single hole punch
narrow ribbon

❧ CRAFT TIP ❧

Save up scraps of coloured paper
to make this groovy stars card.

1 Draw a circle on to paper and cut out. Draw a star to fit inside the circle and cut out. Draw around the star template on to several different colours of card (cardboard) and cut out. Draw around the circle template on to different colours of paper and cut out.

2 Cut a piece of card large enough to fit four circles comfortably and fold it in half. Glue the paper circles on to the front side of the card.

3 With the help of an adult, make a slit in the centre of each star and circle with scissors. Push a paper fastener through the centre of each star, then push it through one of the circles. Open out the fastener so that it sits flat.

4 Make a round or label-shaped gift tag to match the card. Punch a hole at one end of the tag to thread a piece of ribbon through.

Stained Glass Card

Place this lovely card by a window so that the light shines through the tissue paper.

MATERIALS

scissors
black card (cardboard)
pencil
paper for template
white crayon
tissue paper in various colours
PVA (white) glue and brush
glitter glue (optional)

3 Cut out coloured pieces of tissue paper, slightly bigger than the openings in the card. Begin gluing them in place on the inside of the card.

4 Continue gluing the pieces of tissue paper, alternating the colours. Allow the glue to dry. Decorate the design with dabs of glitter glue, if you wish.

1 First make the backing for the greetings card. Cut a square of black card (cardboard), fold firmly in half, then open out. Following the main photograph, draw the Christmas tree design on plain paper and cut out to make templates. Using a white crayon, draw around the templates on the left side of the black card.

2 With the help of an adult, use scissors to cut out the Christmas tree from inside the design.

GOLD STARS

Cover a plain sheet of gift-wrap with stencilled stars, twinkling with shiny dots.

MATERIALS

pen or pencil
paper for template
scissors
stiff card (cardboard)
coloured card (cardboard)
single hole punch
narrow ribbon or string
sponge
gold paint
sheet of plain wrapping paper
shiny papers in various colours
PVA (white) glue and brush

1 Draw a star on paper to make a template and cut out. Draw around the template on to stiff card (cardboard). Carefully cut out the inside of the star shape to make a stencil.

2 To make a star gift tag, draw around the paper template on to coloured card and cut out. Punch a hole in the tip of one of the points of the star and thread with ribbon or string.

3 Dip the sponge in gold paint. Position the stencil on the paper and dab through it with the sponge. Remove the stencil to reveal the print. Re-position the stencil and repeat.

4 When you have covered all the paper with stars, cut or punch dots from the shiny papers. Glue dots on to the stars on both the paper and the tag.

Snowman Card

The lovable seasonal character on this card is made from fluffy cottonwool and paper.

MATERIALS

white cottonwool
coloured card (cardboard)
PVA (white) glue and brush
white paper
scissors
coloured papers
single hole punch

3 Cut out pieces of coloured paper for the snowman's face, hat and scarf. Glue them down, checking that they are in the right position as you go.

4 Punch dots from white paper and glue them on the card around the snowman, to look like gently falling flakes of snow. Leave the glue to dry.

1 Gently mould two pieces of cottonwool into shapes to make the head and body of the snowman. Make sure that you make your snowman nice and fat!

2 Fold a piece of card (cardboard) in half. Glue a piece of white paper on the base at the front of the card, to look like a snowdrift. Glue the snowman's head and body on to the card.

Advent Table Decoration

Glue sweets (candies) on to this terrific decoration and eat one a day in the countdown to Christmas.

MATERIALS

green card (cardboard)
PVA (white) glue and brush
green crepe paper
24 foil-wrapped sweets (candies)
pencil
paper for template
scissors
gold card
green corrugated cardboard
red poster paint
decorator's paintbrush
terracotta flowerpot

3 Glue sweets (candies) on to the tree. Hold them in place until the glue is dry.

5 Cut a rectangle of green corrugated cardboard and roll it up to make a tube. This makes the tree's trunk. Glue along one edge of the tube and hold in place until the glue has dried.

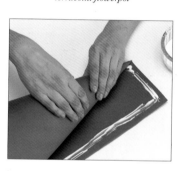

1 Roll a piece of green card (cardboard) into a cone shape, using your hands. Glue along one edge of the card and hold the cone shape in place with your hands until the glue has dried.

4 Draw a star and cut it out to make a template. Draw around the template on gold card and cut it out with scissors. Make a second star in this way. Cut out a strip of card and place it between the stars as shown. Glue the two stars together.

6 Paint a terracotta flowerpot with red paint. When the paint is dry, place the trunk in the pot and balance the tree on top of it. Glue the star on to the top of the tree.

🌿 CRAFT TIP 🌿

Foil-wrapped sweets (candies) are always cheerful and will make your tree look really festive.

2 Tear up plenty of crepe paper and scrunch up. Paint glue on one side and glue all over the cone. Leave until the glue has dried.

FLOWER-STUDDED BAUBLES

Tiny daisy-like flowers look very pretty on the tree.

MATERIALS

scissors
sparkly embroidery thread (floss)
paper baubles
PVA (white) glue and brush
artist's paintbrush
poster paints
sequins
glitter glue

❋ CRAFT TIP ❋

Try decorating these Christmas baubles in different ways. You could use foil sweet (candy) wrappers and artificial gemstones for added sparkle.

1 Cut a length of sparkly thread (floss) and fold it in half to make a loop. Glue the ends of the loop to the top of one of the paper baubles. Hold the thread in place with your hands until the glue has dried. Repeat for each of the paper baubles.

2 Paint the baubles with poster paints. Red, purple and gold paints have been used here but you could use any colours you like. Hang the baubles up by the loops while the paint dries.

3 When the paint has dried, glue a few sequins on to each of the baubles in tiny flower shapes. Allow the glue to dry completely.

4 Using glitter glue, paint little dots between the sequins and in the middle of the sequins. Leave to dry.

CHRISTMAS BUTTONS

Rummage around flea markets to find interesting old buttons for this project.

MATERIALS

felt-tip pen
felt in red and green
scissors
sewing needle
sewing thread in red and green
buttons in red and green
ribbon
PVA (white) glue and brush

3 Turn over one of the circles of felt and glue a folded loop of ribbon to one of the edges.

4 Place one green circle on top of one red circle and join together with glue. Sew around the edge of the circles with running stitch. Repeat for the other circles.

1 Using a felt-tip pen, draw a circle on red and green felt. Cut out the shapes and repeat, so that you have several circles in both colours.

2 Thread a needle with matching sewing thread and sew a selection of green buttons on to the circles of green felt. Sew a selection of red buttons on to the circles of red felt.

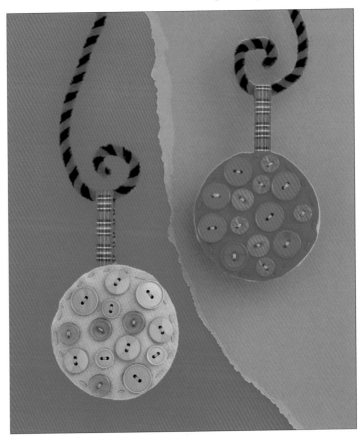

DOVE DECORATIONS

These colourful doves fly on beautifully fanned wings around the Christmas tree.

MATERIALS

pencil
tracing paper
scissors
coloured card (cardboard)
coloured paper
gold (magic) marker pen
single hole punch
narrow ribbon

CRAFT TIP

Enlarge the template on a photocopier to make small and large doves for added interest.

1 Trace the template for the dove's body from the back of the book and cut out. Draw around the template on to coloured card (cardboard). Make a slit in the dove's body for the wings. Cut out the dove shape.

2 Cut out a rectangle of coloured paper and fold it into a fan by turning it over each time you make a fold. This will be the dove's wings.

3 Open out the fan and decorate the edges of the wings with a gold pen. Draw patterns on the dove's body and leave to dry.

4 Fold up the fan and pass it through the slit. Open out the ends so that they meet above the dove. Hold the two sides of the fan together and punch a hole through the paper. Thread ribbon through the hole and tie in a knot to make a hanging loop.

FESTIVE POM-POMS

These unusual decorations are fun to make and children will love to play with them.

MATERIALS

pencil
tracing paper
scissors
thick card (cardboard)
wool (yarn) in various colours

3 Place one blade of a pair of scissors between the two pieces of card and carefully cut around the circle, snipping the wool as you go.

4 Wrap a long strand of wool between the two pieces of card and tie in a knot. Tear off the pieces of card and throw them away. Fluff up the pom-pom and trim loose ends with scissors.

1 Trace the template at the back of the book and cut out. Using the template, draw two circles on card (cardboard) the same size, with one smaller circle in the centre of each. Cut out the circles.

2 Place the two pieces of card together. Knot the end of the wool (yarn) bundle around the card and thread through the hole. Wrap the wool around the whole circle until the centre hole is almost full. Tuck the ends of the wool in, to stop them unravelling.

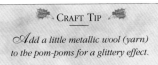

CRAFT TIP

Add a little metallic wool (yarn) to the pom-poms for a glittery effect.

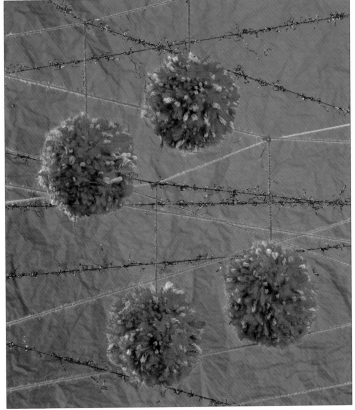

CHRISTMAS ANGEL

This decoration will add a beautiful finishing touch to your Christmas tree.

MATERIALS

thin white card (cardboard)
*double-sided adhesive
(cellophane) tape*
scissors
silver doily
PVA (white) glue and brush
pencil
tracing paper
gold card (cardboard)
small cake candle
paper bauble
artist's paintbrush
poster paints in various colours
yellow wool (yarn)

3 For the angel's wings and halo, draw around the templates on the back of the gold card (cardboard). For the arms and hands, draw around the templates on white card. Pencil in the fingers.

5 Push a pencil into a paper bauble, use an artist's paintbrush to paint the bauble in a skin colour, then leave to dry. Paint the angel's eyes, nose and mouth on the paper bauble.

1 Fold the white card (cardboard) into a cone shape. Stick a strip of double-sided adhesive (cellophane) tape under one of the edges, peel off the backing tape and stick in place.

4 Cut out the body and wing shapes, then glue the angel's arms and wings on to the cone. Allow the glue to dry. Slot a small cake candle between the angel's hands.

6 Cut about 12 strands of yellow wool (yarn) the same length and glue them to the top of the angel's head as hair. Glue the gold halo to the back of the head. Attach the head to the body.

2 Cut a silver doily to fit around the cone shape and glue in place. Leave to dry. Trace the templates at the back of the book and cut out.

🎄 CRAFT TIP 🎄

*This silver angel decoration
doesn't have to go on top of
the Christmas tree. Place it
anywhere special, where
everyone can see her.*

Gift-wrap Advent Calendar

This ingenious design is made out of last year's Christmas cards and a sheet of gift-wrap.

MATERIALS

*sheet of gift-wrap
ruler
pencil
scissors
assorted Christmas cards
PVA (white) glue and brush
number transfers
ribbon
backing card (cardboard), cut to the
same size as the gift-wrap*

3 Cut out pictures from the Christmas cards and glue one picture behind each door. Leave for a few minutes until dry.

5 Using number transfers and a pencil, rub a number between 1 and 24 on the front of each door.

1 Carefully mark 24 doors on the gift-wrap, using a ruler and pencil. Try to choose pretty areas of the gift-wrap for the positions of the doors. You can make the doors different shapes and sizes if you like.

4 Dab a small amount of glue along one edge of each door and close them.

6 Cut a piece of ribbon and fold it in half to make a hanging loop. Glue the ends of the loop behind the top edge of the paper. To finish, glue the backing card (cardboard) to the reverse side of the calendar.

2 Cut out three sides of each door, leaving one side as a hinge so that you can open and shut the door easily.

> ### ❋ CRAFT TIP ❋
>
> *This Advent calendar is a great way to recycle last year's wrapping and cards. Try to use areas of the paper that are not torn or folded.*

METALLIC FOIL DECORATIONS

These dazzling decorations have great folk art appeal and are surprisingly easy to make.

MATERIALS

pencil
paper for templates
scissors
dried-out ballpoint pen
metallic foil in various colours
single hole punch
narrow ribbon or cord

🌿 CRAFT TIP 🌿

Metallic foil is available in sheets from specialist craft shops. It is easy to draw on with an empty ballpoint pen.

1 Draw a heart and a star shape on paper and cut out to make templates. Using a dried-out ballpoint pen, draw around the templates on the back of the metallic foils.

2 Using the ballpoint pen, decorate the hearts and stars with swirly and polka dot patterns on the reverse side of the foil. Try to think of as many interesting shapes and designs as you can.

3 Cut out the decorated shapes with scissors, cutting approximately 3mm/ ⅛in outside the drawn lines.

4 Punch a hole in one point of each star, and in the top of the hearts. Thread a length of ribbon or cord through the hole and tie the ends in a knot for hanging.

Miniature Stockings

Pop a small gift such as a striped candy cane inside these cute decorations

to make them even more appealing.

MATERIALS

pencil or pen
paper for template
scissors
felt in various colours
PVA (white) glue and brush
sewing needle
sewing thread
ribbon
small bell

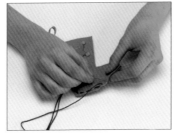

1 Draw a mini stocking shape on paper and cut out to make a template. For each stocking, draw around the template on to two different colours of felt and cut out. Draw stars and dots on contrasting colours of felt.

2 Cut out the stars and dots from the felt and position them on one side of the stocking. When you are happy with the positions, use PVA (white) glue to stick them on to the stocking. Leave to dry completely.

3 Sew the two stocking shapes together, around the edge, using running stitch. Fold a piece of ribbon in half to make a hanging loop and sew into the side.

4 Sew a bell on to the toe of the stocking. Add a scalloped trim to the top of the stocking, using a contrasting colour of felt. Glue in place.

Snowstorm Shaker

Carefully shake the jam jar and watch the glitter snow twinkle!

MATERIALS

*modelling clay in white and
various colours
jam jar with a tight-fitting lid
silver glitter*

1 To make the snowman's head and body, roll two balls of white modelling clay in your hands. Make the ball for the snowman's body slightly bigger than the one for his head. Press the small ball on top of the larger ball.

2 Make the snowman a hat and a scarf out of small pieces of coloured modelling clay. Make him a carrot nose and a happy face.

3 Make sure the jam jar is clean, and has no greasy fingerprints. Fill the inside of the lid with another piece of white clay.

4 Using your fingers, make a shallow hole in the clay on the inside of the lid. Firmly press the snowman into the hole, making sure he feels secure.

--- · CRAFT TIP · ---

Choose a jam jar to suit the size of your snowman. Make a Father Christmas or Christmas tree shaker following the same technique.

5 Pour cold water into the jam jar so that it is three-quarters full. Sprinkle at least 1 tablespoon of the silver glitter into the jar.

6 Carefully screw on the lid, then slowly turn the jar upside down, so that the snowman is the right way up. Add a little more water if needed.

Sunflower Crackers

Colourful sunflowers decorate these unusual tissue paper Christmas crackers.

MATERIALS

small gifts
tissue paper in various colours
toilet-paper tube
pen
small pieces of paper
cracker snaps
PVA (white) glue and brush
pinking shears
paper ribbon
scissors
coloured paper

1 For each cracker, wrap a small gift in tissue paper and place it inside a toilet-paper tube. Write a joke on a piece of paper, roll up the paper and place it inside the tube. Add a cracker snap.

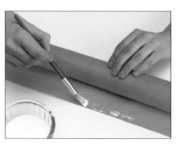

2 Cover the tube with a large sheet of tissue paper and glue the edges together with PVA (white) glue.

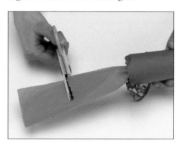

3 Trim both ends of the tissue paper with pinking shears. Glue a contrasting colour of tissue paper around the tube, then tie a long length of paper ribbon around each end. Gently draw the blade of a pair of scissors along the ribbon to make it curl.

4 Using scissors, cut out coloured papers to make a sunflower shape. Glue the sunflower on to the tube section of the cracker.

PARTY PAPER CHAINS

These bright colours and patterns will liven up any room.

MATERIALS

pencil
paper for template
coloured paper
artist's paintbrush
poster paints in various colours
glitter glue
scissors
PVA (white) glue and brush

3 Add a few dabs of glitter glue for extra sparkle. Allow the glitter to dry. Use scissors to cut out the decorated strips of paper.

4 Curl a strip around so that you can glue one end of the strip to the other. Hold it while the glue dries. Thread a second strip of paper through the first loop and glue the ends together. Continue to add the rest of the strips in the same way.

1 Make your own template for the paper chain, as long or as wide as you want. Draw around the template on to a piece of coloured paper so that the strips are next to each other. Don't cut the strips out yet.

2 Paint the strips in bright colours and swirls, stripes and dots. Paint flowers on some of the strips. Allow to dry.

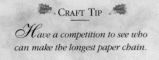

CRAFT TIP

Have a competition to see who can make the longest paper chain.

FELT TREE CALENDAR

This stylized picture is easy to make and a calendar would make an excellent Christmas present.

MATERIALS

pencil
paper for template
felt-tip pen
scissors
PVA (white) glue and brush
felt squares in three shades of green,
brown, red and orange
large piece of felt for the background
mirror-tile sequins
thin card (cardboard)
mini calendar
ribbon

1 Using the picture on the opposite page as a guide, draw separate shapes for each part of the Christmas tree design. Cut out the templates and draw around them on three pieces of green felt, using a felt-tip pen. Cut out the felt shapes.

2 Snip a fringe along the bottom edge of each green section of the tree.

3 Glue all the small felt pieces on to the large piece of background felt to make up the Christmas tree design. Leave to dry.

4 Glue a row of mirror-tile sequins on to each green section of the tree and leave to dry.

CRAFT TIP

If you don't have any mirror tiles, this tree calendar looks great decorated with sparkly sequins or artificial gemstones.

5 Cut a piece of card (cardboard) the same size as the finished picture. Glue it to the back of the background felt and leave to dry.

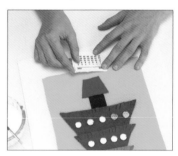

6 Glue a mini calendar to hang below the bottom centre of the picture. Fold a length of ribbon in half and glue to the back of the card at the centre top, to act as a hanging loop.

–	–	–	1	2	3
4	5	6	7	8	9	10
11	12	13	14	15	16	17
18	19	20	21	22	23	24
25	26	27	28	29	30	31

GLITTERY GIFT BOXES

These two spectacular little boxes look very impressive, but are simple to make.

MATERIALS

pencil
small paper bauble
artist's paintbrush
poster paints in brown and black
scissors
felt squares in green and red
PVA (white) glue and brush
2 small cardboard boxes
glitter in various colours
mini pom-pom
small glass beads in various colours

1 Using a pencil, lightly draw the outline of whipped cream on a Christmas pudding (cake) on to a paper bauble.

2 Paint the base of the pudding brown and allow the paint to dry. Paint small black raisins on the brown paint to make your pudding look tasty!

3 Use scissors to cut out two mini holly leaves from green felt, then cut two small circles of red felt for the berries. Using just a tiny dot of glue, glue the holly leaves and berries on to the top of the painted pudding.

4 Glue the Christmas pudding on to the middle of the lid of a box. Allow the glue to dry completely.

CRAFT TIP

To save glitter without making a mess, fold a scrap of paper in half and then open it out and lay it under the project you are working on. When you have finished working, collect the glitter in the paper and carefully pour it back along the paper crease into the glitter tube.

5 Apply glue all around the pudding, then sprinkle on glitter. Lightly tap the lid on the work surface to remove any excess glitter.

6 Another way to decorate a gift box is to glue a mini pom-pom on to the lid, then apply glue around the pom-pom and sprinkle small glass beads all over the lid.

Winter Wonderland

This little scene is really magical and makes a beautiful table decoration.

MATERIALS

fir cone
cork
strong glue
artist's paintbrush
acrylic paint in various colours
PVA (white) glue and brush
glitter in various colours
scissors
coloured card (cardboard)
small cardboard gift box

1 Make sure the fir cone is clean and dry. Glue the base of the cone on to the top of a cork, using strong glue. Firmly hold the cone and the cork together for a few minutes until the glue has dried completely.

❄ CRAFT TIP ❄

Look out for fir cones whenever you're on a woodland walk, or alternatively you can buy them from a florist's shop.

2 When the glue is dry, hold the cork in your hand and gently paint the fir cone with a bright green acrylic paint. Stand the cork upright to allow the paint to dry.

3 Paint the cork in a different colour, this time holding the fir cone. Allow the paint to dry.

4 Once all the paint is completely dry, apply PVA (white) glue all over the coloured fir cone.

5 Sprinkle green glitter over the green fir cone, then tap the cork to remove the excess glitter. Cut a small star out of card (cardboard) and glue it to the top of the cone.

6 If you wish, you can decorate a small gift box by gluing the glittery cone "tree" on to the lid.

FATHER CHRISTMAS PUPPET

Put on your own Christmas show by making your own puppets.

MATERIALS

pencil
paper for template
felt squares in red, pale pink and pink
fabric scissors
wadding (batting) fabric
dressmaker's pins
needle
sewing thread
pom-pom trim
small blue glass beads
small bell

1 Draw a glove puppet shape on paper and cut it out to make a template. Position the template on red felt and cut out two puppet shapes. Cut a beard, moustache and eyebrows from the wadding (batting) fabric and pin them on to one of the puppet shapes.

🌿 CRAFT TIP 🌿

This project shows you how to make Father Christmas, but you can apply the same principles to make all sorts of other puppets too. Why not try making a Christmas snowman or a fairy puppet?

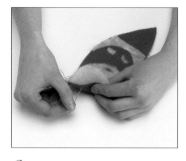

2 Stitch the wadding in place on the puppet. Remove the pins when you have finished sewing.

3 Sew a length of white pom-pom trim in a straight line just above Father Christmas's eyebrows.

4 Sew a blue bead under each eyebrow. Draw a hand shape on pale pink felt and cut it out. Draw two small circles for the cheeks on pink felt and cut them out.

5 Sew the hand in place on the thumb of the glove and sew the cheeks on either side of the face. Place the two puppet shapes together and carefully pin them in place.

6 Sew a bell on to the top of the puppet. Sew around the edge of the glove, leaving the bottom edge open to fit your hand inside. Remove the pins when you've finished sewing.

478

Découpage Santa Tray

This colourful tray makes a great present and you can design it to suit whoever you are giving it to.

MATERIALS

fine sandpaper
small wooden tray
damp cloth
medium and fine artist's paintbrushes
acrylic paint in various colours
scissors
wrapping paper
PVA (white) glue and brush
glitter glue
sequins
water-based clear varnish and brush

1 To prepare the tray for painting, rub it all over with fine sandpaper to make the surface smooth, with no rough areas. Wipe away any dust with a damp cloth. Leave the tray to dry.

2 On a well-covered surface, paint the tray all over using a medium-size paintbrush. Allow the paint to dry. For best results you may need to cover the tray with two coats of paint.

3 Cut out pictures from wrapping paper and position them on the tray. When you are happy with the design, stick them on with glue. Allow the glue to dry completely.

4 Add a few dabs of brightly coloured paint or glitter glue around the pictures to give the tray extra sparkle. Leave the tray to dry completely.

CRAFT TIP

As well as using wrapping paper for your découpage material, you can cut pictures or abstract shapes out of Christmas cards. If you use a lot of cut-outs, you can have them overlapping for a busier design.

5 Using a fine paintbrush and a contrasting colour of paint, paint the edge of the tray with narrow stripes. Try to make the stripes as even as you can. Leave the paint to dry.

6 Glue some sequins on to the tray and leave for several minutes to allow the glue to dry. Using a varnishing brush, paint on a few coats of clear varnish. Allow the varnish to dry.

DRAWSTRING GIFT BAGS

These little bags are ideal for holding foil-wrapped chocolate coins.

MATERIALS

scissors
fabric
ruler
ribbon
pencil
paper for template
felt square
needle
sewing thread
embroidery thread
(floss)
braid
cord
safety pin

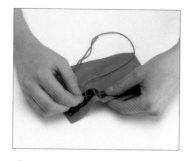

2 Using sewing thread, stitch the ribbon along one edge of the fabric 1cm/½in from the top. Sew along each side of the ribbon but leave the ends open.

5 Turn the bag the right way out. Cut a piece of braid, making sure it is long enough to go around the top of the bag, and stitch it in place.

1 Cut a piece of fabric 20 x 15cm/ 8 x 6in and a length of ribbon 18cm/ 7in. Draw a star on paper and cut out. Place the paper template on the felt, draw around it and cut out.

> ### CRAFT TIP
>
> *If you wish, you can glue the felt star on to fabric instead of sewing it. Felt does not fray so there is no need to turn under the edges whether you glue or sew it.*

3 Sew the felt star on to the fabric, positioning it over to one side.

4 Fold the fabric in half, right sides facing, making sure the corners meet. Sew along the bottom and sides of the bag, using embroidery thread (floss), but leave the top open.

6 Cut a length of cord and attach a safety pin through one end. Thread the cord through the ribbon at the top of the bag. Tie the ends in a knot. Pull the cord tight to close the bag.

Snowflake Candlestick

This folk art design uses a simple resist technique to create the white shapes.

MATERIALS

fine sandpaper
plain ceramic candlestick
scissors
sticky-backed plastic (contact paper)
artist's paintbrush
enamel paints in various colours
gold ceramic paint

❦ CRAFT TIP ❦

A wooden candlestick base would work equally well. Sand it lightly to remove the varnish.

1 Using fine sandpaper, lightly rub down the candlestick to remove the glaze and make the surface smooth. This will make it easier to paint on to the candlestick.

2 Cut out small circles and long strips from sticky-backed plastic (contact paper). Stick the strips around the upper part of the candlestick and the circles on to the main body of the candlestick.

3 Paint the candlestick. Allow the paint to dry completely, then remove the sticky-backed plastic shapes.

4 Paint an asterisk-shaped snowflake inside each circle and allow to dry. Using gold paint, place a small dot in the centre of each snowflake. Allow all the paint on the candlestick to dry completely before using.

GLITTERY POMANDER

Jazz up a traditional pomander with a huge ribbon bow and gold glitter.

MATERIALS

orange
wide ribbon
scissors
cloves
PVA (white) glue and brush
gold glitter

3 Cover all the exposed areas of the orange with cloves by carefully piercing the pointed end of each clove into the orange. Position the cloves in even lines.

4 Brush a thin layer of PVA (white) glue over the cloves and sprinkle gold glitter over the orange, shaking off the excess. Let the glue dry.

1 Holding the orange in your fingers, wrap the length of ribbon tightly around it. Keep hold of the ribbon.

2 Without letting go of the ribbon, twist it and wrap it around the orange in the other direction. Tie the ribbon in a large bow at the top and trim the ends to make "swallowtails".

CRAFT TIP

Place the scented pomander in a warm, dry location where it will gradually dry out naturally.

Party Games

*A*fter Christmas Dinner the traditional way to continue the celebrations is with a favourite selection of party games. We start off here with popular guessing games such as Charades, which usually takes over the whole room, followed by quieter memory games such as My Aunt Went Christmas Shopping. Word and card games include the notorious Chinese Whispers, Old Maid and the amazing Balancing Act. For the younger members of the party there are plenty of boisterous games, including several riotous races around the room. Now that everyone has warmed up, it's time to suggest some team games to bring out a little good-humoured competitiveness. The afternoon ends with a Treasure Hunt, after which it is time for mince pies and Christmas cake.

GUESSING GAMES

Guessing games are perhaps the most enthralling of all family-fireside games, since they involve an element

of intrigue. The rest of the group has to use skill and judgement to unravel a secret known only to one

person, or to members of the opposing team. It is a challenge that is eagerly taken up by young and

older guests alike, and the challenge may come in many guises.

CHARADES

This is a mime game that can be both fun and frustrating. Each person in the group thinks up the name of a book, a play, a TV show, a song or a film, and writes it on a slip of paper. One player picks a title from the pack at random and without saying a word, tries to mime it as a whole, in separate words or in syllables for the others to guess. The first person to get it right takes the centre stage and performs his or her own title mime.

To indicate the category of the title, the player opens out his palms like the pages of a book; mimes drawing back the curtains for a play; draws a square in the air for a TV screen; mimes an opera singer, hand on heart, for a song; and winds an imaginary handle for a film.

He or she then holds up one, two, three or more fingers to indicate the number of words in the title and then indicates which of those words he intends to mime by holding up the appropriate number of fingers. If the mime represents a syllable of the word, then he places one, two, three or four fingers on the forearm. If the title were A Christmas Carol, the player

would hold up three fingers. Then to mime the syllable "mas", he would hold up two fingers followed by placing two fingers on his forearm.

The word "the" is indicated by making the letter T with both forefingers, and "a" or "an" by holding up an index finger and thumb together. If he intends to mime a "sounds like" word, "time" instead of "lime", for example, he cups one ear with his hand.

BELOW: *Ribbons galore, from colourful paper to shiny raffia, comprise a teaser for "How Many, How Long?"*

HOW MANY, HOW LONG?

This is an interlude game which you can pass from hand to hand in a group, or set out on a table with a notebook and pencil for guests to enter their guesses.

To prepare the game, gather together a collection of pieces of ribbon or string. Measure each piece, add up the total, write it on a card and put it in a sealed envelope. Tie the ribbons into double and multi-bows, joining them together in one long, complicated-looking string. The answers to how long is that piece of string are likely to vary wildly from a couple of yards to half a mile! The same game can be played with a jar full of candies, as everyone guesses the number in the jar.

WHAT MANNERS!

This is a game that allows the cheekiest of questions to be met by the most tantalizing responses.

One person in the group thinks up an adverb. It can be a simple one like "happily" or "sadly" or a more obscure one like "self-effacingly" or "bookishly". The others take it in turn to ask the key player to respond to questions, or perform certain activities to questions, or perform certain activities in the manner of that adverb. "Tell me what you thought of the Christmas present I gave you", asks an intrepid player. One can only hope that the chosen adverb wasn't "frankly"! The first one to guess the adverb takes over the key role.

SILENCE, PLEASE!

The players are seated in a circle, on chairs or on the floor. Each one in turn whispers to his left-hand neighbour telling him to do some absurd thing.

When the instructions have gone full circle, everyone stands up and takes a vow of silence. Each player in turn rises and performs his given task and sits down only when someone in the group has guessed his mime. Anyone who speaks or laughs, pays a forfeit (penalty).

ABOVE: *For "How Many, How Long?", choose the most colourful candies you can find and decorate the jar with a ribbon and a sprig of greenery. Provide paper and pencil to the contestants for their estimates.*

PENCIL AND MEMORY GAMES

In theory, pencil and memory games provide a quiet interlude between, say, lunch and tea,

or tea and television, or between noisy team games. But it does not always work out like that,

especially when the answers or results are read out or scrutinized.

PELMANISM

This games requires a little preparation on the part of the host or hostess, so have everything ready to bring in when you judge the moment is right.

Collect 40 or 50 small items from around the home, and place them on a tray. There may be a candle and a coin, a nut and a nail, a key and a kumquat, a cone and a stone, a leaf and a lime, a pottery cat and a cork or any other easily forgettable selection you care to make. Give each player a paper and pencil, and bring in the tray covered with a cloth. Remove the cloth and give everyone, say, 1 minute to study the tray, then 3 minutes to write down as many items as they can remember. Have small prizes such as chocolate bars ready to reward the most accurate memories.

MY AUNT WENT CHRISTMAS SHOPPING

This is another lazy afternoon game. No-one needs to move! One player starts by saying "My aunt went Christmas shopping and she bought ..." It may be that her purchase was a pair of look-alike fun-fur zebras. The next player repeats the line about his aunt's expedition, and her first purchase, and then adds his own. Her next good buy might be a second-hand pink and blue feather boa. And so it goes on. As each player's memory fails or even an adjective is forgotten, he drops out of the game until eventually the only niece or nephew who accurately repeats the list wins.

BEETLE GAME

This is such an old favourite that some families organize beetle-drives on a similar principle to whist drives, four to a table with the winner moving on to the next. The game can be played by three or more players; everyone needs their own pencil and paper. The aim is to complete a drawing of beetle.

This is purely a game of chance, the outcome being determined by the luck of the dice.

Each player takes it in turn to throw the die and cannot start his drawing until he has thrown a six, for the body. With this oval drawn, he can complete the beetle outline, in any order, when he throws a five for the head, a four for each of six legs, a three for each of two antennae, a two for the tail, and a one for each of the two eyes. The player who completes his insect first cries "Beetle!".

THE MINISTER'S CAT

This is a memorizing-out-loud game. It is up to the organizer to keep the game moving. Too many long pauses and you're out!

The first player announces that the minister's cat is an awkward, or an awesome, or an Alpine cat. The next player repeats the "a" adjective and adds one of his or her own, beginning with the letter "b", and so it goes on, around the circle and through the alphabet. Anyone who remembers that the minister's cat is an awesome, batty, cantankerous, dowdy, eclectic, fastidious, gregarious, horrendous, indigenous, jumpy, kinky, lazy, mischievous, notorious, opulent, pernicious, quiet, rowdy, sleepy, tortoiseshell, undisciplined, violent, wayward, xenophobic, yellow, zany cat – starts again! Anyone who does not, is out.

LEFT: *A tray of small items like these can tax even the most alert mind when playing the "Pelmanism" game.*

RIGHT: *Fill a Christmas stocking with an assortment of objects for the memory game, "It's in the Bag".*

IT'S IN THE BAG

Children especially love this rummaging guessing game. Collect a number of small and unlikely items together and put them in a thick pillowcase, cushion cover or even a Christmas stocking. Give each player about 30 seconds to rummage in the bag, but tell them that they must not look. Each one then writes down what he or she felt in the bag. Whoever comes up with the most complete list claims a small prize for the most accurate or the most humorous list.

PICTORIAL SEQUENCES

This is a game that can verge on the bizarre – if it is to be the greatest fun. Divide the company into groups of four and give each player a paper and pen.

Each player draws a human, animal or fantasy head at the top of the paper, folds it over to leave just the neck showing and passes it to the player on the left. He or she draws down to the waist, folds it and passes it on. The next person draws the figure from the waist to the knees and passes it on to the fourth player to add the feet.

WORD AND CARD GAMES

Some word games seriously tax the lexicographers among the group, while others

encourage hilarity and deviousness. There is a place at a family party for both types.

THE MAD MAHARAJAH

This game gives children a chance to act up. They can be theatrically sick, writhe about in seemingly grievous pain and even dramatically drop down dead. But before that they have to remember to spell.

One player stands in the middle of the circle, points to another player, and announces, "I, the mad Maharajah, do not like the letter (for example) P. What will you give me to eat?" The player indicated must offer the Maharajah a food that will not, by including the letter P, poison him. He might serve up a flan but not a pie, an orange or lemon but not an apple or pear, and so on. Easy? Not when the Maharajah demands more and more food as he points to other players and warns them of one poison letter after another.

Each successive food offered must contain none of the poison letters. If it does, the Maharajah is dead, the player who poisoned him is out, and someone else takes the crown.

CHINESE WHISPERS

The chances of the original whisper going full circle around the group are remote enough, without the wiles of mischievous players who deliberately muddy the waters!

The first player whispers a message close to the ear of his or her neighbour in the circle. That person passes it on, to the next person, who whispers it to the next until in theory the message should return unscathed – this rarely happens – to the first player. He calls out the message he has just received, and everyone falls about laughing at how

the message has changed since they passed it on.

Older players may remember the legendary story of the World War I message which was transmitted as "Send reinforcements, we're going to advance", and was ultimately received as "Send three-and-fourpence, we're going to a dance".

BANK ROBBERS

This trick relies on a confident smile and a ready line of patter – younger children are more likely to be amazed.

Take the pack of cards and remove, publicly, the four jacks and, stealthily, four other cards. Fan out the jacks with the other four cards hidden behind them. Place the remaining 44 cards on a table in front of you and hold up the four jacks, explaining that they are robbers who are going to break into a bank and steal its gold. Then place the jacks and, again stealthily, the other four cards face down on top of the pack. Take the top card, concealing its face, and place it into the pack, saying that this is the first robber entering the bank. Take the second, third and fourth cards and place them one by one in the pack. These will of course be the "innocent" cards, not the robbers.

Now tap the pack with a very knowing air and produce the four jacks from the top of the deck as if by magic. Take a bow, to delighted applause.

LEFT: *You might be quite surprised at the final sentence in a game of "Chinese Whispers".*

OLD MAID

Remove the Queen of Hearts from the pack of cards and deal the remainder to the players. Each player sorts his or her hand into pairs, two cards of equal numbers or court (face) value, and places them face down on the table. The first player offers one of his cards to the player on his left. If that player can match it with a card he holds, he discards the pair and passes a card to the player on his left and so on around the table. Players who run out of cards just pass a card from the player on their right to the one on their left. As there is an uneven number of queens, the last card is certain to be one of them.

BEGGAR YOUR NEIGHBOUR

Don't despair! Someone who seems to be winning this game hands down could be declared out in a matter of minutes.

Deal two packs of cards, face down, between the players who stack them in neat piles in front of them. The player on the dealer's left turns over the card on the top of his pack and puts it in the centre of the table. The next player puts his top card face up on the first one and so on around the table.

If a court (picture) card is turned over the player has to pay a forfeit (penalty), placing four cards on the central pile for an ace, three for a king, two for a queen and one for a jack. If, when paying a forfeit, the player turns over a court card, his punishment stops and the player on his left pays the appropriate new forfeit. If only numbered cards are turned over when paying a forfeit, the player takes all the cards in the central

pile and places them beneath his own. He turns up the first card in the next round, and so it goes on. Players drop out of the game when they have run out of cards.

BALANCING ACT

This is another way to amuse the assembled company. Take a card in your hand and attempt to balance an unbreakable glass on its rim. The glass will fall off. Now tell your audience that with a little concentration you can perform this seemingly impossible balancing act. This time produce the two prepared cards in your hand. One has been folded

ABOVE: *With a pack of cards, you're never short of a game at Christmas. The games described here are sure to delight your guests.*

lengthways with one half pasted to the back of the other to create a flap. Show the audience both sides of the apparently single card, making sure that the flap is closed. Work up the anticipation in the audience and, with a deft movement, open the flap towards you so that the two cards present (only to you) a T-shaped edge. Balance the tumbler on this edge with a look of studied nonchalance.

ℬOISTEROUS 𝒢AMES

There are times in every family party when the older members have to put their fingers in their ears and

grin and bear the noise made by the youngsters. And there are times when they can't resist joining in!

FARMYARD NOISES

The title speaks for itself! The players form a circle with one of their number, the farmer, blind-folded in the centre. The players walk around him and, when the "farmer" taps his foot on the ground, they stop. He points at a player (whom he cannot see of course) and asks him to make the noise of a farmyard animal, such as a cow, a pig or a horse. The farmer has to guess who the animal is. If he guesses correctly, the two players change places. If not, the circle moves around again and he points to another player with a request for another impersonation.

MUSICAL MINDREADING

You need someone playing a piano or controlling the volume of a recorded piece of music.

One player goes out of the room and the others decide on a simple act he has to do. This may be rearranging the fruit in a bowl, cracking a nut and so on. The music starts and the player enters and walks around the room. The nearer he gets to his goal the louder the music plays. The further he gets, the softer the music. As the player approaches his goal, the music becomes deafening. The player must guess what the task is and perform it.

AND THE BAND PLAYED ON

This game is noisy in the extreme, but all the more fun for that.

Divide the group into orchestras of four or five players and supply a selection of house-hold items and utensils which

they can use as improvised musical instruments. These items could include empty "mixer" bottles, a jug of water, metal skewer, rubber bands, combs, spoons, rulers and tissue paper. Tell the orchestras to select and create their musical instruments, and give them about 5 minutes to rehearse a tune. This could be an earsplitting time! Then each band gives a polished performance to the others, and everyone votes for the best one. Voting for one's own band is not allowed.

Primitive music can be made in primitive ways. Bottles filled to different levels will produce different notes when struck by a metal skewer or spoon. Rubber bands stretched around a ruler at different tensions will produce a variety of notes when plucked. Paper wrapped tightly around a comb will make an instrument with some of the characteristics of a mouth-organ, and the rounded sides of spoons tapped together sound like castanets, to the untutored ear. Good listening!

FAN RACE

You need a good, clear space to play this game. It could even be played outside on a still, dry afternoon.

Each player is given a small fan and a feather. Everyone stands in a row, toeing the line, with his or her feather on the

LEFT: *Make your own musical instruments from household objects, and when you're ready, give a performance to your guests.*

ground in front of them. At a given signal, the fun begins. Players have to fan their feathers to the finishing line. Anyone who touches his feather with his hands, or blows it, is disqualified. Those not taking part in the race are encouraged to pick a winner and cheer their "horse" to the finishing post.

SPOON A BALLOON

This is a game of gamesmanship. The players each have a spoon and stand in a circle with about a metre (a yard) between each of them. A balloon is placed on one spoon and is then tossed from spoon to spoon around the circle. The other players, without moving from their posts, do all they can, in the way of verbal discouragement, to make the receiving player lose concentration. Any player who fails to catch the balloon on his spoon is out, and the others close ranks.

BALLOON RACE

This game can be played in heats, the winners of each event meeting in the semi-finals and the finals. Each heat consists of three or four players – more if space and the number of participants permit. Each player is given a balloon and a short, thin stick with which he has to pat it across the room and into a bowl on the other side. If he touches the balloon or it falls to the ground the player is disqualified. Onlookers will no doubt wish to cheer on their chosen contestants.

RIGHT: *Spoons at the ready for the "Spoon a Balloon" game in which the players' dexterity is foiled by verbal discouragement from the opposition.*

BELOW: *An assortment of feathers and coloured fans for a "Fan Race". Use a notepad and coloured pens to keep score.*

TEAM GAMES

Bring a little competitive spirit to the party by introducing a few team games.

You don't need a full-size Olympic stadium for these family favourites.

ORANGE RELAY

Divide the group into two teams and then each team into two sections, one at each end of the room. Provide each team leader with an orange wrapped around with an elastic band, and each player with a skewer.

The two team leaders hold the orange on a skewer, threaded through the band, and run to the next member of their team at the other end of the room. They transfer the orange to that player's skewer without using their hands. The two new runners rush to the other end of the room, pass on the orange, and so the game continues until one team has successfully completed the race. If the orange falls to the ground at any stage, that team starts again.

ROPE RACE

The players divide into two teams. Each team is given a length of rope knotted into a large circle (make sure the knot is secure and cannot be "slipped"). On the word "go" the first player in each team passes the rope circle over his or her head, over the shoulders and down to the ground. It is picked up by the next player who does the same, and so on down the line and back again, to the first player in each team. The side which finishes first celebrates vociferously.

CHOCOLATE RACE

You will have to shop in advance for this game, for two large bars of chocolate. Divide the group into two teams and ask each one to form a circle. Place a chair in the middle of each group, with an unbreakable plate, a large chocolate bar, a knife and fork, a hat and a scarf.

Give each team a die and a die shaker. The first one on each side to throw a six rushes to the chair, dons the hat and scarf, cuts off a piece of chocolate with the knife and conveys it to his or her mouth with the fork. The next person to throw a six grabs the hat and scarf from his team-mate, puts them on and proceeds to devour another piece of chocolate in the same way.

ORANGE RACE

This game is all the more fun if you divide the group into two teams, each one evenly balanced with small children and tall grown-ups.

The two teams stand in line. Each team leader is given an orange, which he or she tucks under the chin. On the word "go", the two players attempt to transfer the orange to the chin of the next two players in line. Touching the orange with the hands is the worst form of cheating, punishable by returning the orange to the first in line and starting all over again. The same fate befalls a team if the orange falls to the ground.

The winning team is the one which successfully manoeuvres the orange from the first to the last in line.

LEFT: *To play "Orange Relay" all you need are some oranges – one per team. It's hard not to cheat in this game.*

OBSTACLE RACE

This is a race for two players, and a heap of fun for everyone else. Two players go out of the room while the others prepare two identical obstacle courses, placing two piles of books, heaps of cushions, empty boxes and so on in two lines down the room. The two contestants are brought in, led to the start of the course and told to memorize it. They are then blindfolded, and the rest of the group, the conspirators, silently remove the obstacles.

On the word "go", the two contestants climb and clamber over obstacles that are no longer there, while the conspirators fall about laughing. The first competitor to reach the finishing line with success claims a prize.

TREASURE HUNT

This game involves some preparation by the host and hostess, and a polite request to observe that some rooms are out of bounds, if this is the case.

Divide the party into teams of three or four players, and give each of them a different list of "treasure" to be unearthed, and a box to put it in. Give the teams, say, 10 minutes to go on the hunt. The prize goes to the team who gets closest to finding all the items on their list within the time limit.

Make up the lists with some items that players are likely to have in their pockets or handbags and others which may be found without too much disruption in the kitchen and dining room. Suitable treasure might include a railway season ticket, a bus ticket, a library card, a lipstick, a teaspoon, a salt cellar, a nut, a book of matches, a used envelope and so on.

ABOVE: *Homemade cakes and candies make excellent prizes.*

You Win!

Although it is not absolutely necessary to award prizes for individual or team success, a small token is always appreciated, especially by children.

FOR CHILDREN

Chocolate bar; candies; wrapped gingerbread men and other shapes; wrapped homemade biscuits and small cakes; coat badge; Christmas tree ornament.

FOR ADULTS

Chocolate bar; miniature chocolate liqueur; individually wrapped truffles or pralines; miniature pot of preserve; scented drawer sachet; packet of bath pearls.

You Lose!

Sometimes the forfeits (penalties) that players are asked to pay are as much fun (for the rest of the company!) as the games themselves. Here are some suggestions that should help to spark off other ideas.

- Kiss everyone in the room of the opposite sex.
- Dance gracefully to some imaginary ballet music.
- Whistle the national anthem.
- Mime a given task, such as getting dressed in the morning, or having a shower.

$\mathscr{T}$EMPLATES

Trace the templates directly from the page and then

enlarge with a photocopier if necessary.

ADVENT CALENDAR
PAGE 336

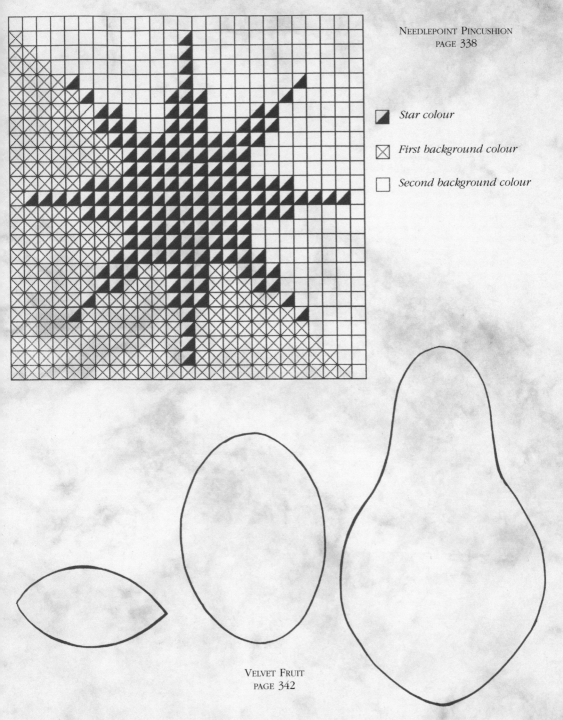

NEEDLEPOINT PINCUSHION
PAGE 338

Star colour

First background colour

Second background colour

VELVET FRUIT
PAGE 342

ANGEL STOCKING
PAGE 350

VELVET STOCKING
PAGE 348

HOLLY LEAF NAPKIN
PAGE 355

HAND-PAINTED PLATE
PAGE 358

SHINY SNOWFLAKES
PAGE 362

GOLD CROWN TABLECLOTH
PAGE 356

ROCOCO STAR
PAGE 368

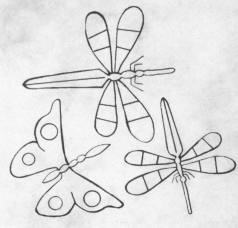

EMBROIDERED DRAGONFLIES
PAGE 371

INDIAN-STYLE DECORATIONS
PAGE 377

PAPIER-MÂCHÉ DECORATIONS
PAGE 381

HERALDIC DECORATIONS
PAGE 380

BYZANTINE DECORATIONS
PAGE 382

WIRE ANGEL
PAGE 386

SHINY TIN DECORATIONS
PAGE 394

VICTORIAN BOOT
PAGE 397

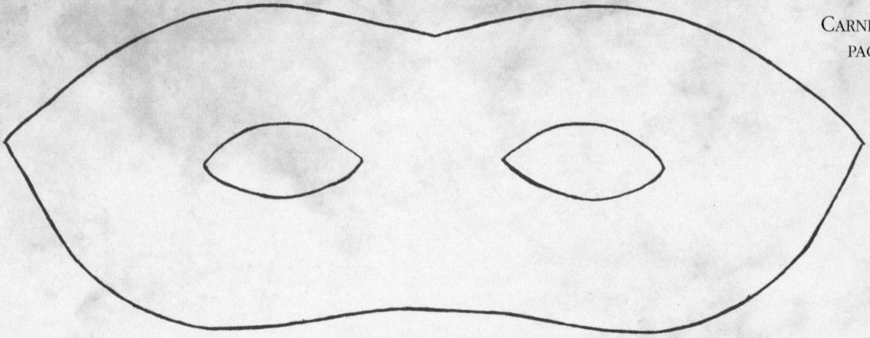

CARNIVAL MASK
PAGE 400

COUNTRY ANGEL
PAGE 404

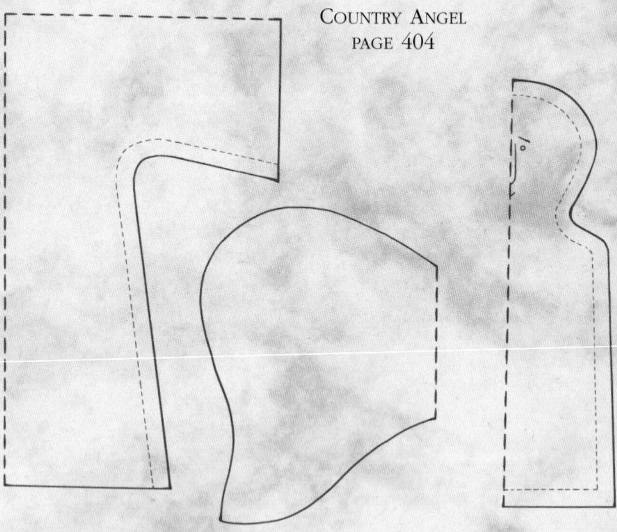

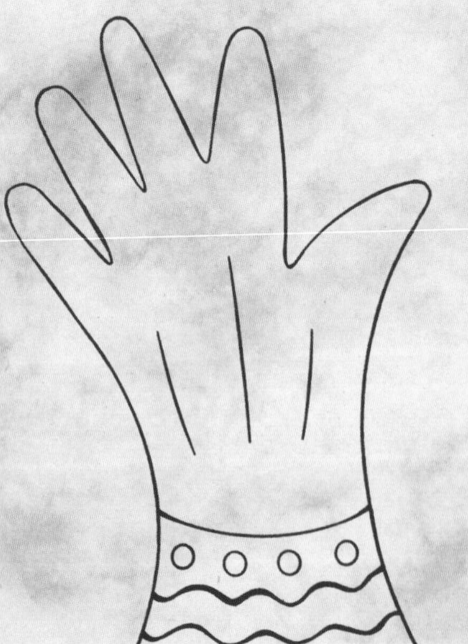

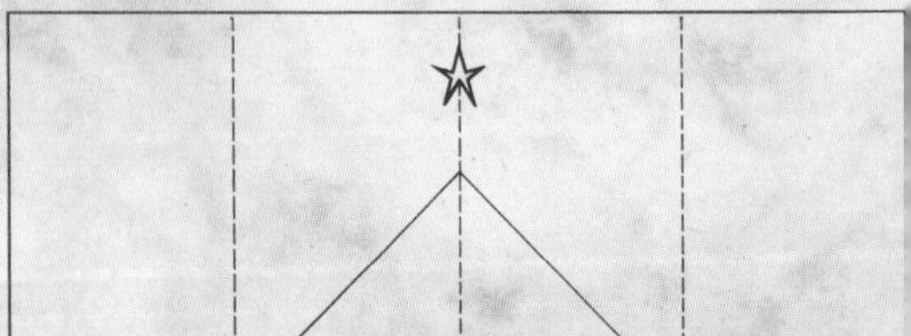

LACY SILVER GLOVES
PAGE 401

CUT-OUT MANGER CARD
PAGE 415

GIANT SNOWFLAKE BOX
PAGE 434

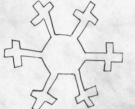

PLACE MARKER GIFT BAGS
PAGE 438

DOVE DECORATIONS
PAGE 460

FESTIVE POM-POMS
PAGE 461

CHRISTMAS ANGEL
PAGE 462

FESTIVE CAT CARD
PAGE 444

INDEX